"The Finer Thread, The Tighter Weave"

William T. Stafford

"The Finer Thread, The Tighter Weave"

Essays on the Short Fiction of Henry James

Edited by
Joseph Dewey and Brooke Horvath

Purdue University Press
West Lafayette, Indiana

05   04   03   02   01   5   4   3   2   1

The paper used in this book meets the minimum requirements of American
National Standard for Information Sciences—Permanence of Paper for Printed
Library Materials, ANSI Z39.48-1992.

Printed in the United States of America

Jeanne Campbell Reesman, "'The Deepest Depths of the Artificial,'" pp. 42–68 is
reprinted from Reesman, Jeanne Campbell, "The Deepest Depths of the Artificial":
Attacking Women and Reality in 'The Aspern Papers.'" *Henry James Review* 19.2
(1998), 148–165. © The Johns Hopkins University Press. Reprinted with permission
of the Johns Hopkins University Press.

Library of Congress Cataloging-in-Publication Data

The finer thread, the tighter weave : essays on the short fiction of Henry James /
edited by Joseph Dewey and Brooke Horvath.
    p. cm.
Includes bibliographical references and index.
  ISBN 1-55753-207-9 (alk. paper)
  1. James, Henry, 1843–1916 Criticism and interpretation. 2. Short story. I. Dewey,
Joseph, 1957– . II. Horvath, Brooke.
  PS2124 .F54 2000
  813'.4—dc21   00-008149

Contents

To the memory of William T. Stafford

In Heaven there'll be no algebra,
No learning dates or names,
But only playing golden harps
And reading Henry James.

—Anonymous

Acknowledgments

This collection would not have been possible without the support and assistance of many people. When we began to contemplate the assembly of a collection of essays in memory of William T. Stafford, we thought perhaps our chances of success might be enhanced if a subvention to defray publication costs was raised. Consequently, friends of Professor Stafford were contacted and asked to contribute to such a fund. We invited donations at four amounts and received a generous response. However, our method of contacting Professor Stafford's colleagues and students was slapdash, limited by whom we could remember and find a ready means to reach. We know there are doubtless many others who would have liked to be a part of this memorial but never had the chance, and we want them to know that only our shabby memories kept them uninvited.

We want all who did contribute to know that their help has been appreciated. Your contributions funded no lavish lunches but were indeed used to help produce the book, and we think a particularly attractive volume has been the result. What follows is grateful acknowledgment of those who helped out, all of whom we consider friends.

Benefactors
> Ruth Ann Stafford
> Joseph Trimmer

Sponsors
> Mark Bourdeau
> Henry Hughes
> Neil Myers
> Dennis Petrie
> Adeline Tintner

Patrons
> Jacob Adler

Richard Anderson
Sam and Bunnie Aubrey
Christopher Brooks
Jonnie Guerra
Martin Light
Virgil Lokke
Alan McKenzie
Frank and Cheryl Oreovicz
Kathleen and Richard E. Shaw
Gary Scharnhorst
Leon and Marguerite Trachtman
Cristof Wegelin

Friends
Timothy Alderman
Ray Browne
Thomas Dukes
Leslie Field
Bruce Harkness
Edward Lauterbach
Mordecai Marcus and Erin Jenean Marcus
Hugo Richard
E. L. Risden
Daniel Ross

We thank, of course, our contributors as well as those who wished to contribute but were prevented for one or another reason and those whose essays could not, because of space and balance requirements, be included here.

Without the help of Kathy Ginther at Kent State University, we would still be typing and photocopying and trying to convert ASCII files into something readable, and we appreciate very much both her skill with office technology and reluctance to lord her superior abilities over us.

A special thanks is due to Irving Malin and Richard Hocks for their invisible assistance throughout this project.

"The Finer Thread, The Tighter Weave"

Joseph Dewey

INTRODUCTION

Lately, I have had cause to think about Henry James and baseball.

Not that James, the career Anglophile, ever deigned to treat our national pastime directly (or even metaphorically, for that matter) in any of his fictions. I should say, rather, that I've been thinking about what an ardent reader of James might have in common with an inveterate baseball fan. The question, of course, is not entirely hypothetical. William T. Stafford, longtime professor of American literature at Purdue University, one of the founding editors of *Modern Fiction Studies*, and the man in whose honor these essays have been gathered, was a lifelong explorer of the Jamesian canon and was, as well, in the closing years of his life, a baseball enthusiast, a passion he channeled particularly into tracking the (in)glorious fortunes of the Chicago Cubs. At the close of a professional career during which he had produced some of the most insightful commentary on James and, as editor of *MFS*, had shepherded into print a stellar catalogue of Jamesian criticism, Bill Stafford came to savor summer afternoons spent away from the office, watching the unfolding of each game with an intensity that became an addiction and absorbing the game's constantly shifting definition, its accidental choreography.

3

But he would relish even more—the day after—the lively rehashing of the game, his trenchant commentary ably supplemented by newspaper and television reportage he would absorb in those dead off-hours between games. In the office or in his favorite off-campus eatery, Bill's tireless reading of the game-text would quickly become the witty interplay of conflicting perspectives proffered by colleagues and cronies who had watched the same game but who had come away with entirely opposite readings, the same game morphing into different (re)constructions fraught with different critical turns and ultimately signifying different meanings—each reading (in)valid, each take determining that the satisfying closure of the Absolute Take on the game would stay wonderfully elusive. Indeed, Cubs baseball itself would become a most exhilarating exercise in (un)reliability—thirty thousand or so (un)reliable narrators gathered in Wrigley Field joined by millions more through the cable links of WGN—each (mis)reading of the game wholly (im)perfect and wholly (in)correct.

Sound familiar? For a career Jamesian, what better environment, a dynamic lexical playfield charged by the interplay of competing takes on a game-text that is both fixed (by stats and videotape) and yet fluid, a game-text whose enduring vitality depended wholly on the participation of reader-fans motivated both by intellectual acuity and by the simple love of the game itself.

It is surely not to trivialize the essays gathered herein to suggest that what we wanted to offer is a heady and noisy "day-after" on the short fictions of Henry James, an animated give-and-take among reader-fans fascinated by the hands-on work/play of textual explication. These are essays that, we are certain, Bill Stafford would have relished. He had little patience with the posturing of so much contemporary critical inquiry that promoted theoretical agendas at the expense of the loving examination of the text itself, that diminished the focus on the text and, in turn, threatened to recode critical explication into inaccessible and hollow theorizing that imported the toxic vocabulary of mathematics and science into what had been by long tradition the joy of one reader illuminating a text for other readers. Bill Stafford relished provocative and lucid essays that turned familiar texts into strange new territories; as a teacher and as an editor, he loved to be shown what he had missed, to be returned to a familiar text stunned by its sudden unfamiliarity; he loved the clash and noise of literary debate—he understood that in the act of agreeing on a text something vital died. He knew that consensus was the ultimate threat to the art and act of reading.

We have gathered, consequently, a contentious lot, essayists who take provocative stands, who dare us to reencounter James and to rethink what James might have been up to, readers who understand what Bill Stafford taught both Professor Horvath and me in graduate seminars: the duty of any reader is to upset. It is a particular challenge with James. Indeed, it might seem incongruous to assert, so near to the close of the century whose literary definition was so largely shaped by the fictional experiments of Henry James, that any part of that writer's vast canon can still be termed "neglected." The sheer industrial-sized output of Jamesian studies is surely a measure of James's imprint, his enduring influence. For nearly a century, in journal articles, chapter studies, book-length investigations, we have charted the intricate turns of James's sensitive consciousnesses who struggle toward—and ultimately with—illumination, and we have charted James's radical willingness to push the techniques of the narrative form he inherited into the experimental arena. And yet in that formidable library of Jamesian criticism, studies of his short fiction account for only a handful of volumes, and many of them are now dated or are collections of previously published articles or focus only on the major tales or provide only a single author's perspective, a monologic model that is necessarily limited.[1] Of course, exemplary work on the short fictions has been scattered about in academic journals and in chapters of studies of James's novels. But still the exegetical record on the vast reach of James's short fictions is curiously underdeveloped—and raises the enticing possibility of new insights into the achievement of James's considerable investment in short fiction. And so we have gathered a colloquium of new essays, the work of both new and established Jamesians that collectively testifies to how much remains to be said about what James termed his "brevities."

Some of this neglect, of course, can be laid to James's own well-documented frustrations over the form and to his abiding sense that the reputation of a writer would rest in the production of heftier texts. In his prefaces, when he addresses his short fictions, he talks with apparent irritation of the necessary "boiling and reboiling" of his material; of the "squeezing" of his subject into the exiguous forms; of his repeated "chemical reductions" of his concepts; of the rigors of his "struggle to keep compression rich," a struggle he compared to a prison warden engaged in "making fast a victim's straightjacket." And yet, over a lengthy career, James never abandoned the form, never stopped producing short fictions, never stopped toying with startling, wholly original ways to give depth to brevity, writing more than a hundred tales (with outlines for a considerable number more), writings that form a substantial element of the James canon and are indispensable today not only if we are to understand fully the achievement of James but if we are to understand as well the evolution of the modern short story, a genre only beginning to find its form at the time James produced his stories. It is the argument of this collection that critical attention trained on some of these lesser-known stories—and even on some of the more visited ones—can yield startling exegeses that lead to provocative insights into James, the very sort of critical work that so intrigued and delighted Bill Stafford.

The organization of such material, of course, is the engineering work of the editors. Taking a cue from (and freely adapting the logic of) James's remark, recorded by his friend William Dean Howells and so often cited in undergraduate short story anthologies, concerning how the rigorous construction of a tale differed from the work of longer fiction (the tale, James commented, is "the labour of a patient weaver, spinning from finer threads, producing a tighter weave"), we have divided our collection into two broad areas—Threads and Weaves. We offer first the Threads—insights into individual tales arranged here following the chronology of the stories themselves. These essays either challenge or completely rethink established readings of the more familiar tales or endeavor to introduce tales long relegated, undeservedly, to the backwaters of critical inquiry. These "Threads" savor the work of close textual interrogation, drawing illumination not only from a variety of scholarly work but more from the painstaking consideration of how James's texts themselves create uncertainties over character definition and reader sympathy. In their able hands, James's "brevities" surprise and intrigue.

To begin, Adam Bresnick, in his investigation of "The Madonna of the Future," suggests that here is not simply a tale of a failed painter or of the dilemma of the artistic endeavor but rather that the severe, dead whiteness of Theobald's ancient canvas is more a telling critique of the "logical impasse of aesthetic formalism" itself, that is, a formal sign of the impossibility of Romantic idealism. Jeraldine Kraver finds "The Author of *Beltraffio*" an unsuspectedly complex text-in-conflict by examining the narrator, who insists on his own marginal role in events while the very narrative he tells testifies to his deep involvement in the sad pathos of the deliberate death of the Ambients' sickly child. Jeanne Campbell Reesman renegotiates "The Aspern Papers" into an intricate investigation into the elusiveness of knowledge itself by charging the American editor's search for, and the eventual destruction of, the dead poet's papers with the polarizing dynamics of language, sexuality, and gender, ultimately finding in James's narrative a significant reworking of the Orpheus legend as well as tantalizing insights into James's much-debated homoeroticism.

Rory Drummond recasts the entire frame of the apparently slight "Brooksmith" by arguing that we are in the hands of a thoroughly class-conscious narrator with a barely concealed contempt for the lower social orders who romanticizes the working class by suggesting that the butler Brooksmith was spoiled by a life spent serving in the Offord salon, a reading of the butler that is subverted, Drummond charts, through the powerful irony of James's narrative strategy of leaving the butler himself oddly silent, thus allowing that character to be wholly shaped by a most unreliable narrative energy. Karen Scherzinger takes apart the bizarre "A Private Life" to discover therein an exercise in deconstructive politics, one that is defined by a tension of readings that shift (un)easily between ghost fantasy and Freudian case study to yield a text that refuses to resolve the dilemma of multiple Vawdreys, which leaves a most unsettling ambiguity that denies legitimacy to the interpretative coherence expected in traditional narrative and that, unexpectedly, anticipates the vigor of so many of the ludic texts of postmodernism. Daniel Kim finds a similar postmodern anticipation in, of all places, "The Altar of the Dead" by recasting Stransom's candled altar itself into a text and further by suggesting that Stransom's reading of that altar is in conflict with that of the anonymous woman, in an exercise that parodies the entire enterprise of realistic fiction by denying the altar itself any stable or objective reading and that ultimately tests the conventions of realism against what would become several generations later the tempered postmodern agenda most prominently explored in texts of Rushdie and DeLillo.

Patricia Laurence takes us into one of James's most slighted fictions, "The Friends of the Friends," that bizarre tale with its nameless (and mostly dead and perhaps made-up) characters and its heavy paranormal overlay, and reclaims it as a precursor of much contemporary fiction that explores the terrifying and uncertain element of silence itself, the strategy of the narrative gap, the use of the blank (page) to suggest the unreveal-ability of our emotional lives and the bittersweet frustration over the narrative enterprise itself. Molly Vaux, in her reconsideration of "In the Cage," finds the nameless telegraphist an apt representation of the nerve and hunger of the writerly imagination, what Vaux calls "creative receptiveness," absorbing others' experiences and wrestling them, via her creative imagination, into an interior narrative all her own, a promising enterprise that collapses only when she leaves "her cage" and attempts to engage experience more forthrightly. Lomeda Montgomery upsets the text of "The Beast in the Jungle" to argue that May Bartram, far from saintly, *is* the beast—a powerful, consuming witch-woman who coldly devours Marcher, who himself realizes the nature of the beast in the tale's disturbingly ambiguous ending. Annette Gilson takes "Broken Wings" and finds within its tale of two pathetic pseudoartists James's painfully personal exploration of the nature of success and of the role of the artist amid the monied class, whose patronage so defined the artistic endeavor in James's circle, and further concludes that here is a story of resurrection, of two artists spoiled but not destroyed by the system and willing by narrative end to pursue creativity, not social position. Earl Rovit takes on the text of "The Jolly Corner" to trace James's careful manipulations of the imagery of incompatible oppositions and persistent doublings—a striking pattern of polarizing imagery that stays true to James's moral vision, where such conflicts and ambiguities are held in balance, evocatively irresolvable. And Michael Pinker, offering our last "Thread," reconstructs the character of Sidney Traffle in James's last published story, "Mora Montravers," to find a deluded romantic, charmed by his niece's scandalous behavior and willing to persist—despite revelations to the contrary and the disapproval of his own wife—in a preposterous faith in Mora's integrity, a reading of character wholly independent of what she actually is.

Although these "Threads" surely stand by themselves, it is tempting, of course, to spin splendid "Weaves"—to pull together themes suggested by each of these takes on James: themes of textual unsolveability, unreliable narration, the uncertainty of appearances, the risk of assuming understanding, the subversive thrust of (mis)perception, the inevitable contradiction of any conclusion made about human conduct. These are stories, we find out, that stay stubbornly open-ended, making (im)possible the defining take. These are stories centered on writers, artists, readers: meticulous observers whose narrative testimony, nevertheless, parodies the very possibility of signification and leaves heavily ironic the notion of privileging any point of view. These fictions are self-conscious tales of the slipperiness of form itself that reveal an abiding ambivalence, as James evolved as a writer, over the dilemma of representation—anxieties and exhilarations that (as several of our contributors point out) extend well into the canon of James's heftier fictions.

Such issues of textuality are as well very much at the heart of the essays by our "weavers," or more specifically by those contributors who have found their argument by threading narratives, what Bill Stafford called the work of tales talking to tales. Brooke Horvath considers "A Landscape Painter" and "The Middle Years" to ask how the portrait of an artist presented in each constitutes the delineation of a failed artist—the only sort of artist James himself said could be the subject of a fiction. Kristin Boudreau weaves a fuller range of reference by placing James within a cultural context that includes Emerson and Hawthorne as she explores how "The Altar of the Dead" examines the Victorian process of grief and loss and specifically how involved language is as the individual moves from historic fact to thought, from an individual to a memory that is itself a complicated construct of words.

We then move to weavers of a larger scale. Phyllis van Slyck opens up her argument to a half-dozen of James's tales of artists to examine the considerable dilemma of how characters come to understand others largely through the evidence of the wildly unreliable energy of perception and how that understanding often finds expression in the infatuation with art objects that represent the ideal that experience can only mock. For van Slyck, these characters ultimately encounter the stubbornly real, confront the very illusions they have nursed, and—in James's more lambent fictions—emerge with a stronger ethic that acknowledges the limits of human understanding by accepting the implications of ambiguity. Joseph Wiesenfarth ranges about a wide selection of James's fictions to highlight those narrative strategies that reveal James's ultimate fascination with the role of the writer as a unifying theme for his short fictions and that suggest his short fictions can be defined largely as metafiction, a vast and roughly coherent critique of the writerly dilemma itself—the struggle for expression, the struggle for perfection, the struggle for success, and the profound discontent with the sorry, sordid, squalid real.

We close with our most massively scaled weave—an exploration (we think fittingly) of what is surely James's most explicated tale, "The Turn of the Screw," performed here by Daniel Schwarz. Fitting to close, we think, because in its willingness to reengage this most (de)/(re)constructed of James's tales, this essay offers what most intrigued Bill Stafford: the radical suggestion that we have only begun to find our way into even the most familiar of James's texts. First, Schwarz weaves ties between James's ghost narrative with its emphasis on seeing and the experimental canvases of late French impressionists and of the early Cubists; then Schwarz ties both the dilemma of the governess's evident sexual repression and James's technical challenge to the conventions of mimesis to other significant modernist experiments in Lawrence, Joyce, Conrad, Wallace Stevens, and (supremely) Mann, along the way touching on the resonant influences of Freud, Darwin, photography, and atomic physics. In its scope, Schwarz's essay, we hope, celebrates what each of our contributors at least indirectly contends: the vast and inexhaustible promise of inquiry itself.

It is not to limit the range of our contributors' insights to note that what we offer in this collection are investigations into perspective itself—all of these threads spin that significant weave. We surely did not solicit essays on this theme; rather in selecting the best of those essays that responded to a year-long call for submissions, we found again and again the best work coming around to touch on this thematic thread. And that theme, we feel, is an important one. In the twentieth century, which James to a large extent inaugurated by his narrative experiments, we too often, too casually accepted the notion of our environment's necessary indecipherability, the stubborn mystery of our closest neighbors, our loving spouse, our most familiar colleagues. It is to a world before Heisenberg so inelegantly made uncertainty a banal principle that James directed his restless, textual conundrums, his patient revelations that revelation itself was a deception, a surprise, a risk. It is how we—characters and readers—handle this anxiety of uncertainty that forms the core of our volume. Whether our contributors expose unsuspected angles of tales or expose characters who must move toward the open-ended, we learn as we move about in these essays that as readers we must accept the necessary (in)adequacy of reading itself, an (in)adequacy that argues, in turn, the splendid inexhaustibility of the act of participatory reading.

But, of course, such freedom threatens to diminish into the precious and narrow enterprise of texts forever generating readings, supporting, like some bloated government bureaucracy, a dependent class of professional readers and savvy academics constructing and then blithely reconstructing careers by endlessly twisting the Rubik's Cube of James's tales. We close this introduction by reminding ourselves what Bill Stafford so ardently impressed on his students. These tales perhaps delight our relish of the academic game of textual reading, reward (as our contributors demonstrate) the deep work of excavating, at times sentence by sentence, James's careful, terraced prose. But it is not to the academic that James turned his wary eye. If these stories delight as lexical playfields, they also disturb because ultimately even the professional reader must close up the text and turn to the contemporary world of shifting reliabilities and indecipherable behavior and must perforce live amid the very shadows and hazy lines that cross James's fictions. It is, in fact, that deadly serious business that makes James the profitable read and that ensures that as each wave of interpretative "ism"—modernism, postmodernism, post-postmodernism, and whatever waves in next—gets into the business of Jamesian explication, the texts themselves will provide endless resource. Much like the patient emerald of the baseball field that awaits each generation to play its variations of the game, the texts of Henry James await each generation of readers, such durability testifying to the enthralling paradox of the texts themselves, which are, like the game of baseball, at once so stable and so flexible. Like those baseball games played during the long summer afternoons at Wrigley and then reanimated in contentious conversation the next day, the texts delight because they excite response, but they persevere because such openendedness is surely the mixed blessing of James's twentieth century. And so we offer the clash and noise of seventeen essays that testify to the resilience, viability, and consequence of short fictions that our contributors find simultaneously disturbing and enthralling in their deadly serious play of unreliable perspective.

Note

1. The seminal study on James's short fictions (Krishna Baldev Vaid's *Technique in the Tales of Henry James* [Cambridge: Cambridge University Press, 1964]) is now more than thirty years old. Other, more recent single-author studies include James Kraft's *The Early Tales of Henry James* (Carbondale: Southern Illinois University Press, 1969); Edward Wagenknecht's *The Tales of Henry James* (New York: Ungar, 1984); George Bishop's *When the Master Relents: Henry James' Titled Story Sequences* (New York: Peter Lang, 1988); Sara S. Chapman's *Henry James's Portrait of the Writer as Hero* (New York: St. Martin's, 1989), and Richard Hocks's *Henry James: A Study of the Short Fiction* (Boston: Twayne, 1990); and W. K. Martin and Warren U. Ober collected much of their previously published work into *Henry James's Apprenticeship: The Tales: 1864–1882* (Toronto: P. D. Meany, 1994). Vivian Pollak edited a 1993 collection with a most limited scope: *New Essays on "Daisy Miller" and "The Turn of the Screw"* (Cambridge: Cambridge University Press); Harold Bloom edited *Henry James' "Daisy Miller," "The Turn of the Screw," and Other Tales* (New York: Chelsea, 1987)—although Bloom's selections were all previously published.

Part One: Threads

Adam Bresnick

THE INELUCTABILITY OF FORM

"The Madonna of the Future"

> "What a droll thing to 'represent' when one thinks of it!"
>
> —*The Tragic Muse*

HENRY JAMES OFTEN CLAIMED that he had learned more about the art of fiction from the works of Balzac than he had from the works of any other writer. In "The Lesson of Balzac" (1905), James writes, "I speak of him, and can only speak, as a man of his craft, an emulous fellow-worker, who has learned from him more of the lessons of the engaging mystery of fiction than from anyone else, and who is conscious of so large a debt to repay that it has positively to be repaid in installments" (66). In his essay of 1875 entitled simply "Honoré de Balzac," James remarks in passing that "what is most interesting in Balzac is not the achievement but the attempt. The attempt was, as he himself has happily expressed it, to 'faire concurrence à l'état civil'—to start an opposition, as we should say in America, to the civil registers" (67).[1] James distinguishes Balzac's French writing from that of his English language contemporaries by way of national typologies. In contrast to the English writers of the nineteenth century, who confine their novelistic attention to the intrigues of the drawing-room or country estate, Balzac, as the exemplar of the French imagination, grapples with a social scene that is incomparably more vast. "The civilization of the nineteenth century is of course not infinite, but to us of English speech, as we survey it, it appears so multitudinous, so complex, so far-spreading, so suggestive, so portentous—it has such misty edges and far reverberations—that the imagination, oppressed and overwhelmed, shrinks from any attempt to grasp it as a whole" ("Honoré de Balzac," 68).

In James's account, nineteenth-century civilization functions for the novelist as a sublime object whose essential characteristics are a mathematical enormity and a dynamic complexity that produce an oppressive feeling of terror in James's English-speaking subject, whose imagination is overwhelmed by its mysterious grandeur.[2] If nineteenth-century society is not infinite in the strict sense, it works as a place-holder for the infinite in James's schematic formulation. Bereft of the capacity to domesticate an unruly reality by confining it to the realm of the represented, the English writer withdraws his attention from the seemingly limitless horizon of nineteenth-century society and restricts it to the more reassuring precincts of the private estate. In James's typological account, the English novelist must forgo the sublime and content himself with the lesser pleasures of the beautiful, representing in his fiction only a tractable part of the social scene, for he cannot muster the sheer aesthetic energy necessary to confront contemporary civilization in its sublime totality. According to James, it is precisely such a totalizing grasp that Balzac exhibits without hesitation: "The French imagination, in the person of Balzac, easily dominates it [nineteenth-century civilization], as he would say, and, without admitting that the problem is any the less vast, regards it as practically soluble" (68). With no trepidation, the ferally confident Balzac confronts the sublimity of nineteenth-century civilization and manages quickly to transform it into what James, by way of a highly suggestive oxymoron, calls "a conventional infinite." With this concise phrase, James precisely indicates the paradoxical fate of the sublime object in postromantic aesthetics, for the sublime object incites a moment of terrifying imaginative failure only to give way to a moment in which the faculty of reason, here conceived as the faculty of what Kant calls "negative presentation" (*negative Darstellung*), is contradictorily ascendant.

Now whereas James believes that it is surely the case that Balzac's sublime grappling results in a form that is grander both in its ambition and in its results than what one generally finds in English and American fiction of the same period, he refrains from allowing his admiration of the French writer to sweep him off his feet. Indeed, James's panegyric to his beloved precursor is all the more remarkable for its readily offering a catalog of the blemishes and deformities of the Balzacian corpus, while at the same time it claims Balzac to be among the handful of genuinely great writers of the nineteenth century, or, more emphatically, of any century whatsoever. "The great general defect of his manner, as we shall see," writes James toward the outset of his essay of 1875, "is the absence of fresh air, of the trace of disinterested observation; he had from his earliest years, to carry out our metaphor, an eye to the shop" (61). Relying on the notion of aesthetic disinterest, one of the key terms in both Kant's *Critique of Judgment* and the romantic aesthetics that comes in its train, this remark gives us to understand that at bottom, Balzac lacks taste, for as Kant argues, taste is contingent on one's being able to forego immediate pragmatic interest for the disinterested pleasure afforded by the aesthetic object. As Kant succinctly puts it, "Taste is the faculty of estimating an object or a mode of representation by means of a delight or aversion *apart from any interest*. The object of such a delight is called *beautiful*" (915).[3] In true Kantian form, James will insist throughout his writings that the writer must eschew immediate pragmatic or even moral interests for the beautiful utopia of what Kant famously calls disinterested pleasure (*interesseloses Wohlgefallen*) in all its prospective imaginary liberty.

Though it is surely the case that in his fiction and criticism James is invariably concerned with the ethical question of literature, his is a moralism of the second degree; that is, he believes the moral mission of art to arise precisely from its immediate rejection of pragmatic interest in the name of the disinterested pursuit of truth and beauty. According to James, it is only by rigorously maintaining its disinterest that art may lay claim to being fundamentally free and essentially ethical. James argues that by turning his eye to the shop, Balzac betrays one of the commandments regulating the artistic enterprise; more severely, James implies that insofar as it lacks disinterest, Balzac's writing does not always qualify for admission into the stringent category of art in the first place. Though this criticism seems damning enough, James does not limit his complaints only to Balzac's lack of taste; rather, he is quick to enumerate what amounts to a virtual catalog of Balzacian aesthetic flaws. Here are some of the choicest bits of James's intermittent diatribe: Balzac is morally and intellectually superficial (72); he must be reckoned "an arrant charlatan" "from the moment he ceases to be a simple dramatist" (72); he often avails himself of a gratuitously "sanguinary" irony at once typically French and ethically dubious (80); he has a touch that "often goes woefully astray in narrative" (82); and he is unusually poor for a writer of his stature when it comes to dialogue (82). In sum, writes James in an extraordinary moment, "He was a very bad writer, and yet unquestionably he was a very great writer"(90). With this statement, James plays both ends against the middle via an irrecuperable paradox, for he claims that Balzac is at once the best of writers and the worst of writers, an artist worthy both of admiration and of derision, a genius and a fraud.

In his critical essays on Balzac, James works out much that is essential in his aesthetic position, just as he pays tribute to and prospectively deposes his master. As these essays indicate, Balzac cast a long shadow on the Jamesian oeuvre, functioning as both good and bad object in James's imagination. Less often remarked is James's fictional grappling with his great precursor, and nowhere is this more observable than in the early tale "The Madonna of the Future" (1873). Here James offers a revisionary homage to Balzac that takes up and recasts many of the central problems of Balzac's *Etudes philosophiques*, the series of highly romantic stories in which Balzac meditates on the aesthetic presuppositions and practice of the *Comédie humaine*. James's story, which details the tribulations of the painter Theobald, an American expatriate in Florence who for twenty years has worked on a painting that would rival the sublime perfection of Raphael's "Madonna in the Chair," is clearly an updated and somewhat altered version of Balzac's "Chef d'œuvre inconnu,"[4] a tale that recounts the tragic career of the great painter Frenhofer, who labors over his masterpiece for ten years only to unveil its abstract "wall of paint" to two shocked onlookers at the end of the story in a moment of unmitigated catastrophe.[5] That James had Balzac's tale on his mind while writing "The Madonna of the Future" becomes obvious when one of its characters remarks that were one to enter Theobald's studio and unveil his mysterious painting, "one would find something very like the picture in that tale of Balzac's—a mere mass of incoherent scratches and daubs, a jumble of dead paint!" (215). Yet as we shall see, this is not exactly the case, for whereas Frenhofer's great botched painting turns out to be a kind of maximalist adumbration of the abstract expressionism that will arrive one hundred years down the line, Theobald's painting will rather parodically anticipate a version of minimalism. As the story's climax makes clear, poor Theobald has never been able to bring himself to put brush to canvas and so has nothing to show for his twenty years of labor but "a mere dead blank, cracked and discoloured by time" (228). His painting remains a "Madonna of the Future" precisely because it never quite exists in the present except as an index of a pure negativity, because it cannot manage to accede to the confines of representation except in a wholly prospective, practically abortive manner. Theobald's painting will present itself precisely as the lack that undergirds all painterly representation, as a blank primed canvas and nothing else. In his tale of a painter's apparent failure, then, James confronts what I shall call the ineluctability of aesthetic form and the inevitable recuperation of the sublime aesthetic object as an object of reason, for in a final irony, the canvas does manage to be grimly representational of Theobald's aesthetic dilemma. As the narrator mysteriously suggests at the outset of the story, "I've known a poor fellow who painted his one masterpiece, and . . . he didn't even paint that" (202). A masterpiece, in short, even more unknown and even more unknowable than Frenhofer's. What kind of masterpiece is this?

On the night of his arrival in Florence, the narrator meets Theobald, an American painter in exile, near Michelangelo's statue of David and the statue of Perseus and the Gorgon's head mentioned by Cellini in his memoirs, both of which stand on the plaza in front of the Palazzo Vecchio. On the one hand, we have Michelangelo's famous statue of the biblical hero who slew the giant Goliath, a figure that has become a virtual synecdoche for the proud vocation of Renaissance humanism; on the other hand, we have a representation of the Greek hero whose story Freud famously read as an allegory of castration anxiety and its subsequent reaction formation. "The Madonna of the Future" will figuratively play itself out between the poles suggested by these two statues, for though Theobald would like to accede to the kind of confident representationalist humanism exemplified by Michelangelo, in the end he will appear as one who has been figuratively turned to stone, reduced to mute inaction by the recalcitrant grandeur of his painterly ambition. As the narrative indicates, Theobald so insatiably clings to an ideal beyond the confines of any particular formalization that he cannot bring himself to begin painting his picture, which must remain in a state of permanent abeyance if it is to have any allure for the painter. His creation, he is quick to inform the narrator, is not just a production "in the vulgar sense" (206) but aspires to something more fundamental. This cavalier remark, which casts aspersion on those artworks that fail to measure up to the stringent ideals Theobald has proposed for himself, obscurely suggests the main problem at stake in James's tale, for Theobald's vigorous wish to avoid vulgarity leads him to forgo aesthetic formalization altogether in a vain effort to maintain his creation in the pristine precincts of his mind. The obviously defensive, narcissistic aspects of Theobald's painterly incapacity do not in any way invalidate the seriousness of the issues at stake in "The Madonna of the Future," for what James is after in this Balzacian tale is a description of the pathos of the aesthetics of the absolute, or, what amounts to the same thing, the pathos and necessary failure of aesthetic absolutism. As if further to impress the narrator with his willingness to sacrifice everything for the glory of Art, the ragged painter proudly remarks, "I've never sold a picture!" (206). Though by this Theobald would point to the sublimity of his creation and its resistance to commodification and the vulgar understanding of his contemporaries, in the narrator's ironic presentation these pronouncements are fraught with an incipient self-parody that lends them an air of dubiety.

Though it is clear that the narrator wishes to interpose an ironic distance between himself and Theobald, when he meets the painter the following day, he finds himself swept into an avid discussion of art and its reception. According to Theobald, there are two modes of aesthetic judgment, which he respectively terms the "critical" and the "ideal." The former concerns itself with the "petty trivialities of art, its vulgar clevernesses, its conscious graces" (207), whereas the latter concerns itself only with "the best of the best" (208) of art, with its sheer affective power. Though Theobald is able to muster a certain grudging interest in the technical problems of art, it is clear that what most impassions him are works of art that wholly absorb the spectator, such as Raphael's "Madonna of the Chair," a painting that hangs on a wall in the Uffizi and to which Theobald returns with the obsessive loyalty of a jealous lover: "None betrays less effort, less of the mechanism of effect and of the irrepressible discord between conception and result . . . it has nothing of manner, of method, nothing, almost, of style; it blooms there in rounded softness, as instinct with harmony as if it were an immediate exhalation of genius. The figure melts away the spectator's mind into a kind of passionate tenderness" (208). This description of the painting suggests that it is a perfect rendition of the Kantian notion of *Nachfolge* in all its quasi-automatism, for it is not so much an imitation of a natural object as an imitation of the very manner in which nature produces its objects. The painting is said to have sloughed off any sign of artifice, appearing as a pure emanation of nature that simultaneously affirms the primacy of human genius in the re-naturalization of the world, for Raphael's genius here allows for the immediate auto-presentation of nature in the form of art. Like nature, Raphael's painting instantiates the happy union of freedom and constraint and as such stands as an immediate embodiment of that toward which the aesthetic culture of humanity strives. The work of genius produces a powerful effect that "melts away the spectator's mind" and thus recalls Kant's sublime with the crucial difference that whereas in Kant's formulation of the sublime, the melting is initially experienced in the mode of terror that depends on a certain masochism, here it is a matter of immediate sensual delectation. We might say, then, that what is at stake here is less the sublime as such than a hyperbolic aesthetics of the beautiful. Indeed, Theobald is so moved by this image that he declares, "Other works are of Raphael: this is Raphael himself. Others you can praise, you can qualify, you can measure, explain, account for: this you can only love and admire" (209). In a prosopoetic rush, Theobald has divined the artist in the image and implies that insofar as Raphael was able to decoct the entirety of his artistic being into the living form of his painting, he continues to live on the museum wall three centuries after the fact.

Though the narrator harbors doubts about Theobald's abilities as a painter, he maintains a certain admiring skepticism toward his interlocutor, for if nothing else, Theobald's wild enthusiasm for the art of painting is remarkable in and of itself. "If my friend was not a genius," the narrator remarks, "he was certainly a monomaniac . . . [he] lived and moved altogether in his own little province of art" (212). Theobald's "little province of art" remains off-limits to anyone other than the painter himself, and the appearance—not to mention the very existence—of the masterpiece "Madonna," a painting that "was to be a résumé of all the other Madonnas of the Italian school" (214), can only be a matter of sheer speculation. That Theobald can at least draw becomes clear when he invites the narrator to come to the abode of the "most beautiful woman in Italy" (216), a woman whom he affectionately calls "la Serafina" and who for more than two decades has been the imaginary model for Theobald's "Madonna," though she has yet actually to sit for him in person. Though the narrator is quick to recognize the beauty of la Serafina's "composition" (218), he is rather taken aback when he discovers that she is "decidedly an elderly woman" who exhibits the signs of a "certain mild intellectual apathy" (218) and who clearly has seen better days. She informs him that Theobald "has a magnificent genius" (219) and promptly unveils an extraordinarily finely wrought drawing the artist made of her son shortly before his death, an image that incites a feeling of enormous admiration in the narrator. Convinced of Theobald's essential genius, the narrator challenges the painter to finish his "Madonna" in one month, and, to sweeten the deal, he offers to buy Theobald's "Madonna" for any amount of money the painter might demand. Shocked to hear la Serafina described as an old woman and to be confronted with his own dawdling, Theobald takes up the challenge, proudly promising the narrator that as a result of his painting, "she shall be eternal!" (222). Shortly thereafter, the narrator surmises that this challenge has perhaps precipitated Theobald into "the vulgar effort and hazard of production" (222), as he does not see the painter for days and assumes he must be feverishly painting in his studio.

The narrator's comment indicates a powerful ambivalence toward the process of aesthetic formalization, an ambivalence that runs throughout "The Madonna of the Future." It is as if the necessity of casting the ideal into a perceptible form were in and of itself an irrevocable fall from the grace of imaginary conception, as if the fabrication of aesthetic objects were necessarily nothing but a gross matter of vulgarization. The fantasy of the ideal artwork that exists wholly within the precincts of the mind depends on a radical forgoing of the very process of formalization through which any artwork must pass in order to exist for others, indeed, to exist at all as an artwork and not simply as a secret affair of mental projection. This fantasy leads to a kind of speculative aesthetic madness that takes romantic passivity to its aporetic limit, for in this scenario the romantic genius, entirely enthralled by the objects of his own imagination, becomes so spectacularly passive that no aesthetic formalization may transpire through him. Here we may glimpse the young James wrestling with the legacy of Balza-

cian romantic aesthetics, for while the artist languishes in solipsistic absorp-
tion, imaginarily communing with and libidinally investing the ideal
image he privately fashions in the interior of his mind, the artwork remains
unbroached and undone. In lines that seem to have been written precisely
to describe the conundrum at the center of "The Madonna of the Future,"
Mario Praz argues that for romanticism, "The essential is the thought and
the poetic image, and these are rendered only in a passive state. The Romantic exalts the artist who does not give material form to his dreams—the
poet ecstatic in front of a forever blank page, the musician who listens to the
prodigious concerts of his soul without attempting to translate them into
notes" (14–15). To add a note of confirmation to his assertion, Praz goes on
to cite Keats's famous lines, "Heard melodies are sweet, but those unheard
/ Are sweeter." Of course, there is a basic paradox to Keats's poetic formulation, for whereas at the lexical level it exalts an ideal sensual silence, this
very idea is embodied in a poetic melody that is heard, or at least read, as
part of a poem that necessarily partakes of the materiality of language and
thus of aesthetic formalization. The central paradox upon which the sense
of Keats's injunction depends has to do with the fact that in order to be presented at all, the fantasy of an ineffable formlessness above and beyond any
aesthetic presentation depends on a formalization that contradicts the di-
rective it expresses merely by virtue of existing at all. It is precisely this paradox that will structure the moment of the unveiling of Theobald's
"Madonna," a moment in which James's narrative represents Theobald's
pictorial nonrepresentation, except that whereas for years the unseen was
sweeter than the seen for the painter, allowing Theobald to be wholly absorbed in a prospective, seemingly unbreachable narcissistic torpor, now
Theobald's painting is reckoned a sour failure both by the narrator and by
the painter himself because it has preserved nothing other than the blankness of a passive desire wholly unable to accede to artistic activity in the conventional sense of the term.

Let us look closely at this revelatory scene. When the narrator, hoping
to catch a glimpse of the painter's secret masterpiece, surreptitiously makes
his way into Theobald's studio, he precipitates the climax of the tale. The
narrator's descriptions of Theobald's bearing and studio are richly indicative of the painter's general aesthetic problem: "On my entering, he looked
up at me blankly, without changing his position, which was that of absolute

lassitude" (228). Theobald's sensory organs seem to have taken flight as he sits alone in a "sordid, naked" room, "a grim ghost of a studio" (228). Blank, naked, ghostly: these three adjectives prefigure the canvas that stands at the center of the room and at the center of James's tale, a canvas that is now revealed to be "a mere dead blank, cracked and discoloured by time. This was his immortal work!" (228). Here we are confronted with a sublime troping of the romantic sublime, for if the latter depends on what Kant calls "negative presentation," that is, on the paradoxical presentation that there are things that lie beyond the possibility of imaginative adequation and so may only offer the transcendental promise of reason, Theobald's blank canvas points to the essential materiality of painting and, in doing so, challenges the transcendental fantasy just as it denies the possibility that the painting may successfully function as an aesthetic fetish object. The grisly revelation of Theobald's abortive painterly endeavor powerfully moves the narrator, who finds himself reduced to silence by the sublimity of the painting's apparent failure, for Theobald's absent "Madonna" is a colossal botch that represents twenty years of nonactivity in the face of an all too redoubtable canvas. Now if, as we have seen, "The Madonna of the Future" consistently evidences a certain loathing of aesthetic formalization, at the same time the story evidences a horror at the very formlessness occasioned by such a hyperromantic aesthetic credo because, as the narrative makes clear, such an experience of formlessness cannot but prove threatening to the sanctity of the artistic personality. Jonathan Auerbach has suggested that for James, "the alternative to form's coercion would seem to be sheer formlessness, a dreaded state that threatens to dissolve the first person's sense of self altogether" (165). And in a series of events that confirms Auerbach's claim, the revelation of this formlessness does in fact occasion Theobald's final dissolution because now that the secret of Theobald's nonpainting has become public knowledge, the painter becomes gravely ill with brain fever and shortly meets his demise. With no aesthetic form to ballast it, with no formalized object to bind its cathexis, the artistic ego dissolves into nothingness. The revelation of this formlessness is properly traumatic in the Freudian sense of the term. As Samuel Weber cogently remarks, "Trauma, for Freud, cannot designate any particular, objective reality, for what it entails is precisely the inability of the psyche—or more specifically, of the ego—to determine, its inability to bind or to cathect an excess of energy that therefore tends to overwhelm it" (53). Trauma, on this account, would be that which follows upon the failure of the aesthetic fetish and the fracturing of absorptive disavowal. Within the imaginary economy of James's tale, it is only logical that the overwhelmed Theobald should quickly pass from the moment of the revelation of his painting's formlessness to the formlessness of his death. To put this equation otherwise, we might say that the very unboundedness of Theobald's imaginary identification overwhelms him at this instant, leading him to the unboundedness of his death and the denouement of the narrative.

At the level of narrative form, however, there can be no such thing as formlessness, for insofar as James's tale presents a narrative embodiment of a story of the lack of pictorial embodiment, it cannot but participate in the process of aesthetic formalization that provides the key to the odd plot of "The Madonna of the Future." It is also the case that, were one to shift one's critical parameters, Theobald's "Madonna" might be recuperated as a success in its very failure, even though the characters in the story consider it an unmitigated catastrophe, for finally its blank minimalism manages to be allegorically representative of the absolute severity and impossibility of Theobald's desire. Indeed, in this remarkable revelatory moment, James's tale gives us to understand that even in its sheer pictorial silence, Theobald's abortive artwork cannot escape the confines of the representational: its cracked, dead whiteness ironically formalizes and negatively presents Theobald's "weakness and poverty and nullity" (228). By way of a marvelous paradox, Theobald's "Madonna" finally reduces to a grimly successful adequation of form and content, an allegorical representation of Theobald's magnificent failure to represent. In the end, then, James's tale attests to the very impossibility of aesthetic formlessness precisely at the moment of its apparent unveiling in Theobald's painting, which is also a nonpainting, a painting that exists by not existing. Within the register of its awful irony, James's tale makes it clear that there is no escaping the confines of the representational, that the romantic dream of an absolute beyond all representation cannot but be embodied within the confines of a representative form, whether its content be wholly negative or not. Even the most extreme formalism, a formalism that is entirely emptied of pictorial content, ends up being a formalism for and about somebody. So it is that Theobald understands that even in its apparent absence, his Madonna remains exemplary:

"'*That's* mine!' And he pointed with a gesture that I shall never forget at the empty canvas" (229). And indeed, the canvas is Theobald's and Theobald's alone because in its hyperbolic assumption of two decades of fantasy it can now be seen to bear the marks of Theobald's uniquely nonexistent painterly identity. Like Balzac's *Etudes philosophiques,* "The Madonna of the Future" points to the ineluctability of the aesthetic, to the impossibility of escaping the formalizing imperatives of the mind in a narrative that turns around an artwork that asymptotically skirts the limits of conventional representation.

The unveiling of the painting, then, may be said to mark the point of its completion, a completion that can only come about because paint has never touched Theobald's canvas. "I'm the half of a genius!" exclaims Theobald, "Where in the world is my other half? Lodged perhaps in the vulgar soul, the cunning, ready fingers of some dull copyist or some trivial artisan who turns out by the dozen his easy prodigies of touch!" (229). Theobald is no copyist; indeed, he only has one painting in him, and it is the awful fate of that painting to exist solely as a nonrepresentation of lack. Here James broaches the limit of romantic idealism in a moment of great representative pathos, as the agonized Theobald finally recognizes his painterly miscarriage. "Well for me if I had been vulgar and clever and reckless, if I could have shut my eyes and dealt my stroke!" (229), he exclaims, shortly before lapsing into the attack of brain fever that will take his life within a week and usher in the end of James's tale. Theobald's absolute reticence before the unmarked canvas is a result of his aversion to a mimetic art that would reduce itself to a typology, for though he would have his painting be a summation of all the Madonnas that preceded it, Theobald cannot bear the idea that his version of la Serafina might be perceived as little more than a type, as just another in a long series of Madonnas. Yet in a sense, Theobald's painting may still be read as a perfect summation of all the Madonnas of the world because just as the ideal product of the combination of all colors is white, so the whiteness of his canvas may be read as an ironic approximation and perverse idealization, the superimposition of all preexistent painted Madonnas in the world. Theobald's painting is "The Madonna of the Future," in short, for it blindingly indicates, in its own lack of existence, not only the end of a particular career but also the end of a genre, indeed, the romantic end of all painterly genres. In its complete lack of conventional idealization, in its apparent formlessness, Theobald's "Madonna" ruthlessly exposes the blank canvas upon which the tradition of the painted Madonna reposes, just as it exposes the essential impossibility of a hyperromantic aesthetics of the absolute.

There is another artist-figure who turns up at the end of James's tale, however, who relishes the typologies to which Theobald is so averse and who produces satirical statuettes, not of human beings—at least in the conventional mimetic sense—but of cats and monkeys, and does so with astonishing facility. The man shows the narrator his collection of figurines, each of which is made out of a "peculiar plastic compound" (226) that he has invented. He accompanies this display with a running commentary: "What do you say to my types, signore? The idea is bold; does it not strike you as happy? Cats and monkeys,—monkeys and cats,—all human life is there! Human life, of course, I mean, viewed with the idea of the satirist!" (226). The narrator is taken aback by these sculptures, which are "at once very perfect cats and monkeys and very natural men and women" (227). The narrator perceives the statuettes as representations of men and women not in the strictly mimetic sense of the term, but as caricatures. By forgoing the realist's obligation of mimetic approximation, the sculptor grants himself a large compass of representational possibilities and has produced an inordinately large number of works. "It is not classic art, signore, of course," he continues, "but between ourselves, isn't classic art sometimes rather a bore?" (226). But the narrator cannot bring himself to like these "peculiarly cynical and vulgar" statuettes and even goes so far as to say that he finds their "imitative felicity" entirely "revolting" (227). Indeed, the man appears to the narrator to be himself little more than an "exceptionally intelligent ape" (227), for in comparison to Theobald's striving for a painterly absolute, the man's tiny caricatures induce a feeling of nausea in the narrator. This nausea is only compounded when the man remarks that he no longer knows "whether the cats and monkeys imitate us, or whether it's we who imitate them" (227). With this statement, the sculptor would prospectively overthrow the Aristotelian mimetic hierarchy by which man is to be distinguished from all other animals by virtue of his general capacity to imitate and represent. Here the mimetic capacity, rather than being a proud index of man's unique position in the animal kingdom and the human likeness to God, the original artificer, is exposed as that which is most deeply animalistic in humanity.

Though the narrator respectfully declines to purchase any of the sculptor's seemingly infinite variations on the cats and monkeys theme, it is perhaps not surprising that the story's final words should echo his disturbing formulations because the narrator does at least partially buy into the sculptor's cynical pronouncements. In closing, he remarks that for some time after Theobald's demise, whenever he was taken with "some peculiarly poignant memory of Theobald's transcendent illusions and deplorable failure, [he] seemed to hear a fantastic, impertinent murmur, 'Cats and monkeys, monkeys and cats; all human life is there!'" (232). Given the logic of the story, we may surmise that in the long run it makes little difference whether one devotes one's life to an impossible ideal of absolute realism and fails even to begin its painterly formalization or whether one fabricates animal burlesques of human activity with nary a worry about realistic mimetic verisimilitude: either way, it is the mimetic aspiration that gets brutalized in the end, as it is revealed to be the very stuff of human *bêtise*. By way of such paradoxes, James confronts his great precursor Balzac in "The Madonna of the Future," carving out a place for his postromantic prose by pushing the romantic aesthetic of the absolute to its parodic breaking point. A deceptively complex tale, "The Madonna of the Future" offers a gently subversive critique of the logical and practical impasses of aesthetic formalism. By writing a tale of an artist who cannot begin to formalize his work as a result of a sublime desire for an unbreachable absolute, James opens a space for his post-Balzacian writing.

Notes

1. Although it is perhaps unwise to quibble with as assiduous a reader and writer of French as James, I would suggest a briefer, more direct translation of Balzac's legendary phrase: "to compete with the civic register."
2. In the preface to *Roderick Hudson,* James famously insists on the overwhelming vastness of the social: "Really, universally, relations stop nowhere, and the exquisite problem of the artist is eternally but to draw, by a geometry of his own, the circle within which they shall happily *appear* to do so." James goes on to remark the sublime challenge of such a task: "a young embroiderer of the canvas of life soon began to work in terror, fairly, of the vast expanse of that surface, of the boundless number of its distinct perforations for the needle" (260–61).
3. Slightly earlier in this paragraph, Kant remarks, "Everyone must allow that a

judgment on the beautiful which is tinged with the slightest interest, is very partial and not a pure judgment of taste."

4. Although there is little doubt that Theobald and his story revise Balzac's tale, Philip Grover has suggested that James's painter has another antecedent: he points to the painter Tebaldeo in Musset's arch-Romantic *Lorenzaccio*. See Grover, 24.

5. For a psychoanalytic and philosophical reading of Balzac's great tale, see Bresnick.

Works Cited

Auerbach, Jonathan. *The Romance of Failure: First Person Fictions of Poe, Haw-thorne and James*. New York: Oxford University Press, 1989.

Bresnick, Adam. "Absolute Fetishism: Balzac's 'Unknown Masterpiece.'" *Para-graph* 17.4 (1994): 134–51.

Grover, Philip. *Henry James and the French Novel*. New York: Harper, 1973.

James, Henry. "Honore de Balzac." 1875. In *The Art of Criticism: Henry James on the Theory and the Practice of Fiction*. Ed. William Veeder and Susan M. Griffin, 59–90. Chicago: University of Chicago Press, 1986.

———. "The Lesson of Balzac." 1905. In *The House of Fiction: Essays on the Novel*. Ed. by Leon Edel, 60–85. London: Hart-Davis, 1957.

———. "The Madonna of the Future." In *The Tales of Henry James*. Ed. Maqbool Aziz. 2:202–32. Oxford: Clarendon, 1978.

———. Preface to *Roderick Hudson*. 1907. In *The Art of Criticism: Henry James on the Theory and the Practice of Fiction*. Ed. William Veeder and Susan M. Griffin, 259–70. Chicago: University of Chicago Press, 1986.

Kant, Immanuel. *The Critique of Judgment*. Trans. James Creed Meredith. Ox-ford: Clarendon, 1952.

Praz, Mario. *The Romantic Agony*. Trans. Angus Davidson. 2nd ed. New York: Oxford University Press, 1950.

Weber, Samuel. *The Legend of Freud*. Minneapolis: University of Minnesota Press, 1982.

Jeraldine R. Kraver

ALL ABOUT "AUTHOR-ITY"

When the Disciple Becomes the Master in
"The Author of *Beltraffio*"

I

ALTHOUGH NOT FREQUENTLY DISCUSSED, when it is, "The Author of *Beltraffio*" (1884) is considered among Henry James's "tales of the literary life" (Edel, 143).[1] A handful of critics have focused upon the role of the narrator in "*Beltraffio*." Some dismiss him as merely an observer of the events of the weekend—for example, Frank Kermode, who explains that the conflict between the Ambients "called for an observer" (13), or Joseph Warren Beach, who characterizes the narrator as "an observer not concerned personally, or but slightly concerned, in the incidents recorded . . . simply the narrator and interpreter of all that we are offered" (68–69). Sara S. Chapman identifies him as "the first of James's meddlesome narrators" (29).[2] However, to dismiss the narrator as a mouthpiece for James or as a mere "meddlesome" observer is to neglect a character whose actions within the story he tells are key if we are to understand both the events of the weekend and the place of the "Author of *Beltraffio*" among James's master-disciple stories.

Three decades ago, Donald H. Reiman and James Scoggins engaged in a spirited debate concerning the role of the unnamed young American visitor who narrates "The Author of *Beltraffio.*" Reiman, suggesting that the story "[raises] the question of the reliability of narrators in Jamesian fiction," concludes that the narrator of *"Beltraffio"* is unreliable, in part, because he fails to recognize his complicity in the tragic events of his visit. The visitor is, Reiman argues, "the prime mover in the tragedy," and his fateful actions are the result of his "limited sensibility which can grasp only the superficial aspects of his master's doctrine" (505, 507). The disciple, in effect, misunderstands or distorts the message of the master and therein lies the seeds of tragedy. Taking issue with this interpretation, Scoggins argues that in Reiman's essay the young American "is made responsible for too much" and Mark Ambient for too little. Suggesting that, because there is no calculation in the narrator's actions, he is a Jamesian "fool" (266–67), Scoggins defers to James, who explains: "In themselves nothing, fools are the very agents of action. They represent the stupid force of life and are the cause of trouble to the intelligent consciousness" (quoted in Scoggins, 266). Scoggins seizes upon the symbolic significance of Ambient's name and contends that, by creating an "enveloping atmosphere . . . in which events take place and the characters are defined," Ambient effectively authors the tragic events: it is the master, not the disciple, who is to blame.

Central, then, is the degree of the narrator's culpability. Scoggins suggests that he is manipulated by Ambient and that this at least mitigates his guilt. Reiman contends that the narrator has misunderstood Ambient's doctrine and, as a result, in his determination to "force upon [life] the arbitrary, formal patterns of [art]," he authors the tragic events of the tale (507). Such an "either-or" choice ignores the true complexity of James's narrator and, hence, the brilliance of the tale.

To understand the nature of the narrator's role in "The Author of *Beltraffio,*" we must discern just how "present" he is in the story that he tells. As Gerard Genette neatly explains in *Narrative Discourse,* although "absence [from a narrative] is absolute . . . presence has degrees" (245). In classifying first-person narrators, Genette distinguishes between two types: a narrator who is absent from the story he tells, what Genette terms a *heterodiegetic* narrator, and a narrator who is present in the story he tells as a character, a *homodiegetic* narrator. However, because "presence has degrees," within this latter type he distinguishes two variants: the narrator as observer or witness, referred to as a *homodiegetic narrator,* and the narrator as the hero of his narrative, an *autodiegetic narrator*. The complexity of *"Beltraffio"* rests in two opposing views of the narrator's relationship to the text: the narrator's belief in his status as a mere witness to the events versus the narratee's realization that he is, in fact, the central character in the story he narrates. Essentially, the narrator and the narratee assign different levels of importance to the narrator's role in the story. Thus, there are two stories to *"Beltraffio"*: one told by the narrator and one that the narratee must discover. For the narrator, only by maintaining his status as witness (a variant of the homodiegetic narrator) can he minimize his role in the tragic events of his stay with the Ambients. As narratees, once we realize that the narrator is a central actor in the tragedy (hence an autodiegetic narrator), only then can we recognize the twist in the master-disciple relationship that is at the core of James's story.

The diligent reader must observe the "observer" in order to assess how his vision of his role in the story affects his narration. James's narrator clearly has an emotional and psychological investment in his particular version of the events that he narrates. Examining the narrative voice in *Beltraffio* reveals a pattern of deception that is central to James's tale. This deception informs not simply the American visitor's story but also the relationship he seeks to form with his narratees, what Genette calls "the narrating situation." Central to the narrating situation is "the narrator's orientation towards the narratee—his care in establishing or maintaining with the narratee a contact, indeed, a dialogue" (255). Establishing such a contact involves the narrator's "acting on" (256) the reader, and, in *Beltraffio*, the relationship that the narrator establishes with the narratee is vital to his deception. The narrative pose that he assumes is designed to "act on" the narratee, and the narrator depends upon the narratee's acceptance of him as a witness as part of his attempt to deny culpability.

II

As the narrator presents the story, "The Author of *Beltraffio*" is a morality play. The young American visitor recounts the struggle between the pagan Mark Ambient and his puritan wife, Beatrice, for the soul of their innocent young son, Dolcino. He perceives Ambient as a sensualist, an advocate of "the gospel of art" whose call for art for art's sake is "a kind of aesthetic war-cry" that the narrator altogether embraces ("The Author of *Beltraffio*," 30). Beatrice Ambient is "in no great intellectual sympathy" with her husband

and, the narrator concludes, seeks to stifle his creative life force in the form of his artistically perfect son.

The attentive reader quickly realizes that Ambient is not quite as committed to his aesthetic gospel as the narrator thinks and as the narrator apparently is. As a result, it is the narrator and not Ambient who tends to view all the mundane elements of life in terms of art. He notes, for example, that Ambient's house "is like one of his pictures" (39) and explains: "It was not the picture, the poem, the fictive page, that seemed to me a copy; these things were the originals and the life of happy and distinguished people was fashioned in their image" (33). The narrator's devotion to Ambient (he has read *Beltraffio* five times in three years and has enshrined the author's portrait on his mantel) results in a distorted vision both of Ambient and of his aesthetic. The American visitor fails to recognize that, beyond a few bohemian tendencies, Ambient is without any obvious signs of the devout aestheticism with which he credits him: "he was addicted to velvet jackets, to cigarettes, to loose shirt collars, to looking a little disheveled" (32). In fact, Ambient appears quite conventional: he chats about chrysanthemums with the vicar's wife—a "superficial communion" that surprises the narrator, who views Ambient's writings as implying "so much detachment from that institution" (36); he has an "extreme dread of scandal" (48); and he reads England's periodical institution, *The Observer*.

An important aspect of Ambient's character, one the narrator fails either to recognize or to comprehend fully, is his realization that, in order to survive, life must be a series of compromises (thus, his ability to chat amicably with the vicar's wife). This is especially true in his relationship with his wife; as he explains to his visitor, "'The difference between us is simply the opposition between two distinct ways of looking at the world'" (58). Despite such oppositions, Ambient indicates that the couple has come to accept their disagreements and differences.

This philosophy of compromise informs both Ambient's literary and personal life. Discussing his work, Ambient remarks that he now recognizes that his earlier works were limited by his youth and his inexperience with "Life": "'It isn't till one has been watching her [Life] for some fifty years that one finds out half of what she's up to. Therefore one's earlier things must inevitably contain a mass of rot'" (56). Ambient attempts to explain what he has learned, but the narrator either misunderstands or ignores Ambient's new wisdom:

"I want to be truer than I've ever been. . . . I want to give the impression of life itself. No, you may say what you will, I've always arranged things too much, always smoothed them down and rounded them off and tucked them in—done everything to them that life doesn't do. I've been a slave to old superstitions."

"You a slave, my dear Mark Ambient? You've the freest imagination of our day!" (56)

Perhaps, at one time, Ambient believed that life unfolds in an artistically perfect order, but no longer. He tells his young visitor, "My dear fellow, if you could see the surface I dream as compared with the one with which I've to content myself" (57). His eager listener fails to arrive at the same conclusion and cannot understand Ambient's assertion that in his next work he will try to capture life's "peculiar trick": "'This new affair must be a golden vessel, filled with the purest distillation of the actual. . . . When I see the kind of things Life herself, the brazen hussy, does, I despair of ever catching her peculiar trick'" (56).[3] The narrator's limited sensibilities can only grasp superficially Ambient's meaning and message. Although Ambient can reflect back upon his early work as flawed, the narrator tells us that "now," at the time of the narrative and "with his riper judgement," he still admires *Beltraffio* "as much as ever" (29).

The young American, completely misunderstanding Ambient's mature statements about the mimetic function of art, interprets his desire to write a fiction that is closer to "Life herself" as a desire to have a life that imitates the perfection of art, and he tells us, "Mark Ambient revealed to me more and more the consistency of his creative spirit, the spirit in him that felt all life as plastic material" (57). It is the narrator's misguided goal of making Ambient's imperfect life a reflection of his perfect art that sets into the motion the tragedy of "The Author of *Beltraffio*."[4]

III

The narrator's effort to create for Ambient a world that reflects the perfection and beauty of art is a destructive one that culminates in his urging Beatrice to read her husband's work. He well knows, having been told by Gwendolen, Ambient, and Beatrice herself, that Beatrice disapproves of her husband's work. Gwendolen is quite clear in her description of Beatrice's response to Ambient's work: "'she has a dread of my brother's influence on the child. . . . It's as if it were a subtle poison or a contagion—something that would rub off on his tender sensibility when his father kisses him or holds him on his knee. If she could prevent Mark from even so much as touching him'" (53). Indeed, Beatrice has asserted that she would rather send her son early to heaven than expose him to what she believes to be the pagan, even immoral, content of her husband's writing. Nonetheless, the narrator continually goads and provokes her, urging her to view Ambient's work more favorably. When she does finally read her husband's work, she responds as she herself had predicted: denying her son medical attention, she effectively kills him. Or does she?

Whether the narrator takes any responsibility for the events of the weekend, and the extent to which he does so, is central to determining his relationship to the narrative. In narrating the story of his visit with Ambient, the young American consistently minimizes his own role. By denying the magnitude of his part in the tragedy, he seeks to maintain the posture of observer. By establishing himself as a disciple of the master storyteller Ambient and aligning himself so completely with (his mistaken sense of) Ambient's notions of art, the narrator's actions, even his interferences, seem in accordance with Ambient's own desires. Here, the narrator's failure to understand the mature Ambient is critical because despite Ambient's protests, the young American continues to perceive the author of *Beltraffio* as desiring a perfection in life that mirrors the perfection of art. And he assumes the intrusive task of seeking to make it so.

In order to minimize his role in the tragedy, the narrator must emphasize his status as a disciple. He describes himself as an "undisguised disciple" who, during his conversations with the "master," strove to prove "I was worthy to listen to him" (65, 47). An aspiring writer, in the moments before the fateful delivery of the manuscript to Beatrice, he wanders in Ambient's study, wondering whether "I might learn to write as well as the author of *Beltraffio*" (69). By establishing himself as a disciple, the narrator seeks to lose himself in Ambient's shadow and thereby to minimize his own presence and influence (hence, his responsibility). This enables him to portray himself as an observer of events. Only if we accept the narrator's vision of himself as observer can we concur with his vision of his role in the tragedy as a minor one—that he is a mere extension of the real hero and prime mover, Mark Ambient. However, once we recognize the magnitude of the narrator's misapprehension and his subsequent actions, we not only question his perception, but also assess blame.

The moment that the narrator places the manuscript into the hands of Ambient's reluctant wife, his relationship to the story changes. Explaining his actions, the narrator writes that he had a "vision of reconciling Mrs. Ambient with her husband, of putting an end to their ugly difference" (67). This might be a logical artistic resolution to the Ambients' troubled marriage; however, it is a resolution that Ambient himself would reject. Earlier Ambient had remarked, "'I've always arranged things too much, always smoothed them down and rounded them off and tucked them in—done everything to them that life doesn't do'" (56). Nonetheless, the narrator, confusing the relationship between life and art, tries to force upon the Ambients' life the formal perfection of art. No longer simply an observer of events, the young American becomes a central actor: in the language of Genette, he can no longer pretend to the witness variant of the homodiegetic narrator; he has become an autodiegetic narrator.

By refusing to assume responsibility for his integral role in the tragedy, the narrator's interpretations of events are ultimately unreliable. At the time of Dolcino's death, he rejects any insinuation that he might be in some way responsible. When Gwendolen observes that, as Dolcino lay dying, Beatrice "'held his hand in one of hers . . . and in the other—what do you think?—the proof-sheets of Mark's new book," the narrator's response is an angry one: "'What has that to do with it? I don't understand you. Your accusation is monstrous'" (76).[5] Recalling the events later, the narrator remembers not the significance of Gwendolen's observation but rather a "vulgarism" in her speech:

> "In the other [hand] what do you think?—the proof-sheets of Mark's new book! She was reading them there intently: did you ever hear of anything so extraordinary? Such a very odd time to be reading an author whom she never could abide." In her agitation Miss Ambient was guilty of this vulgarism of speech, and I was so impressed by her narrative that only in recalling her words later did I notice the lapse. (73)[6]

Even upon reflection, the narrator fails to realize his own role. Although he reveals that, when Gwendolen first related these events, he was "impressed" by her narrative, he quickly shifts the focus from the proof-sheets to Gwendolen's vulgar lapse in an attempt to divert attention from his role in the tragedy. He is clinging desperately to his pose as a homodiegetic narrator.

As readers, however, we recognize the narrator's role and his guilt. By urging Beatrice to read the manuscript, he becomes a prime mover in the tragedy. And despite his attempts to suggest that Gwendolen Ambient is erratic, her assertion that "'It was the book that finished [Beatrice]—it was that decided her,'" is precise. Even Beatrice's own words when she collects the manuscript implicate the visitor; she tells the young American, "'I mean to take *your* advice'" (69, emphasis added). Nonetheless, the narrator persists in trying to distance himself from the tragic event. A curious example of just how far he will go in order to retain control of the narration occurs when Gwendolen relates her encounter with Beatrice in Dolcino's sickroom. Initially, it is Gwendolen who relates the details of the event; however, after the reference to the proof-sheets and the narrator's remark about Gwendolen's "vulgarism," Miss Ambient does not resume her narrative. Rather, the narrator continues her story and, for the first time in his narrative, relates the details of an event at which he was not present: "Mrs. Ambient had looked up from her reading with her finger on her lips—I recognised the gesture she had addressed me in the afternoon—and, though the nurse was about to go to rest, had not encouraged her sister-in-law to relieve her of any part of her vigil" (73). Having usurped the narrative from Gwendolen, he then proceeds to dispute her conclusions about Beatrice's actions. Gwendolen suggests that some change must have taken place that compelled Beatrice to deny her son necessary medical attention; the narrator's conclusion is quite different:

> This was the moral of Miss Ambient's anecdote, the moral for herself at least. The moral for me, rather, was that it *was* a very singular time for Mrs. Ambient to be going into a novelist she had never appreciated and who had simply happened to be recommended to her by *a young American* she disliked. (73, second emphasis added)

Two very important things occur in this passage. First, the narrator shifts all possible blame to Mrs. Ambient and her negligence of the gravely ill child. Second, in seizing the narrative from Gwendolen, he removes himself from the events completely by referring to himself as "a young American." By offering us a third-person account of the events in Dolcino's sick-chamber, he effectively reduces the importance of the message by denying it a first-hand rendition; he also ensures that there is no hidden accusation in the narrative. Retaining the narrative privilege is central to the American visitor's view of himself as an observer, thus he refuses to relinquish the narrative privilege even to one who was present at the actual event. Indeed, he becomes the one who announces, with proper sympathy, that Dolcino's state "was far from reassuring" (73).

Immediately after his conversation with Gwendolen, the narrator increases the distance between himself and the event and the reader and the event by shifting from story time to narrative time: "I must be sparing on the minor facts and the later emotions of the sojourn—it lasted but a few hours—and devote but three words to my subsequent relations with Ambient. They lasted five years—till his death" (73). By inserting, at this odd point, the mention of Ambient's death five years after the story, the narrator again deflects our attention away from Dolcino's death and the influential manuscript toward his role as a master storyteller in control of the narrative.

Not only do these machinations deflect any possible assignment of guilt to the narrator; they also provide an opportunity for the narrator to fulfill his wish to "write as well as Ambient" (69). In telling of the event, the young American is elevated from disciple to master. It is a movement that effectively parallels the difference between the homodiegetic and the autodiegetic narrator. By giving the manuscript to Mrs. Ambient, the young American visitor has, in effect, produced a story he can both narrate and direct.[7] Ambient and his family become characters in two stories contrived by the narrator. Most clearly, they are characters in the story of the events observed by the homodiegetic narrator during his thirty-six-hour visit. However, they are also characters in a tale that features the autodiegetic narrator, whose act of giving the manuscript to Mrs. Ambient directs the course of action in the story of the visit. By involving himself intimately in the events of the weekend, the narrator provides himself with a story to tell. The disciple has become empowered, has switched roles with the master and wrested "author-ity" from the master storyteller, Ambient, all the while pleading his innocence to the narratee.

The narrator's authority over Ambient is both literal and figurative, for more than simply creating a situation that provides him with a story to tell, the narrator exerts actual control over Ambient. For example, despite Gwendolen's assessment of the gravity of Dolcino's situation, his own assertions that "the boy's state was far from reassuring," and Beatrice's refusal to permit the doctor access to the sick child, the narrator prevents Ambient from going to his son, advising him that "Women know; women should be supreme in such a situation. Trust a mother" (73, 75). He then remarks upon his success at calming the agitated Ambient, boasting "I tried to soothe and comfort him, and marvelous to relate, I succeeded" (75). By distracting Ambient, the narrator's actions again serve to seal young Dolcino's fate. Even after the tragic events of the weekend, the narrator has extracted a promise from Gwendolen that she will not mention the manuscript to her brother and will thus allow Ambient to "form his own theory of his wife's conduct" (77). The manuscript becomes "a secret from him which I guarded to the end" (73). The narrator thus denies Ambient access to the complete story of the tragedy and suggests, in a most patent case of denial, that had Ambient known that Beatrice possessed the manuscript, he would hold himself accountable for the death of Dolcino. Conveniently, this guilty secret protects the narrator as much as (if not more than) it does Ambient.

At the conclusion of his narrative, the narrator coyly calls upon the reader to pass judgment on his actions: "And, apropos of consciences, the reader is now in a position to judge of my compunction for my effort to convert my cold hostess. I ought to mention that the death of her child in some way converted her" (77). By characterizing Beatrice as "cold," he places the burden of responsibility on her. His mention of her ultimately reading her husband's work is at best boast and at worst tasteless. In suggesting that the narratee ultimately judge his conduct, the narrator depends upon the relationship that he has sought to create with his reader. Throughout his narrative he presents himself as a "rash youth" (31), a "juvenile pilgrim" (45), and "a candid young American" (47). He tells us that Ambient and Beatrice both recognized his youth and inexperience and that Ambient had commented on more than one occasion that "'You're very young after all'" (43). By presenting himself to the narratee as one who is both young and naive, the narrator seeks to avoid any blame for the events of the weekend. He explains, "looking back . . . I find it important to avoid the error of appearing to have at all fully measured the

situation" (41). His success in presenting his case depends upon how successfully he has "acted upon" the narratee. If we accept the American visitor as
witness and disciple, then we do not portion blame. If, however, we are *not*
"acted upon" but recognize his role as author of the events—both figuratively
and literally—we know that the cost of his story was a dear one, the "perfect
little work of art," the Ambient's young son, Dolcino.

Notes

1. Edel suggests that the story is less about literature and the literary life than it
   is about "a difficult marital situation" (143). The idea originated, Edel
   explains, with James's learning of the relationship between J. A. Symonds and
   his wife. She, like Beatrice Ambient, disliked her husband's writings.
2. W. R. Macnaughton, in his brief discussion of the tale, also suggests the importance of the narrator. Commenting upon all Jamesian narrators, he notes that
   they are "rarely 'disinterested' either in the sense of being emotionally unin-
   volved in the actions which they describe, or able to judge these actions with
   anything approaching total objectivity" (145).
3. The "golden vessel" will of course be central to James's 1904 novel *The Golden
   Bowl*. Here, its symbolic significance prefigures that of the later and more
   famous golden bowl. For a thorough discussion of the significance of the bowl,
   see Mary Cross.
4. Ironically, it is Beatrice Ambient who warns that one should not cultivate and
   enjoy beauty without extraordinary precautions. Mark Ambient explains,
   "'she is always afraid of it, always on her guard'" (59). Ultimately, she will be
   accurate in her fears because it is the narrator's urge for artistic perfection—
   not only for Ambient, but for himself—that inspires his destructive acts.
5. Although the narrator perceives Gwendolen's words as an accusation, there is
   really little hint of any such accusation in them. Indeed, in the discussion that
   precedes any mention of Ambient's book, Gwendolen characterizes the
   young American as "sympathetic" (75). The narrator does, however briefly,
   wrestle with a sense of his own guilt. Considering Gwendolen's words, he
   remarks, "they came amazingly straight, and *if* they did have a sense I saw
   myself too woefully figure it in. Had I been the proximate cause?" (76, emphasis added). All too quickly he concludes that Gwendolen's observations are
   part and parcel of her habitual posture as a prophet of ill who does not possess
   any depth of insight: "I am now convinced that she hadn't in her nature those
   depths of unutterable thought which, when you first knew her, seemed to
   look out from her eyes and to prompt her complicated gestures" (44). Ultimately, he remarks to Gwendolen, "'You're a very strange woman and you

say incredible things'" (76). To dismiss Gwendolen Ambient thus is to dismiss her observations and their implied accusations.

6. As Dr. John T. Shawcross so graciously explained to me, the "vulgarism of speech" to which the narrator refers is relatively insignificant: "What is being said is that 'she could never tolerate,' but 'abide' has come to mean that only in later times. It should mean only 'await' or 'remain' (from 'bide' as in 'bide' one's time). The narrator first misses the 'lapse' because it is so commonplace. . . . There are many such vulgar uses of words that James would cite: 'caliber' (to mean 'worth' when it really means only the diameter of the bore of a gun) or 'enormous' (to mean 'large' when it means something like 'elephantine')."

7. In terms of Genette's notions, by giving the manuscript to Mrs. Ambient, the narrator "produces" a story in which the Ambient family is victimized. In this way, he provides himself with a story to tell. His actions during the course of the weekend will greatly alter the lives of the Ambients and create an opportunity for him to author a story about the "author of *Beltraffio*."

Works Cited

Beach, Joseph Warren. *The Method of Henry James*. New Haven: Yale University Press, 1918.

Chapman, Sara S. *Henry James's Portrait of the Writer as Hero*. New York: St. Martin's, 1989.

Cross, Mary. *Henry James's The Contingencies of Style*. New York: St. Martin's, 1993.

Edel, Leon. *Henry James: The Middle Years*. New York: Avon, 1962.

Genette, Gerard. *Narrative Discourse: An Essay in Method*. Ithaca: Cornell University Press, 1980.

James, Henry. "The Author of *Beltraffio*." In *Eight Tales from the Major Phase*. Ed. Morton Dauwen Zabel, 29–78. New York: Norton, 1958.

Kermode, Frank. Introduction to *"The Figure in the Carpet" and Other Stories,* 7–30. New York: Penguin, 1986.

Macnaughton, William R. *Henry James: The Later Novels*. Twayne's United States Authors Series 521. Boston: Twayne, 1987.

Reiman, Donald H. "The Inevitable Imitation: The Narrator in 'The Author of *Beltraffio*.'" *Texas Studies in Language and Literature* 3 (1962): 503–9.

Scoggins, James. "'The Author of *Beltraffio*': A Reapportionment of Guilt." *Texas Studies in Language and Literature* 5 (1963): 265–70.

Shawcross, John T. E-mail to the author, 5 March 1997.

Jeanne Campbell Reesman

"THE DEEPEST DEPTHS OF THE ARTIFICIAL"

Attacking Women and Reality in "The Aspern Papers"

In "The Art of Fiction," Henry James tells us that we should strive to make ourselves people "on whom nothing is lost" for "the effort really to see and really to represent is no idle business in face of the constant force that makes for muddlement" (167). What is one's "duty" in trying "really to represent" (173)? As Martha C. Nussbaum puts it, James's characteristic "ellipses and circumnavigations" of language and thought work to convey not truth but "the lucidity of his characters' bewilderment, the precision of their indefiniteness" (149). In the end, the greater the narrative ambiguity the clearer the sense of a fundamental truth, just out of reach. "The Aspern Papers" (1888, 1908) enacts in a particularly dramatic way James's problem of knowledge: as the devious editor/narrator moves closer and closer to the truth he hopes the papers of long-dead poet Jeffrey Aspern will reveal, the reader finds that "truth" grows more and more elusive, for the narrator's notions about reality and those conveyed to his reader are really quite opposite, centering on how the word is or is not made flesh. In this tale of the "publishing scoundrel," the poet Aspern, and the two women who guard "The Aspern Papers," "the word" and "the flesh" are gendered values that reveal a rupture in reality. Through his metaphorical conquest of the female body and its attendant spaces (the house, the garden, the cabinet), the narrator homoerotically hopes to penetrate the truth about his idol, to find the words that will resurrect the idealized Aspern to "reality." Yet "The Aspern Papers" is about a *relational* model for knowledge; it repudiates singularity as a mode by making the singular conquests of the narrator laughable, lonely, and tragic. As in "The Beast in the Jungle," truth in "The Aspern Papers" lies where—or in whom, that is—the protagonist least expects to find it, and it comes too late.

The narrator's polarizing of word and body, male and female, could be described through a Lacanian model (particularly as extended by theorists of *écriture féminine*) that defines the Word (the literal) as a "masculine" value and the Unconscious ("babble") as a prelinguistic "feminine" state. But James's work sharply resists Lacanian theorizing: in "The Aspern Papers" the literal is the realm of the female body, and the male body is, in contrast, unreachable, undefinable, and unsayable. The story's attempts at reality interrogate art and its engendered nature. Which is "real" in the story? That is to say, which, for James, is art: woman in her actuality or man in his elusiveness? The dynamics of language and sexuality in this story recall Hawthorne's experiments in *The Blithedale Romance* and elsewhere as they reenact the anxieties about authorship Hawthorne and James typically address directly in their prefaces. But "The Aspern Papers" dramatically engenders and sexualizes these authorial anxieties.

James tells us in his preface that it was easy for him to recover the impulse behind the writing of "The Aspern Papers." The "seeking fabulist" was like Columbus finding San Salvador: the idea for the story was placed by Nature "to profit" by the "fine unrest" of the explorer of literary history "because he had moved in the right direction for it—and also because he knew, with the encounter, what 'making land' then and there represented" (v). James relates the story of Jane ("Claire") Clairmont, half-sister of Shelley and for a time the mistress of Byron. James heard that she was still living in Florence and had been pursued by a fanatical admirer of Shelley, who hoped to obtain her papers. James's project attempts to recover her, the poet and his poetry, the last century, Italy itself. But Italy James calls "the great historic complexity" where "penetration fails"; we only "scratch at the extensive surface" and "hang about in the golden air" (vi). And so, he continues, "I delight in a palpable imaginable *visitable* past—in the nearer distances and clearer mysteries," a "common expanse" that is "firm and continuous" with our own (x). Thus arises the impulse to make the survivor from the past a New England poet.

Having argued that "nine tenths of the artist's interest in [facts] is that of what he shall add to them and how he shall turn them" (ix), James goes on to justify what some might see as a less than romantic choice of nationality. Fearing he would be accused of having "no warrant" for creating a distinguished American poet of the last century, James insists upon the reality of his creation as "the tone of the picture wrought round him," a

> harmless hocus-pocus under cover of which we might suppose him to have existed. . . . This tone is the tone, artistically speaking, of "amusement," the current floating that precious influence home quite as one of those high tides watched by the smugglers of old might, in case of their boat's being boarded, be trusted to wash far up the strand the cask of foreign liquor expertly committed to it. (xiii–xiv)

There may be no "'link' with reality," James concedes, but "only a link, and flimsy enough too, with the deepest depths of the artificial: the restrictive truth exactly contended for" (xiv). He concludes this defense by admitting that it all hinges on the question of "whether or no the false element imputed would have borne that test of further development which so exposes the wrong and so consecrates the right. My last word was, heaven forgive me, that, occasion favouring, I could have perfectly 'worked out' Jeffrey Aspern" (xiv).

Like most of James's fiction, "The Aspern Papers" is about what kind of knowledge of people is essential and what kind is misleading, or worse. What we are to know of the "truth" versus the "artificial," as the question is framed in the preface, is the particular concern of James's tales of art and artists. The preface raises the major issues that the text will confront: resurrecting the past, using and abusing literary history, questioning the nature of art and the desire for art. It is important to see these impulses together; when Wayne Booth faulted "The Aspern Papers" for not adequately living up to its goal of bringing back the past, he lost sight of the story's complexity.[1] James's choice of an American poet only creates the *illusion* that because this past is closer, it can perhaps be restored. The land discovered by Columbus is a puzzling metaphor for the past because it is, after all, the "New" World, and what Columbus and other early explorers thought they had found was wrong. They had, from a modern perspective, found much more. Truth presented itself in the guise of accident, as James's smugglers also allow the vagaries of the tide to carry their treasure ashore: the waves are the medium for "truth," not the cask itself. James is drawing a complicated analogy to his art, to the "deepest depths of the artificial." Certainly if Jeffrey Aspern *had* been further "worked out," the story would have lost the charm of this epistemological "hocus-pocus," but it would have revealed some sexual secrets James treats with brilliant ambivalence.[2]

The Ground of the Feminine

As land is often portrayed metaphorically as a woman's body (Michie, 8), the site of discovery in the tale will consistently be presented in terms of female spaces. Women's bodies metaphorically provide access to the "truth," to the "past," to the "real thing," as James was fond of calling it, but in the end it seems this *medium* takes over from what is to be "discovered," the "content" of art. James's narrator desperately wishes to shake Juliana Bordereau's hand so that he can have touched Aspern's, but her own immediacy entirely escapes him until he is discovered rifling through her cabinet. Tina's humanity continues to haunt him; but even in the end he never treats with her as though she is real. Besides the elusive Jane Clairmont, another woman seems to have been a "medium" for the story, and she is identified in the preface by James in direct connection with the present/past "land" of America, an embodiment of the "visitable past": James's Great-Aunt Wyckoff, whom he calls in *A Small Boy and Others* an "image of living antiquity." Leon Edel speculates: "Was she, the Small Boy wondered, really, as she seemed, so tremendously old? And the old man, writing this reminiscence, mused that 'It was the Past that one touched in her, the American past of preponderant unutterable queerness'" ("'The Aspern Papers': Great-Aunt Wyckoff and Juliana Bordereau," 394).[3]

Edel offers us another important feminine source in his biography. He relates that James went to Venice in February 1887 to be the guest of Katherine De Kay Bronson. His rooms he found uncomfortable, but he wrote to William Dean Howells that he was glad to be there, as he had been chased from Florence "by the amiable effort that was manifested to retain me" expended by his friend Constance Fenimore Woolson, fellow writer and grand-niece of James Fenimore Cooper (quoted in Edel, *Henry James: The Middle Years,* 226–27). Woolson was James's neighbor, and she never lost an opportunity to seek out his company. (As became clear following her suicide in 1894, she harbored feelings for James that he not only did not share but had willfully ignored.) His stay in damp, cold Venice was unhappy: besides not writing, he became very ill with jaundice. He was persuaded to return to Florence by Woolson's offer to rent him rooms in her villa, the Brichieri. He wrote happily of his breezy hilltop, calling Florence "as beautiful and somehow as *personal,* and as talkative! as a lovely woman. . . . As soon as I can stop making love to it I shall go back to England" (quoted in Edel, *Henry James: The Middle Years,* 214). Woolson he (ambivalently) called his *padrona,* and he downplayed their living under the same roof and occasionally taking their meals together, and, as the above quotation indicates, transferred the feelings she expected to the "hilltop" instead. He "accepted with pleasure," Edel notes, "all the attention and admiration Fenimore gave him and offered a kind of disinterested and aloof affection in return" (226–27). In short, his egotism took as a matter of course the devotion of a lonely, deaf older lady. Perhaps he was drawn to her by her connection with Cooper (who would have been in Italy during Jeffrey Aspern's sojourn); during James's own "Italian phase" he wrote some of his best tales, including "The Aspern Papers." Edel draws a clear parallel: "The narrator [of "The Aspern Papers"] may have told himself 'I had not given her cause'—but the reader knows that he had" (226). James was to hold himself guilty of the same sort of "total failure in awareness" after Woolson's suicide. James carefully retrieved all the letters and papers that mentioned him. Edel retraces his efforts to escort Woolson's relatives to her villa to dispose of her possessions: "His task was opposite the narrator's in 'The Aspern Papers': To make away with, rather than preserve, certain documents, must have been a part of his goal in undertaking what at best was an irksome and lugubrious task for a busy man of letters" (365).[4]

In their female characters, Hawthorne and James explore what Helena Michie has identified as the "uneasy and shifting place at the intersection of the body and its representation." In the indisputably male tradition, women's bodies are made to be metaphors for the unknown; "they are not so much vehicles of epistemological consolation as they are sources of change, disruption, and complication." The tradition of defining male sexuality as "obvious, uncomplicated, and iterable" makes female sexuality "mysterious." Women are both unwilling "metaphors for the unknowable, and metaphors for metaphor, their bodies figures of figuration" (7–8). The tradition from Locke to Derrida links them with metaphor and rhetoric, with language and textuality. Both Claude Lévi-Strauss and Gayle Rubin have identified women as only "signs" or "tokens" of male culture, but an equally long and complex tradition identifies woman with the body and the physical. Thus woman is *both* language and body, as Michie argues: "the representation of the female body is no simple case of *différance,* but a historically aggravated instance of the violent and marked separation of signifier and signified" (7–8). Though, like Hawthorne, James inverts sex roles not so much to comment on the nature of society but to comment on the nature of representation and reality, his gendered "comment" *is* fundamentally also a criticism.[5] The narrator of "The Aspern Papers" attempts to separate signifier from signified, but the Bordereau women resist his effort to draw such lines, and their sheer physicality as well as their words carry out their resistance.

Thus it is not to Hawthorne's male heroes that we should look for precedents in analyzing "The Aspern Papers," but rather to his women: Hester, Hepzibah, Priscilla, Zenobia, Miriam, all keepers of secrets and all guardians of "truth" itself. The secrets kept by Juliana and Tina Bordereau are both literary and personal, but the narrator is so obsessed with his private truth, Jeffrey Aspern, that he misses not only the humanity of Tina but also her own "Aspern" secret, the possibility that she is Aspern's daughter. Is he merely suffering from a profound romanticism, or is there something else going on that complicates the narrator's use of the women to get at Aspern? What is going on is that James's narrator is not being honest about his own befuddlement. He is specifically in conflict with his homoerotic attraction to Aspern, sublimated through the women. James's ambivalence toward this sort of attraction has been the subject of extensive critical speculation.[6] Robert McLean has surmised that the narrator's inability in this story to understand and appreciate people (especially women) parallels his inability to evaluate art. To the end, says McLean, he is "unaware of the drama in which he was involved" (266). Yet James's ambiguity will naturally take this absence of self-awareness and make it the theme itself, as in "The Beast in the Jungle" and many other tales. Such an absence pointedly summons that which is being willfully ignored, or, at the least, misunderstood, which is precisely the pressing reality of the women. Dimmesdale, Hollingsworth, and Coverdale are models for the self-deluding narrator of "The Aspern Papers."

Though he does not give us his name, the narrator reveals himself to us—"Hypocrisy, duplicity are my only chance" (12)—with an unsettling honesty, but in the end, predictably, he does not know his own mind: like Coverdale in the conclusion of *The Blithedale Romance,* who suddenly discovers that he is in love, "With Priscilla!" the narrator confesses, "I can scarcely bear my loss—I mean of the precious papers" (143). As he prepares to "pounce" on Juliana, his prey (the Aspern papers) escapes. The narrator wavers wildly in the last sections of the story between making up his mind to marry Tina and feeling disgust with her, rejecting her as a "ridiculous pathetic provincial old woman" (92). But what he really misses is not Juliana, or Tina, or even the papers, but himself. As Bernard Richards observes, the narrator

> spin[s] out romances from his brain and comes to assume, without subjecting them to sufficient skepticism, that they are true.... The trouble is that the narrator works on hypotheses, many of which satisfy his sense of aesthetic rightness, and they are promoted almost immediately to certainties. (125)

Not only does the narrator express what Sister M. Corona Sharp calls a "condescending opinion of women's lack of speculative intellect," only to be "singularly punished by the experimental, opportunistic, and self-interested practical intellect of Juliana, and the simple-mindedness of her niece" (23), but his dismissal of them loses him everything. Tina is punished by her confider more than James's earlier confidantes, but she is both dupe and avenger; she and her "women's world" that defeats the narrator clearly connect her with the later characters May Bartram and Milly Theale.

So it is not surprising that when the narrator insists upon seeing Juliana as a "grinning skull" or as merely pecuniary in her interests, he forgets that she and he join in their hero worship of Jeffrey Aspern, that they share both their romantic and their mercenary natures, that they are in a sense competitors. He cannot see her as Aspern's lover. He says, "One doesn't defend one's god: one's god is in himself a defence" (5), but he does defend Aspern from the charge of treating Miss Bordereau badly: "I judged him perhaps more indulgently than my friend; certainly, at any rate, it appeared to me that no man could have walked straighter in the given circumstances" (7). Indeed, Jeffrey Aspern is the "property of the human race" (63), and it is up to the narrator to assure that the property is made available to those who understand how to "frame" it, not just to Juliana. The narrator believes that sometimes "battered and tarnished frames . . . were yet more desirable than the canvases themselves" (16), that is, the "framing" that editors do, but he believes he acts "in the service of art" (43). He sees the women of the old Venetian palazzo acting only against it. " 'You talk as if you were a tailor,' said Miss Bordereau whimsically" (90).

The conflicts and confusions of knowledge in "The Aspern Papers" present themselves between appearance and reality, beginning with Juliana and Tina's hidden abode, with its garden, dark hallways, and meandering *salas*. The women are living like nuns walled up in their cells ("We've no life," Tina says [36]); the narrator says that "I had never met so stiff a policy of seclusion; it was more than keeping quiet—it was like hunted creatures feigning death" (40). Next we are arrested by the elder Miss Bordereau's unseen eyes, and images of seeing and not seeing pervade the text. In contrast to the plain Tina's "candid" and "clear" face (17), Juliana's face is hidden by the mask of a "horrible green shade" she wears over her eyes (23). When they are eventually revealed, her eyes hit the narrator "like the sudden drench, for a caught burglar, of a flood of gaslight; they made me horribly ashamed" (118). The narrator had earlier "turned [his] eyes . . . all over the room, rummaging with them the closets, the chests of drawers, the tables" (105), but earlier still Juliana cried out to him and Tina, " 'I want to watch you—I want to watch you!' " as they converse (99). In the end the narrator *is* watched, is exposed—and he never comes near seeing the treasure. Even when he tries to contemplate the miniature of Aspern that hangs above his writing-table, he is confronted with the "one look" Tina gives him after turning her back on him for good (143).

Watching in the Garden

James's "green shade" is of course an allusion to Andrew Marvell's poem "The Garden," which includes the stanzas:

What wond'rous Life in this I lead!
Ripe Apples drop about my head;
The Luscious Clusters of the Vine
Upon my Mouth do crush their Wine;
The Nectaren, and curious Peach,
Into my hands themselves do reach;
Stumbling on Melons, as I pass,
Insnar'd with Flow'rs, I fall on Grass.

Mean while the Mind, from pleasure less,
Withdraws into its happiness:
The Mind, that Ocean where each kind
Does streight its own resemblance find;
Yet it creates, transcending these,
Far other Worlds, and other Seas;
Annihilating all that's made
To a green Thought in a green Shade

        · · ·

Such was that happy Garden-state,
While Man there walk'd without a Mate:
After a Place so pure, and sweet,
What other Help could yet be meet!
But 'twas beyond a Mortal's share
To wander solitary there:
Two Paradises 'twere in one
To live in Paradise alone.

James's allusion carries sexualized nuances of vision and knowledge, blindness and ignorance. Believing that Juliana represents "esoteric knowledge; and this was the idea with which my critical heart used to thrill" (44), the narrator is surprised and taken aback that "the divine Juliana" seems most interested in "pecuniary profit" (71). Seeing her this way removes her as an opponent worthy of Aspern himself. Yet, as earlier noted, he does not see that he also is interested in "gain": he has laid out for himself a certain sum he is willing to invest in obtaining the papers, and when he feels that Juliana is asking too much he plans to "make it up by getting hold of my 'spoils' for nothing" (28). Even when he fantasizes about "touching" Jeffrey Aspern by touching her hand, it is only to seal their "contract"; when Miss Bordereau refuses, Tina's hand is the substitute. The narrator does not know he is perhaps more nearly shaking Aspern's hand at that moment! Knowledge is again the center, and Juliana's green shade is the mate to his blindness. It is the most arresting ocular image of all in the story, and one is led to ask of it: what is it she does not want to see after all these years? Her shameful past? The present, with its new pretender to Aspern's hand? Marvell's use of "green shade" speaks of the pleasures to be had in the garden by Man who "there walk'd without a Mate." One who can "live in Paradise alone" is truly blessed: the Mind's "green shade" has withdrawn, "annihilating" all the world to find its peace. Behind the green shade, Juliana's peace, if we can call it that, is disturbed by the narrator, who, like a modern Adam, speaks of "work[ing] the garden"; he will resurrect the past and its "Mate." Yet while his true desire is to walk without women, his punishment is to walk alone.

If the "green shade" represents the characters' problems of vision, the garden is an image of isolation that brings to bear complex relations among gender, history, and art; it is an enclosed tangled world that gives the narrator his pretext for entering the female space of the Bordereau palace to cross, in effect, the border between himself and the sexualized past that he treasures. He is the would-be penetrator of the past, and he must pass through the women who block his access to his beloved Aspern—he hopes with as much dispatch and as little money as possible. The narrator's practicality extends to his rationalizations of his actions, his attempted rifling of the house, of Juliana's cabinet, of her "drawers." Sexual conquest and editorial conquest are here conjoined, and the descriptions of the rooms, the cabinet, and the garden that goes from barren to flower-bedecked speak for the sexuality (and for him, whorishness) of these spaces. The narrator says he "would batter the old women with lilies—I would bombard their citadel with roses. Their door would have to yield to the pressure when a mound of fragrance should be heaped against it." In the moonlit garden, "its wild rich tangle, its sweet characteristic Venetian shabbiness" (45) transformed by him into an orderly, cultivated English garden, he tries to make love to Tina, but the imagery all points to his revulsion at her, potential ally though she may be. He notes the "odour" of the canal in the "breath" of the garden, and the air around him trembles—

he thinks of Romeo's vows "when he stood among the thick flowers and raised his arms to his mistress's balcony" (52). But, as he quickly reminds himself, "Miss Tina was not a poet's mistress any more than I was a poet." Furthermore, the windows of the palace at which he gazes in the dimness are, for him, Jeffrey Aspern's windows, not a "mistress's." When Tina approaches him out of a dark bower, he fears that she will throw herself in his arms, but "I hasten to add that I escaped this ordeal and that she didn't even then shake hands with me" (53).[7] In a curious section at the end of part 4, James speaks directly to the reader, engendering past and present, Europe and America. The narrator sits in the arbor recalling that Aspern's works portray Juliana as one who "had not always adhered to the steep footway of renunciation." Her "perfume of impenitent passion" induced "her singer" to betray her by "giv[ing] her away, as we say nowadays, to posterity" (48). He muses upon the nature of beauty preserved in art, and upon the romance of going abroad in the 1820s that has disappeared in the present age, when "photography and other conveniences have annihilated surprise" (49). Aspern is prized by the narrator for his Americanness *and* for his residence in Europe, for being new and being old:

> a period when our native land was nude and crude and provincial, when the famous "atmosphere" it is supposed to lack was not even missed, when literature was lonely there and art and form almost impossible, he had found means to live and write like one of the first; to be free and general and not at all afraid; to feel, understand and express everything. (50)

Twice-fallen Juliana, once intemperate and American and now old, ugly, greedy, and European, is unhappily the link to the happy past. Fitting, then, that she was twice-killed in the service of art, given away to "posterity" the first time, and to futility the second.

The narrator knows Juliana has "everything" (78), and he wants everything, but he does *not* want to link Aspern her lover and Aspern the poet. That these "witches" (7) and "Maenads" (10) block his access to Aspern seems unfortunate, but he is prepared to deal with them and to preserve Aspern's godlike purity. One way to deal with the "subtle old witch" (93) and her niece is to cast them in desexualized language (a "ridiculous pathetic provincial old woman" [137] and a "piece of middle-aged female helplessness" [126]). The other route to dominating her is to make love. But he carries through neither design. Thus he is unprepared for Tina's careful burning of the papers at the end and even less for her subtle transfiguration into forgiveness, a worse blow, perhaps, than the loss of the papers. Trying to preserve the pure Aspern from the impure women, he has become, in his eyes, their next victim.[8]

Thus, women in the story are the keepers of the literal object as they are the keepers of the secrets of their bodies. The males, the love objects, in contrast, are out of reach. As suggested in the beginning of this essay, we can best appreciate the significance of their difference if we cast it as a reversal of the Lacanian model of the Law of the Father (symbolic order and language) versus the Feminine, the realm of the Imaginary (the unsaid, the Unconscious, prelinguistic babble) as extended by Hélène Cixous, Luce Irigaray, and Julia Kristeva. Though these critics obviously have important things to say about how women's bodies mediate transactions among men, here they are less than helpful. Nowhere to be found in "The Aspern Papers" are Lacan's notion of phallogocentrism, Cixous's nonunitary women's body and language, Irigaray's rehearsal of the fluidity of feminine discourse, or Kristeva's definition of the prior semiotic realm versus symbolic order and the disruption of the "nameable" by the semiotic realm. The narrator wants the *truth,* the poetry attached to Aspern's body he keeps trying to touch. Lacan tells us, "The Other with a big 'O' is the scene of the Word insofar as the scene of the Word is always in third position between two subjects. This is only to introduce the dimension of Truth, which is made perceptible, as it were, under the inverted sign of the lie" (*Speech,* 269). Yet Lacan's assigning of language and power to the Father has led his critical adherents to underestimate the literal role of female characters, their *possession* of words (small "w," no "the") and their function as "others" who are not erased into "Otherness." Juliana and Tina refuse to be linguistic substitutes or precursors for Truth, and the narrator is not, in the Lacanian sense, able to seize the papers, the Word, the phallus, and unmask the women as powerless (phallus-less).[9] The male artists and editors in "The Aspern Papers" resoundingly fail in the quest for the unrealizable fetish (the papers, the phallus), which remains absent in the (female) world of the story. Because he cannot admit the nature of his desire, he is no match for the women who can and have.[10]

Orpheus and Eurydice

The reversals and revisions of gender, especially as they relate to James's notions of art, are nowhere more richly invoked in "The Aspern Papers" than in a powerful allusion that occurs early in the story and continues to reverberate throughout: the reference by the narrator to the fate of Orpheus. Musing on how "[h]alf the women of [Aspern's] time, to speak liberally, had flung themselves at his head, and while the fury raged, the more that it was very catching, accidents, some of them grave, had not failed to occur," the narrator thinks how this man's poet was victimized like "'Orpheus and the Maenads!'" (7).

As told by Appollonius of Rhodes, Virgil, and Ovid, Orpheus was the son of one of the Muses, a prince of Thrace, and the foremost musician on earth. Everything animate and inanimate followed him. Orpheus journeyed on the hunt for the Golden Fleece and played for Jason and the Argonauts, who rowed to the rhythm of his music on a violent sea; later, he saved them from the Sirens by drowning out their music with his own. He fought both the fury of the sea and the temptation of woman. But he became the passionate lover of Eurydice, whom he lost to death when she was stung by a viper on her wedding day. His final role is solitary wanderer. Orpheus journeyed into Hades in search of her, and he was able to charm even the ruler of Hades and his queen, who released Eurydice with the proviso that he not look back at her until they were safely out of Hell. However, concerned for her safety, he turned back, and so lost her forever. Ovid includes the information in book 10 of *The Metamorphoses* that not only did "Orpheus refuse to sleep with women" after Eurydice's death, but that

> Meanwhile he taught the men of Thrace the art
> Of making love to boys and showed them that
> Such love affairs renewed their early vigor,
> The innocence of youth, the flowers of spring. (275–76)

Orpheus became a solitary wanderer and was finally torn apart by the Maenads. His head was thrown into a river whose course he had once had the power to alter by his music.

The Maenads were frenzied, female Dionysians; because they were so aroused by Orpheus and because he was so oblivious of their desire, devoting himself exclusively to his lyre, they punished him with death. The head of the gentle musician washed ashore on the island of Lesbos, where the sorrowing Muses buried it. To this day, the myth relates, nightingales sing more sweetly there than anywhere else on earth.

A compelling myth that speaks to a theme of love versus mortality, the Orpheus story introduces into "The Aspern Papers" connections between eroticism, creativity, and the sense of the irrecoverable past. Its details offer striking parallels (Venice is named for Venus, goddess of love; and perhaps the "Asp" in Aspern echoes the viper that bites Eurydice on her wedding day). But, more importantly, it illuminates the major themes of "The Aspern Papers" by casting the characters in mythic roles: the narrator as Orpheus come to resurrect his love, Juliana and Tina as, respectively, the (past) dead Eurydice and Tina as the (present) living Eurydice. Juliana goes to her death, but Tina is a woman newly alive with desire and with, perhaps, an awakened sense not only of desire but of self outside desire—a failure, true, but a failure who achieves a kind of self-knowledge still out of reach of the narrator.[11]

If Jeffrey Aspern is the narrator's real love, the two women are at once doorways to the past that contains Aspern *and* obstacles to it; positioned at the portal, they are the real and present guardians of the shadowy unreality he occupies and is.[12] James's web of liminality allows the myth to transform itself in contact with the characters so that they trade roles freely. If the narrator shares features of Orpheus, we still first tend to assign that role to Aspern himself, the divine poet; as we have seen, Juliana calls him "a god," and the narrator worships him. But in an important early scene the narrator calls Aspern back from death:

> I had invoked him and he had come; he hovered before me half the time; it was as if his bright ghost had returned to earth to assure me he regarded the affair as his own no less than as mine and that we should see it fraternally and fondly to a conclusion. . . . "Poor dear, [Aspern cautions,] be easy with her; she has some natural prejudices; only give her time[:]"

"'Strange as it may appear to you she was very attractive in 1820. Meanwhile aren't we in Venice together, and what better place is there for the meeting of dear friends?'" (42–43). In recasting Aspern as the longed-for Eurydice— this time successfully summoned—and the narrator as Orpheus, the scene clearly points to the homoerotic relationship the narrator unconsciously desires. Person characterizes this scene as a compelling instance of how "the narrator's imagination moves through Juliana to Aspern," dissociating her from him. Desirous of taking Juliana's place with Aspern, the narrator is disappointed because "[t]he ideal Aspern becomes increasingly less visible, even imaginatively, as the narrator's plot forces him to confront and acknowledge the real Aspern" ("Eroticism and Creativity," 22).

As Aspern recedes, the narrator is more and more the victim in his own mind, more and more the Orpheus character. He wanders around Venice dazed and agitated following Juliana's death; falling asleep exhausted and resigned, he wakes even more determined than ever to go back into Hell to get the letters. Evan Carton catches this sense of the narrator in his brief analysis of the Orpheus image, which for him comes into play by "drawing art, sex, and money, land and sea, Aspern and the narrator, sublime self-possession and violent self-division" together. To set things going, Carton points out, the narrator rows his gondola up to the "dead wall" of the Bordereau palace on a quest for closely guarded treasure. What is at stake, however, is not the treasure, but self-possession, as the narrator's language reveals when he speaks of "my desire to possess myself of Jeffrey Aspern's papers" (120). Carton concludes:

> At the end Miss Tita's[13] desperate proposal and "flood of tears" produce in the narrator what, in the preface, James's own incautious "immersions" in the "too numerous, too deep, too obscure, too strong" impressions of Italy are said to produce in himself: "a troubled consciousness that heaves as with the disorder of drinking it deeply in." The narrator renounces the papers in order to save himself from immersion in a union with Miss Tita. But then, in one last significant reflexive phrase, he resolves: "I would not unite myself and yet I would have them." With these words, the narrator sentences himself to the fate of Orpheus, for, in a sense, the unified self and the possessed papers can only be one and the same. (120)

Though he is not dismembered, the story ends with the disintegration of the papers, "one by one," as Tina puts it. To make matters even more complex, Tina and Juliana also share aspects of Orpheus, Juliana speaking to the dead and Tina literally turning her back on the narrator at the end.[14]

In the end, James's own sexuality is reflected in the engendering of art in "The Aspern Papers."[15] In his letters, one finds him attributing intensely erotic sensations to reading texts, even in terms of religious ecstasy, as when he praises one of Morton Fullerton's "celestial letters." In his study of eroticism and creativity, Michael A. Cooper is particularly interested in how James's tales of authors and their worshipful admirers "sail the deepest waters of James's fantasies," how the tales of literary life offer the "conceit of the author's having two incarnations, one physical and one textual, each separately capable of being known, interacted with, and mistreated." When the focus is on the author's physical body, the tales "delineate the material conditions enhancing the production of literature and the impediments blocking it." When the focus is on the author's corpus,

> the tales assume it represents 'the quality of the mind of [its] producer' and from there derive rules of engagement with it that mirror ordinary bodily etiquette, for instance that one should feel as embarrassed about reading work of the author's not prepared for publication as one should feel spying on him undressed at home. (69)

Cooper offers as examples "The Author of *Beltraffio,*" "The Private Life," "The Right Real Thing," "The Death of the Lion," and "The Figure in the Carpet," where he notes love triangles of disciple, author, and author's (usually female) lover, with unconscious homosexual attraction present for the two male characters. He could have added "The Aspern Papers," for, as he observes, "Where the threat of the author's death does not constitute one of the events of the plot, it is usually because he dies before they fairly commence. His having died supplies the condition that starts them congealing" (71). In "The Aspern Papers," the death of Jeffrey Aspern becomes the pretext upon which the narrator takes up his assault on the author's textual remains, through the bodies and minds of the two women who guard the tomb. As Cooper notes, "when the incarnation alone persists, even loyal disciples, who would normally distinguish between savoring the author's works and barging into his home, have trouble distinguishing legitimate from illegitimate approaches to and expressions of desire for him" (71). This is certainly the case, as I have argued, with the sexual/textual transgressions of the narrator of "The Aspern Papers."

A second means to understanding James's complicated sexuality is to be found in his use of and identification with female characters and male characters who embody feminine impulses. John Carlos Rowe comments that

> [w]hat makes James's identification with women so successful . . . is his tendency to transform the social psychology of women into the formal esthetics as well as the psychohistory of the author. Even as this identification marks James as singularly sympathetic to the larger so-cial issues of feminism, it is based on James's own inevitable defense: that process by which Henry James, the Master, *uses* feminism, uses the "other sex" as part of his own literary power for the sake of engender-ing his own identity as Author. (91)

William Veeder has taken up Rowe's statement and argued that James as-signed pleasure to the Feminine: men are only safely masculine as long as they "sit tight and expose nothing." Yet James was alive to experience, "affirmative in his responses" and "resilient before setbacks" as well as "daring as an artist" (137); he evolved this freedom through his identifica-tion with the figure of the female orphan, an active woman who can resist anxiety and embrace pleasure.[16] Certainly readers have long responded to James's "masculine" women, women who act, who are in the end able to take responsibility for their lives, even when they fail: Daisy Miller, Isabel Archer, Maggie Verver. At the same time, the femininity of his male pro-tagonists has given them resiliency and wisdom; one thinks especially of Lambert Strether and his education in "Living." But the living is more of-ten done by the women, who dare to "live" in ways the male characters al-most never discover. It is difficult to think of a better example of James's sexual and artistic web of desire than "The Aspern Papers," with its engen-dering of artistic values and roles, its female orphan(s), its pairs—male/male, female/female, male/female—vying for pleasure. No wonder James speculates at the end of his preface on what the *thorough* "working out" of Jeffrey Aspern would have revealed: it would be the narrator's homoerotic attraction to Aspern that the women are designed to prevent and sublimate, and it would reveal too much of the Master at the back of it all.

At the beginning of "The Aspern Papers," the narrator tells Mrs. Prest that he has never been intimate with a woman; she accuses him of being sexually impotent, of "lacking boldness" with the Misses Bordereau, of being unable to push through "a breach ... big enough to admit an army" (38). Juliana also questions his "manly taste" (70) when she says that men do not grow flowers for pleasure. Perhaps this is a clue to the mystery of the narrator's involvement, obsession, rather, with "The Aspern Papers" because it forecasts his search for both his sexuality and for art, for love synonymous with the act of perception. That he does not find either brings us back to the floating cask from the preface, that marvelous image of the fortuitousness of art. We are left only with Orpheus' head washing up on the shore (and preserved in the little miniature frame): as he lost Eurydice by wanting to *see* her, so the narrator of "The Aspern Papers" loses two loves and any claim he has to be a lover of art. Seeking Jeffrey Aspern, the narrator rejects as irrelevant the two women who physically embody his spirit and so loses any hope of finding that spirit within himself.

Notes

I wish to thank David McWhirter of Texas A & M University for his illuminating reading of an earlier version of this essay and Susan Streeter of the University of Texas at San Antonio for editorial assistance.

1. Booth faults James's narrator for not carrying out one of the two stated aims of the story: the narrator does satisfy the first, to reveal his unscrupulous quest and ultimate frustration, but not the second, to evoke the "visitable past," the romantic backdrop for the plot that makes up James's poetic atmosphere. Separate voices (ironic comedy and romantic evocation) conflict, and the story that results is a blur (354–64).

2. Like Hawthorne, that other sojourner in Italy, James in his preface complicates and creates layers of temporal and authorial distance but involves the reader in the writer's epistemological process. With such attention to the anxieties of the author in the preface and tale, perhaps rather than having Byron or Shelley as the model for Jeffrey Aspern, James had Hawthorne in mind. "The Aspern Papers" echoes the sexual and moral conflicts of *The Blithedale Romance;* James's narrator resembles Hawthorne's Coverdale with his drive to pry into the secrets of others, as well as Westervelt, with his sly manipulations. *Blithedale* joins "Rappaccini's Daughter" and its garden as precursors to "The Aspern Papers"; and whereas "The Minister's Black Veil" points to Juliana's green shade, the hidden papers of *The House of the Seven Gables* forecast Aspern's papers. The haunted pasts of the "Custom-House" preface and of *The Scarlet Letter* itself also resonate in "The Aspern Papers." James's peculiar combination of gothicism and irony is certainly a Hawthornian device. But

the most significant debt "The Aspern Papers" owes to Hawthorne is its meditation upon the nature of reality in art, the same question that haunted Hawthorne's Coverdale, Prynne, Holgrave, and Donatello.

Several critics have emphasized the Hawthornian connection. Hutner
finds that like James's, Hawthorne's novels and stories "chronicle the experience of confronting the half-known life that the right application of sympathy
can illuminate or change." In works such as "The Aspern Papers," we are reminded of Hawthorne's "'deeper psychology,' the anxiety of interpreting history, the play of language, the distinction between novel and romance, the
ambiguities of social life and dangers of intimacy" (189). Scharnhorst argues
that "The Aspern Papers" was inspired by James's research into the life of
Nathaniel Hawthorne for his 1879 monograph in the English Men of Letters
Series: "Like Hawthorne, Aspern (the surnames distantly echo) was a strikingly handsome man and a prominent New England romantic author." Like
Hawthorne he died prematurely, and his fame declined after his death for a
decade or so. James claimed that Hawthorne was "thoroughly American"
(James, *Hawthorne,* 47), and he has the narrator of "The Aspern Papers" say
that Aspern's muse was "essentially American" (186). James had imagined
how "Hawthorne must have felt" when "he made the acquaintance of the
denser, richer, warmer, European spectacle" in the 1850s (James, *Hawthorne,*
43), while the narrator of "The Aspern Papers" tries to "judge how the Old
World would have struck" Aspern during the first years of his expatriation
(186). More to the point, although James believed that the posthumous publication of six volumes of Hawthorne's private notebooks violated Hawthorne's
request that no one write his biography, he later qualified his misgivings in
writing *Hawthorne.* Scharnhorst interestingly compares Juliana Bordereau to
Julian Hawthorne, Hawthorne's son, who, like Juliana, impeded the investigation of the would-be biographer—having failed to accede to James's request
for more of his father's papers. Juliana declares, "'I don't like critics'" and refuses to help them "'rake up the past'" (213). James portrays Juliana as crassly
pecuniary; Julian sold his father's mementos and manuscripts piecemeal to
collectors and in 1874 published a biography replete with family documents
and disparaging statements by Hawthorne about various contemporaries. Re-
viewers faulted Julian for his bad taste, and James satirizes him directly in *The
Reverberator* (1888). Perhaps it is then the spirit of Hawthorne that rebukes the
narrator at the end of "The Aspern Papers" (211–17).

3. Edel notes that James "cultivated elderly females," such as Fanny Kemble,
"considering them 'windows on the past'" ("Great Aunt Wyckoff," 393). He
expands upon Great-Aunt Wyckoff:

> Henry James, in his own life, had found the most vivid "*visitable* Past" in
> the New York of the 1850's between his sixth and twelfth years. We are

not surprised therefore when we find him explaining, a few lines after his definition of the near-Past, that, in writing *The Aspern Papers,* "I thought . . . it was natural, it was fond and filial, to wonder if a few of the distilled drops mightn't be gathered from some vision of, say, 'old' New York . . . could a recognizable reflection of the Byronic age, in other words, be picked up upon the banks of the Hudson?" (394)

Looking for the romance of this past, James turns to his great-aunt:

> The Small Boy, in Manhattan of the mid-century, had reached over, making his little arm as long as possible and caught the old lady out of the 18th century with her 'large face in which the odd blackness of eyebrow and of a couple of other touches suggested the conventional marks of a painted image . . . so rich and strange is the pleasure of finding the past—the Past above all—answered for to one's touch, this being our only way to be sure of it. (394–95)

4. James moved the Jane Clairmont story from Florence to Venice, an ironic choice given the Woolson parallel. The Venetian setting may also be seen as a comment on the fluid and shifting nature of reality in the story—a statement on the dual nature of America James would later convey so fully in *The Ambassadors.* The American scene in "The Aspern Papers" is present and absent; two of the Americans on hand, Juliana and Tina Bordereau, say they "used to be" American, and the narrator implies that he is an American "by chance" (19). Edel describes the appropriateness of Venice to James's view of modern America, given the "chink of ducats" in Venetian history, and as evidenced by James's meditation on the statue of the *condottiere* Bartolommeo Colleoni, the great hero and "would-be pirate," who presumably shared the narrator's "predatory impulses" (Introduction, 10). But it is also characterized by a "queer air of sociability, of cousinship and family life," like a "splendid common domicile, familiar domestic and resonant" ("Aspern Papers," 139–40) not unlike James's New England or New York. "Aspern" itself is the name of the town in Austria where Napoleon had his first defeat (Edel, *Henry James: The Middle Years,* 224).

5. Elizabeth Allen underscores this:

> [T]he importance of central female consciousness in James's novels lies in the development of the conflict of the woman as sign and as self. There is a sense of female potential repressed by the signification of it as part of the feminine, in a manner more intrinsic than definitions of class or occupation. The rendering of woman as object makes her visible and therefore vivid as object of study in the text. (7)

6. Person goes so far as to assert that "many recent scholars . . . have brought

James and James studies out of the closet to the point where we can almost take James's homosexuality for granted" ("James's Homo-Aesthetics," 188). Person is referring to such influential readings of James's life and works as Sedgwick's "The Beast in the Closet: James and the Writing of Homosexual Panic," in which Sedgwick rereads "The Beast in the Jungle" in such a way as to "subject [it] to a change of Gestalt and of visible saliencies"; she interrogates assumed heterosexual male norms previously used to read the story (162). She believes "to the extent that Marcher's secret has *a* content, that content is homosexual" (169). She identifies in James's life a "pattern of homosexual desire . . . biographically unobliterable" (164). Similarly, Kaplan details James's relationships with John Addington Symonds, Jonathan Sturges, Morton Fullerton, Hendrik Anderson, and Jocelyn Persse, among others, and believes these relationships figure in the tales of artists and writers; Kaplan is particularly interested in the literary, epistolary nature of these relationships, in which James seemingly found erotic satisfaction through the sublimation of homoerotic desire into acts of aesthetic pleasure (see especially 452–53). Person himself is interested in how homoerotic desire figures in James's tales, sometimes mediated by women, sometimes "homo-aesthetically through works of art," and sometimes "circulated narcissistically through another man as a self-creating, auto-erotic force" ("James's Homo-Aesthetics," 189). See also Butler's discussion of melancholy as the experience of the loss, not of the desired object, but of the desire (i.e., forbidden homoerotic desire) itself, and see Hall, Martin, and Sarotte for other discussions of homosexuality as it enters James's writing.

7. Gargano writes that "The wealth of omission in the narrator's interpretation of the garden scene suggests a fine case of monomania that makes for comedy." The story's many hiatuses are due to "total self-preoccupation," which also keeps the narrator from noticing the nature of Tina's "vaguely aggressive womanliness." He is a "disappointing" narrator, for "[h]is unconcern . . . is nothing less than amazing" (5–6). But contrary to Gargano's assumption, he *does* notice her "womanliness"—he is repelled by it.

8. Person has argued that the narrator "cannot accept his own sexuality and the sexuality of women" and thus fails in his quest for the papers because he refuses to become "a sympathetic reader of the text he seeks" ("Eroticism," 20). With Tina, he wants the letters without "paying the price" ("Aspern Papers," 25) of being human. The narrator makes a fetish of Aspern, "an introjected object" of his own self who epitomizes success in love and art. But he must censor this image. The narrator remains ambivalent because his behavior divorces eroticism from creativity, "the letters from their meaning" (Person, "Eroticism," 25). When he first meets with Juliana, when she catches him in her cabinet, and when Tina makes her proposal to him, the narrator is chal-

lenged to read his true text but does not. In the discovery scene the nature of the letters is itself closest to being discovered; and, significantly, "it is at the moment of touch that the narrator's movement is interrupted," and he is made "horribly ashamed" (118). As he is about to press the "button" of the cabinet, he is trapped by an acute sense of guilt confronting Juliana's "paralyzing" eyes. Presented with Tina's proposal, he finds his attitude to the papers changes abruptly, as he now calls them a "bundle of tattered papers" and "crumpled scraps" (137) the very thought of which is now "odious" (138). In the end, instead of reading the erotic/creative text he longs for, notes Person, "the narrator sits at his writing desk contemplating an image of Aspern that has not quite achieved its 'mature powers'" ("Eroticism," 29).

Similarly, Stein believes James mocks the narrator as an American Don Juan. As imagery attached to him argues for his rejection of women, so developed his vicarious enjoyment of the imagined eroticism in Aspern's papers. Allusions are made to the Venetian Don Juan, Casanova, and to Lady Hamilton and other famous lovers; all of this shows the narrator's "disordered imagination," his erotic transference, and perhaps even a note of sadism. Inflamed by his passion for Aspern's letters, he has unwittingly acted the role of lover. Because he cannot give up his narcissism, he rejects emotional salvation: "he could not lay aside his mask of self-deception—the love of self of which Aspern was a fetish" (175–78).

Such a view of the women's power and the narrator's weakness makes it ultimately difficult to agree with Rivkin in her study of ethics and representation in "The Aspern Papers." The protagonist is not, as she argues, the victor in this battle of the sexes. I concur that Juliana of the lyrics is "killed" and "resurrected" twice, once in becoming a text and again as she "comes to represent—and thus to resurrect—Jeffrey Aspern himself." But as is the case with several of James's women, especially May Bartram, here the critic is in danger of underestimating their power. Though "wronged," Juliana is not "sublimated into poetry"; she is quite literal and "recoverable," but not the "poetry," not Aspern. No one with Juliana's eyes can really be "sublimated" (139–40)!

9. Homans summarizes Lacan's conception of how representation and gender issues become attached in the process of subjectivity: "The phallus, the first mark of difference, will always stand as the primary signifier, for the apparent owner of the phallus, of the marker of difference, is he who speaks." But woman's absence makes possible the construction of language and culture, for it is precisely "a powerful androcentric myth [that] requires her absence and silence" (6–7, 2, 11). Through a Freudian/Lacanian reading of "The Aspern Papers," Joseph Church envisions Aspern's life and work enabling the narrator to "organize his [life] along a certain 'signifying chain' (Lacan), and thus . . . maintain an adequately satisfactory identity, one that carefully avoids

complications, uncertainties, ambiguities, and women, that might disrupt his sense of himself" (25). The narrator must accordingly get control of language from the women, for as the Lacanian concept of the formation of subjectivity tells us, women inhabit only a "mythic" position behind writing. This misguided effort helps us understand why the narrator calls the women maenads, witches, and sphynxes. "The phallus, one might say, is in the wrong place and he must recover it," says Church (28). To overcome the "phallic woman" is to become her lover and to unmask her castration. As Terry Eagleton has it, the need to seduce and to degrade women is the attempt to negate their power. By this light Aspern and the narrator are guilty of the creation of a fetish, the substitute for the "missing" female phallus, "an object which, by plugging that alarming gap, will block the male's fantasy of his own possible mutilation" (59). "In the absence of woman, the male artists generate one another, their 'figuration' founded on woman's occupying a negative site codified in a 'symbolic' order" (32–33). Despite its insights into the attack on the realm of the female in the artistic process, Church's analysis fails to account for the *literal power* of the Bordereau women.

10. As David McWhirter has pointed out, "Love is made problematical in James's fiction, not by its peripheral importance or absence—as some critics have suggested—but by its insistent and often painful centrality" (5). McWhirter distinguishes between love, which James makes the subject of his final novel, *The Golden Bowl*, and desire, which always remains unfulfilled,

> for it only wants to perpetuate itself *as* desire (as wanting and therefore lacking). . . . Caught in the solipsistic labyrinth of its own endless wanting, desire pursues an impossible dream of escape from the limitations and imperfections of life, especially from the facts of time and death. (6)

"The Aspern Papers" would make an instructive contrast to *The Golden Bowl*, as both are about recovery, but one of desire and one ultimately of love.

11. Crowley stresses that Tina is less the evanescent, transcendent Other than she is a flesh and blood woman with her own needs, which she carefully sets out to gain in the story.

12. Korg's thesis that "The Aspern Papers" do not exist at all, explaining important problems in the text, is suggestive here (378–91). In a different context, Hartsock sheds light on the unreality of Jeffrey Aspern: "If one must single out a thesis for "The Aspern Papers," it is that the past has a continuity and a beauty to which the imaginative man must be sensitive; but he cannot light all his candles for the dead. . . . [H]e must turn at last to seeing and living and loving" (68).

13. "Tita" is the name given in the earlier version of "The Aspern Papers."

14. Boren argues that James's work is best understood in terms of its absent/

present quality of an Other, specifically, an anima figure, "a lyrical, feminine mysticism" that breaks through "only in moments of surprise, shocks of intuitive recognition" that make themselves felt, "even within the limitations of a language that is basically inadequate to the task." She uses Orpheus's recovery and loss of Eurydice as a metaphoric context for this figure, but does not, oddly, discuss "The Aspern Papers," and she accepts Lacan's assignment of language to the Father. Yet she admits, "If language is culture bound, to the extent that an artist like James appropriates and identifies with the 'feminine' stance he also engages in a dialogue with the 'masculine' forms and assertions of that culture." Boren concludes that in James's narrative "the act of perception is analogous to an erotic act of lovemaking" (2–3, 15, 81, 85, 88, 105), but she does not see the lovemaking as directed at Aspern. The use of Lacan is from *Four Fundamental Concepts of Psycho-Analysis,* 2–32.

15. Graham's brilliant and sensitive biographical analysis of how James's formation of (homo)sexual identity (or rather, his failure until late in life to recognize it) is framed both by his complex relationship with his brother William and the turbulent historical context of homosexuality in his day. She is especially effective in delineating some of the possible reasons for his celibacy and the way his sexuality was channeled into his friendships and his art. The patterns she outlines are evident in stories such as "The Jolly Corner" and "The Beast in the Jungle" (see especially 66–68, 74–75, 85–89), but she could also have included "The Aspern Papers."

16. Veeder underlines the importance of the anima to James, noting Leon Edel's remark (quoted in Jean Strouse's biography of Alice James) that

> All his life [James harbored within] the house of the novelist's inner world the spirit of a young adult female, worldly-wise and curious, possessing a treasure of unassailable virginity and innocence and able to yield to the masculine active world-searching side of James an ever-fresh and exquisite vision of feminine youth and innocence. (50)

Similarly, drawing on James's letters, Graham sees the "most persistent feature of James's incorporation of a feminine identity" in his writing as "the extent to which he identified artistic creativity with pregnancy" (73).

Works Cited

Allen, Elizabeth. *A Woman's Place in the Novels of Henry James.* New York: St. Martin's, 1984.

Booth, Wayne C. *The Rhetoric of Fiction.* Chicago: University of Chicago Press, 1961.

Boren, Lynda S. *Eurydice Reclaimed: Language, Gender, and Voice in Henry James.* Ann Arbor: UMI Press, 1989.

Butler, Judith. *Gender Trouble: Feminism and the Subversion of Identity.* New York: Routledge, 1990.

Carton, Evan. "The Anxiety of Effluence: Criticism, Currency, and 'The Aspern Papers.'" *Henry James Review* 10.2 (1989): 116–20.

Church, Joseph. "Writing and the Dispossession of Women in 'The Aspern Papers.'" *American Imago* 47.1 (1990): 23–42.

Cooper, Michael A. "Discipl(in)ing the Master, Mastering the Discipl(in)e: Erotonomies of Discipleship in James's Tales of Literary Life." In *Engendering Men: The Question of Male Feminist Criticism.* Ed. Joseph A. Boone and Michael Cadden, 66–83. New York: Routledge, 1990.

Crowley, John W. "The Wiles of a 'Witless' Woman: Tina in 'The Aspern Papers.'" *ESQ* 22.3 (1976): 159–68.

Eagleton, Terry. *The Rape of Clarissa: Writing, Sexuality and Class Struggle in Samuel Richardson.* Oxford: Blackwell, 1982.

Edel, Leon. "'The Aspern Papers': Great-Aunt Wyckoff and Juliana Bordereau." *Modern Language Notes* 67 (1952): 392–95.

———. Editor's Note to "The Aspern Papers" by Henry James. In *Henry James: Selected Fiction.* Ed. Leon Edel. New York: Dutton, 1953.

———. *Henry James: The Middle Years, 1882–1895.* Philadelphia: Lippincott, 1962.

———. Introduction to "The Aspern Papers." In *The Complete Tales of Henry James.* Ed. Leon Edel. Vol 6. Philadelphia: Lippincott, 1963.

Gargano, James W. "'The Aspern Papers': The Untold Story." *Studies in Short Fiction* 5.1 (1973): 1–10.

Graham, Wendy. "Henry James's Thwarted Love." In *Eroticism and Containment: Notes from the Flood Plain.* Ed. Carol Siegel and Ann Kibbey, 67–75. New York: New York University Press, 1994.

Hall, Richard. "Henry James: Interpreting an Obsessive Memory." *Journal of Homosexuality* 8.3–4 (1983): 83–97.

Hartsock, Mildred. "Unweeded Garden: A View of 'The Aspern Papers.'" *Studies in Short Fiction* 5.1 (1967): 60–68.

Homans, Margaret. *Bearing the Word: Language and Female Experience in Nineteenth-Century Women's Writings.* Chicago: University of Chicago Press, 1986.

Hutner, George. *Secrets and Sympathy: Forms of Disclosure in Hawthorne's Novels.* Athens: University of Georgia Press, 1988.

James, Henry. "The Art of Fiction." In *The Art of Criticism: Henry James on the Theory and Practice of Fiction.* Ed. William Veeder and Susan Griffin. Chicago: University of Chicago Press, 1986.

————. "The Aspern Papers." In *The Novels and Tales of Henry James,* 12:3–143. New York: Scribner's, 1908.

————. *Hawthorne.* New York: Harper, 1990.

————. *The Letters of Henry James.* Ed. Percy Lubbock. Vol. 2. New York: Scribner's, 1920.

————. Preface to "The Aspern Papers." In *The Novels and Tales of Henry James,* 12:v–xxiv. New York: Scribner's, 1908.

Kaplan, Fred. *Henry James: The Imagination of Genius.* New York: Morrow, 1992.

Korg, Jacob. "What Aspern Papers? A Hypothesis." *College English* 23 (1962): 378–81.

Lacan, Jacques. *Four Fundamental Concepts of Psycho-Analysis.* Trans. Alan Sheridan. New York: Norton, 1976.

————. *Speech and Language in Psycho-Analysis.* Trans. Anthony Wilden. Baltimore: Johns Hopkins University Press, 1968.

Martin, Robert K. "The 'High Felicity' of Comradeship: A New Reading of *Roderick Hudson.*" *American Literary Realism* 11 (1978): 100–108.

McLean, Robert C. " 'Poetic Justice' in James's 'The Aspern Papers.' " *Papers on Language and Literature* 3 (1967): 260–66.

McWhirter, David. *Desire and Love in Henry James: A Study of the Late Novels.* Cambridge: Cambridge University Press, 1989.

Michie, Helena. *The Flesh Made Word: Female Figures and Women's Bodies.* New York: Oxford University Press, 1987.

Nussbaum, Martha C. *Love's Knowledge: Essays on Philosophy and Literature.* New York: Oxford University Press, 1960.

Ovid. *The Metamorphoses.* Trans. Horace Gregory. New York: Viking, 1958.

Person, Leland S., Jr. "Eroticism and Creativity in 'The Aspern Papers.' " *Literature and Psychology* 32.2 (1986): 20–31.

————. "James's Homo-Aesthetics: Deploying Desire in the Tales of Writers and Artists." *Henry James Review* 14.2 (1993): 188–203.

Richards, Bernard. "How Many Children Had Juliana Bordereau?" *Henry James Review* 12.2 (1991): 120–28.

Rivkin, Julie. "Speaking with the Dead: Ethics and Representation in 'The Aspern Papers.' " *Henry James Review* 10.2 (1989): 135–41.

Rowe, John Carlos. *The Theoretical Dimensions of Henry James.* Madison: University of Wisconsin Press, 1984.

Sarotte, Georges-Michel. *Like a Brother, Like a Lover: Male Homosexuality in the American Novel and Theater from Herman Melville to James Baldwin.* Trans. Richard Miller. New York: Anchor-Doubleday, 1978.

Scharnhorst, Gary. "James, 'The Aspern Papers,' and the Ethics of Literary Biography." *Modern Fiction Studies* 36.2 (1990): 211–17.

Sedgwick, Eve Kosofsky. "The Beast in the Closet: James and the Writing of Homosexual Panic." In *Sex, Politics, and the Nineteenth Century*. Ed. Ruth Bernard Yeazell, 148–86. Baltimore: Johns Hopkins University Press, 1986.

Sharp, M. Corona. *The Confidante in Henry James: Evolution and Moral Value of a Fictive Character*. Notre Dame: University of Notre Dame Press, 1963.

Stein, William B. "'The Aspern Papers': A Comedy of Masks." *Nineteenth-Century Fiction* 14 (1959): 172–78.

Strouse, Jean. *Alice James: A Biography*. Boston: Houghton Mifflin, 1980.

Veeder William. *Male Novelists and Their Female Voices: Literary Masquerades*. Troy: Whitson, 1981.

Rory Drummond

THE SPOILS OF SERVICE
"Brooksmith"

As told by what K. B. Vaid calls its "sympathetic first-person narrator" (49), the story of "Brooksmith" goes something like this: Mr. Oliver Offord, a retired diplomat, holds a regular salon at which some of the best conversation in London is to be heard. Brooksmith, Offord's butler and companion, is "the artist" (*Complete Tales,* 8:16)[1] responsible for creating the atmosphere in which the good talk flourishes, and he enjoys the results as much as any of the guests. When Offord sickens and dies, the salon comes to an end, and the butler is forced to leave the house with no savings and only eighty pounds as a memento from his late master. Unable to reconcile himself to homes in which elegant conversation has no place, he goes through a series of disappointing employments before finally disappearing, presumably to his death. "He had indeed been spoiled" (8:31) is the narrator's conclusion.

Most of the tale's few commentators have agreed with the narrator's version of the butler's fate.[2] One of the shortest of James's often protracted short stories—representing for its author a pleasing example of what could be done with the "single incident"—"Brooksmith" has been reported as

69

among the least complex: a charming character study (Wagenknecht, 51–52) whose moral is the importance of knowing one's place in a society organized on strict class lines. But, as Susanne Kappeler both states and demonstrates with reference to "The Aspern Papers," however convincing a narrator's account of events, for "readers of Henry James, it is only the beginning" (23). In "Brooksmith," no less than in the more celebrated cases of "The Aspern Papers," "The Turn of the Screw," or *The Sacred Fount,* the first-person narrative falls short of being the whole story and requires skepticism on the part of the reader. This is all the more the case because, given the tale's clear concern with issues of class, to rely solely on the narrator is to endorse a privileged point of view and to risk arriving at only the most reactionary of readings. It is because he takes the narrator to be "sympathetic" that K. B. Vaid argues that "it will not do to read into the tale strictures against a class society" (53–54). But is this not precisely the view a member of the leisured classes would want to have circulated?

Two critics have seen in "Brooksmith" more than is provided directly by the narrator. In his recent biography of James, Fred Kaplan calls the tale "a subtle indictment of the British class structure" (367) but does not elaborate. In a much earlier book, however, S. Gorley Putt does pursue a similar line of thought, writing of the tale that "there is acid social criticism, below the surface, of the perfunctory interest of the well-to-do in the private lives of their devoted servants who, when their patron's sun sets, just creep away to die. So far from branding James as a Tory, 'Brooksmith' is a wonderful advertisement for Social Security" (281). Questioning what others have taken for granted—the integrity of the "Brooksmith" narrative—Putt produces a reading unusual in the whole body of James criticism in its political specificity. Until very recently, indeed, critics have been reluctant to bring to bear on James's work any but the broadest of historical or economic forces. Their emphasis has been on aesthetics, and imaginative working-class characters like the anonymous telegraphist of "In the Cage" or Mr. Gedge of "The Birthplace" have more often been seen as versions of the artist than as members of particular professions and social groupings. It is in this spirit that Leon Edel writes of Brooksmith that he is "really an artist" (8) and Vaid refers to him as a "special case" (54). But this tendency, which isolates art from the rest of life and suppresses the frictions inherent in the English class structure, is precisely what "Brooksmith" is about. Though the butler does express some of the aspirations attributed to him, the narrator's decision to view him as the "artist" of the Offord salon is only slightly justified by any verifiable facts. The fancy is maintained less because its subject warrants it than because, by characterizing Brooksmith as exceptional, his social superiors evade the awkwardness and responsibility that accompany the business of employing servants. For the narrator, Offord, and others of their class, there is something to be gained—"spoils," to use a pun James favored (see Kappeler, 37, for the use of this pun in "The Aspern Papers")—from regarding Brooksmith as "spoiled."

The case of "Brooksmith" is complicated by the fact that James's own accounts of the tale seem in accord with the narrator's viewpoint. In the preface to volume 18 of the New York Edition, he recalled the germ for the tale as the anecdote of a housemaid who had "tasted of conversation and been spoiled for life" (*Literary Criticism,* 1282), and he referred elsewhere to the "hapless butler Brooksmith, ruined by good talk, disqualified for common domestic service by the beautiful growth of his habit of quiet attention, his faculty of appreciation" (*Literary Criticism,* 1096). Moreover, the narrator's romanticized portrayal of the butler represents a tendency James himself occasionally indulged. In his 1879 essay about Hastings, "An English Winter Watering Place," for instance, the young James visits a hotel and describes a waiter who "had been in the house for forty years and who was not so much an individual waiter as the very spirit and genius, the incarnation and tradition of waiterhood. He was faded and weary and rheumatic, but he had a sort of mixture of the paternal and the deferential, the philosophic and the punctilious, which seemed but grossly requited by a present of a small coin" (*Collected Travel Writings,* 228). And in "The Great Good Place" (1901), a story with which "Brooksmith" has much in common, George Dane's retreat from the world is figured, in part, as a move from the "merciless ... domestic perfection" of his servant Brown, to the sanctuary's "soundless, simple service ... a triumph of art" (*Complete Tales,* 11:13, 32). The romantic view of service in this tale is partly responsible for its utopian mood, something also attributed to "Brooksmith," which Q. D. Leavis called "a whimsical expression of James's social ideal, and nothing more" (223).

But James was equally capable of expressing a democrat's impatience with those who, underprivileged, nevertheless act only to serve and to reinforce the English social hierarchy. His preface, for instance, to "In the Cage" bemoans the fact that "you may starve in London, it is clear, without discovering a use for any theory of the more equal division of victuals, which is moreover what it would appear that thousands of the non-speculative annually do" (*Literary Criticism,* 1169). It can be no part of a "social ideal" that Brooksmith suffers precisely this fate despite, or even because of, the imaginative speculation attributed to him. Rather, the butler's fate is to be regarded in much more pragmatic terms. A note James made on 18 October 1895 reveals his conception of the English class system:

> the idea of the picture, fully satiric, in illustration of the Moloch-worship of the social hierarchy in this country—the grades and shelves and stages of relative gentility—the image of some succession or ladder of examples, in which each stage, each "party" has something or someone below them, down to extreme depths, on which, on whom, the snubbed and despised from above, may wreak resentment by doing, below, as they are done by. They have to take it from Peter, but they give it to Paul. Follow the little, long, close series—the tall column of Peters and Pauls. (*Complete Notebooks,* 136)

Though no published story corresponds directly to this scheme, it does accurately characterize the version of English social order operating in "Brooksmith." The butler may have stepped up a few rungs from the position into which he was born, but his glimpses of what he calls the "fireworks" (8:26) do not amount to a substantial bridging of the social gap. Rather, his climb only confirms the existence of a ladder for those at the bottom of which the narrator has little but contempt. The narrator's eulogy on Brooksmith serves to reinforce class division, the sense of the tale being that romanticized views of the working class are one of the means by which the status quo is maintained.

As a character study, "Brooksmith" owes a lot to literary tradition. Vaid writes that "the English butler is something of a myth in literature" (54), and the neglect the tale has suffered may be due, in part, to the fact that the mythology is familiar to the point of cliché. In his excellent book *The Servant's Hand: English Fiction from Below,* Bruce Robbins complains that the same can be said of all literary representations of domestic staff:

> The problem is that, forced into the mold of character, servants reveal

so little worth investigating. Criticism on the subject is like a stroll down an endless gallery of look-alikes: each portrait is the same all-too-loyal retainer, sharing his master's conviction of natural hierarchy and aiming complaints only at his own somewhat ambiguous place in it. (34)

It is Robbins's argument that this consistency goes hand in hand with fiction's historical failure to depict the working classes with any great degree of accuracy or sincerity. By portraying servants in such a way, writers operate a safety valve: including in their fictions characters who are nominally of the working class but who serve rather than oppose the "natural hierarchy." This device has the effect of diffusing class-based tensions. "The presence of servants," as Robbins put it, "signifies the absence of the people" (27). For James, however, the borderline status of servants makes them an appropriate means of tackling class issues. His attempts to introduce the "people" into his fiction in *The Princess Casamassima* (1886) were not successful. In "Brooksmith," he comes at the subject from the other side, disclosing in detail, not the anarchist plots of a discontented mass, but the assumptions by which the privileged classes keep hold of power. It is as the representative of the working class within the leisured world that Brooksmith appeals to James.

In a further point, Robbins recalls that the word "character" was once used to designate what we now call a reference: the communication between employers about the merits or otherwise of prospective staff by which their working lives were decided. Characterization, in this sense, is an exercise of power. The relevance of this argument to "Brooksmith" is clear, particularly given the narrator's involvement in the butler's attempts to find a suitable position after Offord's death. James voices the generic conventions that govern the characterization of servants in order to expose the power such stereotypes give to those of the dominant class. The seemingly benign "character" given to Brooksmith by the narrator is actually a means of social control. Moreover, Robbins has a word to say about those critics, like most commentators on "Brooksmith," who settle for the generic representation of servants. "Criticism's demand for 'character'" he writes, is itself "a demand for social immobility" (36).

It is with Offord, the "sovereign" (8:13) liable to benefit most from social immobility, that the characterization of Brooksmith as "artist" originates. The narrator quotes the butler's master as saying of him that "'what he likes is the talk—mingling in the conversation'" (8:17) and claims not, at first, to have seen much evidence to substantiate the claim. Similarly, the idea that Brooksmith is "spoiled" by his contact with Offord's salon is one the narrator rejects when he first hears it from those who will not employ the butler but finally comes to accept. This is the force of the "indeed" in his concluding "he had indeed been spoiled" (8:31). The narrator is, it seems, rather impressionable and particularly prone to the influence of Offord. His relations with Brooksmith after Offord's death are a way of taking this man's place. He talks of "emulating Mr. Offord" (8:21) by taking the butler into his own service and echoes the dead man's patronizing words in calling Brooksmith "my poor child. . . my dear fellow" (8:25). But the butler's despairing wish—"if you could give me some one *like* him!" (8:25)—is not to be granted. The narrator cannot fill Offord's shoes any more than Brooksmith can by continuing as host of the salon: "my service was not worth his being taken into" (8:23), he says, alluding, presumably, to financial constraints. His would-be identification with Offord is replaced by a much closer tie with Brooksmith himself, based on their mutual loss and the narrator's own indulgent sense of having been removed from his rightful place in society. He talks of "the uncertainty of *our* future" (8:21) and, of a dinner party where Brooksmith serves as waiter, remarks, "we had been in Arcadia together, and we had both come to *this!*" (8:27).

Told in retrospect, "Brooksmith" begins as a nostalgic reverie on the part of its narrator, about the Offord salon in terms that are both celebratory and somewhat defensive. He makes much, for instance, of the unusual fact that this conversational haven owed its foundation to a man: "Mr. Offord had solved the insoluble; he had, without feminine help (save in the sense that ladies were dying to come to him and he saved the lives of several), established a *salon*" (15). There is glee here in the way the narrator figuratively leaves a number of ladies to die, just as there is to be a lack of compassion in the language with which he presents Brooksmith's death. Like the narrator of "The Aspern Papers," he has what Susanne Kappeler calls a "prejudice against women" (29); like the "great good place" where everyone is known as "Brother," Offord's salon is a predominately male zone. But the narrator's hostility to women and his view that they "have not the skill to cultivate" (8:14) the art of conversation, are surely not sentiments with which James would concur. "Brooksmith" itself—like many of his other fictions—has its origins in an anecdote told him by a female conversationalist, albeit one about a maid and her mistress, details of sex that James deliberately changed. Rather, the attitude to women is the narrator's own and may reflect the quality of conversation on offer at Mansfield Street. Certainly, this is how some of Brooksmith's later prospective employers regard the case, one deciding "that she couldn't take a servant out of a house in which there had not been a lady" (8:26).

Further evidence of the nature of the salon is provided by an episode the narrator presents as proving Brooksmith's interest in the elevated conversation of his superiors:

> I shall never forget a look, a hard, stony stare (I caught it in its passage), which, one day when there were a good many people in the room, he fastened upon the footman who was helping him in the service and who, in an undertone, had asked him some irrelevant question. It was the only manifestation of harshness that I ever observed on Brooksmith's part, and at first I wondered what was the matter. Then I became conscious that Mr. Offord was relating a very curious anecdote, never before perhaps made so public, and imparted to the narrator by an eye-witness of the fact, bearing upon Lord Byron's life in Italy. Nothing would induce me to reproduce it here, but Brooksmith had been in danger of losing it. If I ever should venture to reproduce it I shall feel how much I lose in not having my fellow-auditor to refer to. (8:18-19)

Far from expressing an ideal, James is allowing his narrator to give himself away here. Brooksmith's interest in the anecdote may be genuine—though the look he gives the footman could have any number of meanings—but this is hardly indicative of sophistication because Byron remained a figure of great fame and controversy throughout the nineteenth century and was popular across the range of classes. The "curious" and decidedly private anecdote the narrator teasingly refuses to reproduce—though not, as he would have believed, because he was not really listening to it—would appear to be the kind of salacious gossip about Byron's sex life that Victorians seemed never to tire of hearing. As in the case of the fictional Jeffrey

Aspern, interest in Byron was less in his work than in his life. Small blame to Brooksmith, then, if he does not want to miss the punchline, but no credit at all to the narrator's attempts to dignify both butler and salon. Again, this passage is echoed during Brooksmith's later demise. The narrator complains that in one of the butler's new homes "there was not a word said about Byron" (8:27)[3] and finally despairs that the work the unfortunate servant does represents "the mercenary prose of butlerhood; he had given up the struggle for the poetry" (8:30). This, of course, is the distinction of a man who knows nothing of financial struggles.

The tale is unusual in the James canon for the number of other writers it names, the narrator attempting in this way to convey the literary credentials of the salon. The implication that it is an acquaintance with literary culture gained through Offord that "spoils" Brooksmith for other positions is a further means of emphasizing the quality of conversation on offer: the talk must be really "good" so as to captivate the butler. But as the narrative subtly reveals, Brooksmith does not enjoy literature on the same terms as his superiors:

> I know Mr. Offord used to read passages to him from Montaigne and Saint-Simon, for he read perpetually when he was alone—when they were alone, I should say—and Brooksmith was always about. Perhaps you'll say no wonder Mr. Offord's butler regarded him as "rather mad." However, if I'm not sure what he thought about Montaigne I'm convinced he admired Saint-Simon. A certain feeling for letters must have rubbed off on him from the mere handling of his master's books, which he was always carrying to and fro and putting back in their places. (8:18)

In typical embarrassment over the status of the servant, the narrator cannot decide whether Offord at home with his butler is Offord "alone,"[4] whether Brooksmith hears what his master reads because it is read "to him" or because he is "always out." The attempted certainty of the following sentences aims to clear up this awkwardness, but, as before, the narrator's proofs of the butler's taste do not convince. Rather, it is Brooksmith who is put in his place by the detail about the books because a clear divide is drawn between the master who reads them and the servant who carries them around. In this light, the narrator's remark that "I'm sure he admired Saint-Simon" reads as a sneer: the 1829–30 edition of that author's *Mémoires* ran to twenty-one volumes. The feeling most likely to rub off on the porter of such a burden has nothing to do with education and everything to do with resentment. The *Bookman* reported, at around this time, "an outcry against three-volume novels . . . from the powdered menials who have to carry the novels from Mudie's counter to the carriage and find it an exhausting labour" (*Bookman*, 28).

The narrator is able to speculate so freely about Brooksmith because of the very quality on which the butler's service is most frequently judged, what James called his "habit of quiet attention" (*Literary Criticism*, 1096). Brooksmith speaks only very rarely, and almost all the information the reader acquires about him comes directly from the narrator in passages that, as I have tried to show, are not to be relied upon. The butler's silence is itself the starting point for one of the most alarming of these:

> His notion of conversation, for himself, was giving you the convenience of speaking to him; and when he went to "see" Lady Kenyon, for instance, it was to carry her the tribute of his receptive silence. Where would the speech of his betters have been if proper service had been a manifestation of sound? In that case the fundamental difference would have had to be shown by *their* dumbness, and many of them, poor things, were dumb enough without the provision. Brooksmith took an unfailing interest in the preservation of the fundamental difference; it was the thing he had most on his conscience. (8:22–23)

I do not want to argue that any of this is necessarily a false representation of Brooksmith's sentiments, simply that it is impossible to verify, and all too neat in its concurrence with the narrator's own position. Like Isabel Archer, the butler is made a "convenience" of (*The Portrait of a Lady*, 782). A few years later, in "In the Cage" (1897), James created a working-class center-of-consciousness who entertained just such a romantic interest in the "fundamental difference," albeit alongside much more violent class hatred. "Stay where you are!" (10:199) the telegraphist demands of Captain Everard when their relationship threatens to transgress hierarchical bounds.[5] But in "Brooksmith" there is no direct access to the consciousness of the butler, and the narrator's right to speak for that individual's "conscience" is questionable, particularly when he finds in it so much to reinforce his own privileged social status. James's right to speak for the telegraphist might also be questioned, of course, and a number of critics have regarded "In the Cage" as a piece of propaganda for the upper classes, but the narrator of "Brooksmith" tends to indulge romanticism where James critiques it. To step back from the narrative—to look, as Putt writes, "below the surface"—is to see in "Brooksmith" just such a critique. The tale is one of James's frequent studies of what the over-imaginative mind can do with an insufficient amount of hard information. James profits by Brooksmith's silence only insofar as it allows him to isolate for attention the narrator's voice.

What that voice does is persistently to reinforce class division through apparent eulogy of one member of the service class. Though, as I have shown, his remarks often have the indirect effect of putting Brooksmith in his place, the butler is not really regarded by the narrator as representative of his fellow workers. He is "untainted with flunkeyism" (8:16), as much the "intimate friend" (8:13) of Offord as his butler, and as such an exception to the rule of strict hierarchical difference. On the issue of his height, in particular, he contravenes prevailing economics:

> The utility of his class in general is estimated by the foot and the inch, and poor Brooksmith had only about five feet two to put into circulation. He acknowledged the inadequacy of this provision, and I am sure was penetrated with the everlasting fitness of the relation between service and stature. If *he* had been Mr. Offord he certainly would have found Brooksmith wanting, and indeed the laxity of his employer on this score was one of many things he had had to condone and to which he had at last indulgently adapted himself. (8:16)[6]

The narrator's contempt for the working class is adequately demonstrated by the fact that, far from questioning the "relation between service and stature," he attributes the acceptance of such a harsh custom to one of those most likely to suffer by it. With Offord's death, Brooksmith is put back into "circulation" and rejected by prospective employers for reasons among which his height is one.

The narrator's claim that it is because he has been "spoiled" that Brooksmith fails to find anything suitable is a continued refusal to look economics in the face. His attitude to the unemployed Brooksmith is characterized by what Putt calls the "false delicacy of the narrator which makes him too 'gen-

tlemanly' to help him" (280). He refuses to take the butler on himself and actually turns down on his behalf opportunities that might at least make him
a living. In particular, the staple businesses of the retired servant—the shop
and the public house—are regarded as below Brooksmith. The narrator
jokes about the possibility of the "Offord Arms" (8:22) and, when Brooksmith receives a small inheritance from his dead master, remarks: "Eighty
pounds might stock a little shop—a *very* little shop; but, I repeat, I couldn't
bear to think of that" (8:24). It is the narrator, then, who maintains and enjoys the notion of Brooksmith as superior to his fellow workers, permanently removed from his class by his contact with Offord's salon. He is
capable of characterizing one of Brooksmith's fellow servants as "a personage who evidently enjoyed the good fortune of never having quitted his natural level" (8:27) but not of encouraging, even allowing, Offord's former
butler to sink below the standards of his previous employment.

The narrator's snobbery is made perfectly clear toward the end of the
story when Brooksmith's aunt, "an elderly, dreary, dingy person" (8:28), visits him with the message that the former butler is ill. His subsequent excur-
sion to the "short sordid street in Marylebone" (8:28) where Brooksmith lives
is described in terms typical of late-Victorian writing about London slums.
The proliferation of "grimy infant life" (8:28) and smell of boiling laundry
come straight off the pages of Arthur Morrison, and Brooksmith's room offers as little seclusion as the public-house he can see from his window: "Several times the door of the room opened, and mysterious old women peeped
in and shuffled back again. I don't know who they were; poor Brooksmith
seemed encompassed with vague, prying, beery females" (8:28). It is a neat
point that Brooksmith has nobody to protect his privacy as it was once his job
to do for the sickly Offord. But the prejudices on display here are the narrator's own, and the link between the working class and alcohol is stereotypical. When the opinion is expressed that the former butler "would come
round if he could only get his spirits up," the narrator punningly insinuates
of Brooksmith's aunt that "in her own case she knew where to go for such
purposes" (8:29).

The pun is repeated a few pages later, at the tale's close, when the butler's aunt repeats her visit to the narrator to bring him news of Brooksmith's disappearance and presumed death: "As my depressing visitant also
said, he never *had* got his spirits up. I was fortunately able to dismiss her

with her own somewhat improved" (8:31). A whole class is dismissed in these words, whereas, for the narrator, Brooksmith's fate confirms his separation from his family's materialistic existence. The apparent circumstances of the former butler's death are of no concern to him as he completes his mythologizing account: "Somehow and somewhere he had got out of the way altogether, and now I trust that, with characteristic deliberation, he is changing the plates of the immortal gods" (8:31). Like his Arcadia, and George Dane's "great good place," the narrator's projection of heaven is as a place of perfect service and, by implication, the eternal "preservation of the fundamental difference" between the classes (8:23).

Notes

1. The text cited throughout is that included in *The Complete Tales of Henry James*, edited by Leon Edel. Edel takes his text from the tale's first book publication in *The Lesson of the Master* (1892). James amended the tale for volume 18 of the New York Edition, and I point in endnotes to a few of his changes.
2. Edel, for instance, finds "Brooksmith" simply the story of a "butler, who in perception and feeling has moved outside his backstairs and can't move back" (8).
3. The New York Edition text has "there wasn't a word said about Byron, or even about a minor bard then much in view" (367), an addition that emphasizes the fact that the narrator's impatience is directed at his hosts' disregard of fashion rather than their lack of sophistication, the point being that he doesn't know the difference.
4. The New York Edition adds to the narrator's difficulty by removing a personal pronoun. James altered "he read perpetually when he was alone—when they were alone, I should say" to the more fraught "he read perpetually when alone—when *they* were alone, that is" (355–56).
5. It is impossible to know (and one would not want to follow the narrator into speculation) whether Brooksmith ever feels anything like this sentiment: "What twisted the knife in her vitals was the way the profligate rich scattered about them, in extravagant chatter over their extravagant pleasures and sins, an amount of money that would have held the stricken household of her frightened childhood, her poor pinched mother and tormented father and lost brother and starved sister, together for a lifetime" ("In the Cage," *Complete Tales,* 10:153).
6. By the time of the New York Edition, Brooksmith has grown an inch, standing at "five feet three" (353).

Works Cited

The Bookman. October 1891, 28.

Edel, Leon. "Introduction: 1891–1892." In *The Complete Tales of Henry James,* 8:7–12. Philadelphia: Lippincott, 1963.

James, Henry. "Brooksmith." In *The Novels and Tales of Henry James,* 18:347–72. New York Edition. New York: Scribner's, 1909.

———. *Collected Travel Writings: Great Britain and America*. Library of America. Cambridge: Cambridge University Press, 1993.

———. *The Complete Notebooks of Henry James*. Ed. Leon Edel and Lyall H. Powers. Oxford: Oxford University Press, 1987.

———. *The Complete Tales of Henry James*. Ed. Leon Edel. 12 vols. Philadelphia: Lippincott, 1962-64.

———. *Literary Criticism: French Writers, Other European Writers, the Prefaces to the New York Edition*. Library of America. Cambridge: Cambridge University Press, 1993.

———. *The Portrait of a Lady*. In *Henry James: Novels, 1881–1886,* 191–800. Ed. William T. Stafford. Library of America. New York: Literary Classics, 1985.

Kaplan, Fred. *Henry James: The Imagination of Genius*. Sevenoaks: Sceptre, 1993.

Kappeler, Susanne. *Writing and Reading in Henry James*. London: Macmillan, 1980.

Leavis, Q. D. "Henry James: The Stories." *Scrutiny* 14 (1947): 223–29.

Putt, S. Gorley. *A Reader's Guide to Henry James*. London: Thames and Hudson, 1966.

Robbins, Bruce. *The Servant's Hand: English Fiction from Below*. New York: Columbia University Press, 1986.

Vaid, K. B. *Technique in the Tales of Henry James*. Cambridge: Harvard University Press, 1964.

Wagenknecht, Edward. *The Tales of Henry James*. Literature and Life Series. New York: Ungar, 1984.

Karen Scherzinger

THE (IM)POSSIBILITY OF "THE PRIVATE LIFE"

IN "THE PRIVATE LIFE," James explores in terms of both subject-matter and narrative technique the troubling divisions wrought upon the artist and the text by the aesthetic enterprise. This tale is dismissed by James himself as no more than a "little conceit" (*Complete Notebooks,* 60), a response that suggests that its intriguing narrative maneuvers are not entirely deliberate; his readers have, in general, tended to concur with his assessment.[1] It might be argued, however, that this text characterizes many aspects of James's concerns with aesthetic failure, particularly in the ways in which it systematically and simultaneously generates and disputes its central premise. In "The Private Life," James's intricate interweaving of the possibility and impossibility of his main topic is mimicked by a corresponding doubling of the tale's realist, self-effacing narrative with disruptive metafictional devices.[2]

My contention that "The Private Life" is a metafictional text that calls attention both to itself as an aesthetic construct and to its contestable pretensions of verisimilitude is influenced by two important conceptual paradigms. First, Shlomith Rimmon-Kenan's definition of ambiguity as the "'conjunction' of exclusive disjuncts" (12) and her claim that James's texts "teach us the nearly impossible lesson of being capable of belief and doubt at the same time" (16) provide important steps in exposing the ways in which the narrative strategies of "The Private Life" render it both self-effacing and, *at the same time,* self-revealing. Second, my discussion of "The Private Life" seeks to remain alert to the deconstructive possibilities generated in the text, which, in turn, shed light on James's complex problematics of aesthetic failure. "The Private Life" dramatizes the ways in which a deconstruction of the opposition between presence and absence (in which each term is shown to be inhabited by traces of, and denied superiority over, the other) causes disruptive effects in the artist and in the work of art.

Jacques Derrida describes the functioning of semiological relationships and the "interweaving" of presence and absence this way:

> The play of differences supposes, in effect, syntheses and referrals which forbid at any moment, or in any sense, that a simple element be *present* in and of itself, referring only to itself. . . . [N]o element can function as a sign without referring to another element which itself is not simply present. This interweaving results in each "element" . . . being constituted on the basis of the trace within it of the other elements of the chain or system. (*Positions,* 26)

In Clare Vawdrey, James presents a figure whose public presence is diminished by a bewildering absence of artistic genius (he is "always splendid, as your morning bath is splendid, or a sirloin of beef, or the railway service to Brighton. But he's never rare," says the narrator [209–10]). At the same time, his private life is all effaced presence, able to function only within an environment of solitude and exclusion. Although it seems on the face of things that the artist "is double" (211), that doubling does not imply a surfeit of wholeness: the presence of each of Vawdrey's personae is riven by absence and lack. The private diminishes in public; the public and social becomes mute and "in the dark" (205), in private. In one sense, the relationship between the public and private in this tale becomes synonymous with the relationship drawn by Derrida between presence and absence, in that each term can only be conceived of *because* it is different and deferred with reference to—and thereby always textured by the "trace" of—its opposite. As the narrator remarks, "one of them couldn't carry on the business without the other. Moreover mere survival would be dreadful

for either" (215). In his preface to the New York Edition of the tale, however, James attempts to gloss over the semiological connections that join the
public and the private, the present and the absent. The theory that lay behind "The Private Life" was, he writes,

> of two distinct and alternate presences, the assertion of either of which
> on any occasion directly involved the entire extinction of the other.
> This explained to the imagination the mystery: our delightful incon-
> ceivable celebrity was *double*, constructed in two quite distinct and
> "water-tight" compartments—one of these figured by the gentleman
> who sat at a table all alone, silent and unseen, and wrote admirably
> deep and brave and intricate things; while the gentleman who regu-
> larly came forth to sit at a quite different table and substantially and
> promiscuously and multitudinously dine stood for its companion.
> They had nothing to do, the so dissimilar twins, with each other; the
> diner could exist but by the cessation of the writer, whose emergence,
> on his side, depended on his—and our!—ignoring the diner. (*Art of the
> Novel*, 250–51)

James's reading of his own tale betrays what Paul de Man would call a
"constitutive discrepancy ... between the blindness of the statement and the
insight of the meaning" (*Blindness*, 110). On the one hand, James argues
that the two selves of the artist are "distinct and 'water-tight'" and have
"nothing to do ... with each other." But in order to make this claim, James
uses a vocabulary of dependence, reliance, and relationship: the "assertion"
of one "*directly involved* the ... extinction of the other. ... the diner *could exist but by* the cessation of the writer, whose emergence, on his side, *depended*
on his ... ignoring the diner" (emphases added). It becomes clear that one
mode of existing is made possible only by means of a process through which
it is deferred and rendered different from its opposite number: exclusion
relies on inclusion as a constitutional necessity. Because James's aesthetics is
informed by a desire for the achievement of perfection and wholeness, he
must insist, blindly, on the impervious distinctions between the artist and
the public man. However, the play of *différance* that propels signification
unsettles his logocentric poetics and causes him to assert, insightfully, independence in the language of reliance.

An important aspect of *différance* is that it marks a resistance to closure and to synthesis. Once terms of binary oppositions are shown to be shot through with traces of one another, the element previously regarded as inferior and negative (such as absence) cannot simply be turned into the superior term. As Jonathan Culler explains, a "scrupulous theory must shift back and forth" (96), and the will to hierarchical metaphysics must be withstood. This teleological resistance, along with the "irresolvable alternation" (96) of aporia, is enacted throughout "The Private Life," in which presences and absences are placed within a dynamic economy; "economy" here being "a metaphor of energy . . . not a reconciliation of opposites, but rather a maintaining of disjunction" (Spivak quoted in Derrida, *Grammatology,* xlii). In Lord Mellifont, James presents a vivid dramatization of the aporia between the opposing terms of presence and absence in the artist. Mellifont, that "plenitude of presence" (213), is only able to figure so forcefully in public because he must, as some kind of constitutional necessity, become a "plenitude" of *absence* when he is in private: "there isn't so much as one, all told, of Lord Mellifont" (211). In another example of an artist whose identity is constituted by the "irresolvable alternation" between opposing values, Blanche Adney is "beautiful without beauty and complete with a dozen deficiencies" (198).

A clue to the disruptive effects that this economy of *différance* has on the creative product is given by James's depiction of the art works that emerge from his two artists. Considerable doubts are cast on the existence of Vawdrey's manuscript, and although we do learn at the end of the story that a play is finally written, its success is uncertain, as Blanche is "still, nevertheless, in want of the great part" (227). Furthermore, Lord Mellifont's painting is imprinted by a telling absence:

> As I again considered this work of art I perceived there was something it certainly did lack: what else then but so noble an autograph? It was my duty to supply the deficiency without delay. . . . (222–23)

The narrator's vocabulary here (he speaks of "lack" and "deficiency") suggests that the work of art is incomplete and—if we bear in mind James's comments about the "ideal of faultlessness" (*Art of the Novel,* 177) to which the triumphant work of art must strive—thereby flawed, a failure. Both Vawdrey and Mellifont are caught up in an existential aporia in which neither the public nor the private, presence nor absence, is ever granted complete authority. And these incomplete duplications and disruptions are echoed or are caused by (the relation of cause to effect is appropriately uncertain) similar traces of omission and dissatisfaction in their aesthetic productions.

Deconstructive tendencies in "The Private Life" do not rest here, however, but course through the narrative of the tale itself, which "simultaneously asserts and denies the authority of its own rhetorical mode" (de Man, *Allegories,* 17). The path these tendencies take and their effect on the tale will be the subject of the rest of this essay.

Most readers of "The Private Life" agree that it is, at a fairly elementary level, a story about the impossibility of attaining satisfactory closure and unity within the aesthetic enterprise. In "The Lesson of the Master," it is suggested that the pleasures of St. George's marriage, children, and Summersoft are obtained at the price of artistic triumph, and James tests, with not a little ambiguity, the value of the doctrine of renunciation as an alternative for the perfection-seeking artist. Now, in the figure(s) of Clare Vawdrey, James develops this theme by calling attention to the existential schism wrought in the artistic persona by the conflicting demands of public, social requirements and private, aesthetic creation.

Quite what this presentation of a split-and-doubled persona implies in terms of establishing the narrative and generic status of the tale, however, is a problematic issue. Critics have tended to read "The Private Life" variously as a tale of the supernatural, an allegorical figure, an account of personal artistic rivalry, or a combination of two or three of these. Tzvetan Todorov, along with Edel (211), Matthiessen (110), and Blackmur (194), takes his cue from James's description of "The Private Life" as a "rank fantasy" (*Notebooks,* 60) and groups the tale along with James's other ghost stories. Todorov also claims that it comes close to "pure allegory," an "[a]llegorical interpretation of [a] supernatural event" (182).

Shlomith Rimmon-Kenan agrees that "The Private Life" is allegorical but finds that the allegory strips the tale of any complexity or pertinence to her definition of ambiguity as it operates in James's work:

> Allegory, in fact, can destroy a potential ambiguity, as Henry James's "The Private Life" amply proves. Although the happenings in this story—the physical disappearance of Clare Vawdrey when in society and of Lord Mellifont when left to himself—are supernatural, no

question arises as to their reality because we immediately translate them into the language of allegory, taking the story to be about the absence of real personality on the part of the man of society and the absence of a social façade on the part of the writer. (14)

But Rimmon-Kenan dismisses the story a little too hastily. First, she misreads the text at a fundamental level. Vawdrey does not *physically* disappear when in society at all: it is only his private or artistic self that does not emerge in social situations, leaving his banal public persona to disappoint his fellow guests. Second, she fails to see that the story's status as a simple, unproblematic allegory is called into question by the text's forceful and insistent mimetic impulses.[3] And although Rimmon-Kenan acknowledges in a note to the above remarks that "[s]ometimes an ambiguity results from the uncertainty as to whether we should take the narrative literally or allegorically" (237–38)—a remark that has special pertinence with regard to "The Private Life"—she does not recognize this tale as a case in point. In fact, Rimmon-Kenan's theory of ambiguity can be most persuasively applied to "The Private Life" and is seminal in defining it as a self-effacing/self-revealing text in which we are asked to "take the narrative literally" *as well as* to embrace the narrative procedures that disrupt such a reading.

Although some readers stress the story's allegorical properties, others concentrate upon the autobiographical and psychoanalytical resonances in "The Private Life." Ross Posnock regards the story as a reflection of James's ambivalent feelings about Robert Browning, taking his cue from James's declaration to that effect in the tale's preface (*Art of the Novel*, 249–52).[4] James admits to a certain bewilderment concerning Browning's apparent lack of artistic personality in social encounters—what he terms in "The Private Life" the "Manfred attitude" (225). Far from seeing the tale as a fantasy, Posnock denies that there are two Clare Vawdreys and offers instead a psychoanalytic reading that, in tracing the web of "[d]eception and unabashed trickery" (42) in the story, suggests James's ambivalence toward Browning and his sexual fear of the poet. Posnock maintains that the narrator/James is obsessed with the mistaken notion that there are two Vawdreys, an obsession stemming from acute anxiety concerning the artist, and one that makes him incapable of detecting Blanche Adney's duplicity and the evidence of her affair with Lord Mellifont.

Fantasy or Freud? Realism or allegory? Autobiographical expurgation or supernatural whimsy? The problem with all of these readings is that they hinge upon an either/or equation: the story is allegorical and therefore not to be taken literally; or it is a ghost story and therefore lacking in seriousness; or it is autobiography and therefore unproblematic. All of these views stem from a fundamental uneasiness with the presentation of Vawdrey as double. Such a notion is, they argue, anathema to our sense of what is real; therefore the figure must be allegorical, or supernatural, or the construction of an overwrought psyche plagued by artistic rivalry.

A far more persuasive reading of "The Private Life" comes from Adam Bresnick, who skillfully demonstrates how the story begins in a realist mode but swiftly changes course into allegory. Bresnick argues that James "allows his story to hover in a kind of disquieting generic undecidability. It is not too much to say that in the end 'The Private Life' aims to problematize the very possibility of practically distinguishing realism and allegory" (93). Drawing extensively upon Freud's theory of the uncanny, Bresnick's central thesis is to show how this "generic undecidability" results in a riven affective response in the reader of the tale:

> The reader's experience of the uncanny is the result of the internal doubling of his or her own reading experience in which everything that was initially read as figurative now gets read as literal, and so takes on an entirely different meaning than that which we at first grant. (93)

This powerful argument substantially problematizes the generically limited responses that "The Private Life" has occasioned. But although Bresnick's reading persuasively undercuts the generic, either/or oppositions presented by the story, his discussion remains fixed within the rhetoric of realism/allegory as terms of classification. A more detailed examination of the story's narrative strategies reveals that the tale is not only an allegory of the split in the aesthetic subject, but that the narrative itself comprises complex doubling and mirroring strategies, which are common traits of a metafictional, self-revealing text.

The problem with reading "The Private Life" as a ghost story or as a rather bland allegory is that the insistence on realism in the tale serves to create a sense of verisimilitude that bolsters the probability of the events taking place. Here, I refer to realism quite simply as a narrative device that presents fiction as a mimetic pursuit that effaces its own existence-as-a-text and demands that what it describes is a recognizable and comprehensible truth. Realism is woven into the fabric of "The Private Life" by means of frequent references to a commonly recognizable, external reality (such as London, the Oberland, or Switzerland) and by appeals to the reader that suggest that the figures in the tale have an existence beyond the fictional paradigms of the text. An aside from the narrator assumes a cozy familiarity among himself, the reader, and a shared social world: "you remember how genuine [Adney's] music could be" (193). Furthermore, the indication that Blanche Adney can (apparently) verify that another Clare Vawdrey does exist, and that the dichotomy between Vawdrey's private and public lives is paralleled by a similar-but-different dichotomy in Lord Mellifont, tends to contradict any supposition that the narrator is hallucinating or is subject to a ghostly visitation.

Additional support is given to the credibility of the theory that Vawdrey has a "private life" in which his aesthetic endeavors take place by the fact that it is not only Vawdrey who demonstrates this peculiar self-replication. Other characters, albeit in differing degrees, also exhibit this tendency. The obvious parallel with Vawdrey is Lord Mellifont, who is suspected by the narrator and by Blanche Adney (and, possibly, by Lady Mellifont) of having no private persona at all and of disappearing completely when he believes himself to be alone. But James also hints that the other artists in the group, such as Blanche and the narrator, also have alternative identities. The narrator, himself a would-be playwright and a "searcher of hearts—that frivolous thing an observer" (202), reveals this possibility in an apparently insignificant encounter. The narrator is about to leave his dining companions to fetch Vawdrey's manuscript:

> my errand was arrested by the approach of a lady who had produced a birthday-book—we had been threatened with it for several evenings—and who did me the honor to solicit my autograph. She had been asking the others, and she couldn't decently leave me out. I could usually remember my name, but it always took me some time to recall my date, and even when I had done so I was never very sure. I hesitated between two days and I remarked to my petitioner that I would sign on both if it would give her any satisfaction. She said that surely I had been born only

once; and I replied of course that on the day I made her acquaintance I had been born again. I mention the feeble joke only to show that, with the obligatory inspection of the other autographs, we gave some minutes to this transaction. (203–4)

In spite of the narrator's self-effacement here and his dismissal of the event as serving little purpose to his story, he—unconsciously perhaps—suggests that he also might have two selves, born, as it were, on different days. This doubling of the self mimics that other allusion to Vawdrey's predicament in which it is noted that Vawdrey has two names, Clare and Clarence, the latter used "only on the title page" (190).

Blanche Adney, on the other hand, is an actress whose occupation demands a professional combination of the public and private life, whose life is dedicated to the convincing presentation of alternative identities. Considered the "greatest (in the opinion of all) of . . . theatrical [glories]" (189), trained in the very art of concealment, effacement, mutability, and pretense, Blanche Adney permits no *observable* existential schism. Any indication of the difference between her private and public life would betray the illusion upon which her career depends. She is all performance, and her private self has been stage-managed to cohere with her public self: "[t]he perspective of the stage made her over, and in society she was like the model off the pedestal" (198). When she calls upon her musician husband to "play up!" in order to ease off the *"contretemps"* (201) presented by Vawdrey's inability to relate the contents of his play to his companions, her response, predictably, invokes the theatrical tradition of the musical interlude. It also becomes evident that Adney himself performs in this story as the actress's manager and lackey, providing her with the firm basis from which she can indulge in her flights of fancy and in the cultivation of her overweening, publicly artistic self. Adney's ineffectiveness and his meek responses to his wife's imperious treatment almost parody the artist in the supporting role. His creative, private self has been entirely effaced into his rather forlorn, public, but nearly invisible position as a musician in the orchestra pit.

The possibility and physical existence of Clare Vawdrey's private self is given credibility, then, by suggestions of alternative presences that are traced, to a greater or lesser extent, in the other major figures in the story. Vawdrey's private self is no fantastic ghost or trick of the narrator's imagination but an extreme manifestation of the dichotomy inherent in an artistic existence. This notion is reinforced by the narrator's continued restatement of the solution to his initial problem of the absence of the "Manfred attitude" in Clare Vawdrey. Until the last lines of the story, his conviction that he has indeed seen Vawdrey's private self never wavers, and his certainty lends a convincing effect to his account.

Contributing toward the realistic values in the text is its apparently coherent structure. Like a play (true to James's response to the "ever-importunate murmur, 'Dramatise it, dramatise it!'" [*Art of the Novel*, 251]), the story seems to be divided into neat acts, each of which presents a linear progression of the action. What one could call act 1 (189–95) introduces the characters and states the central concern to be investigated. Act 2 presents the characters at dinner and includes Vawdrey as the "tame lion" roaring "out of tune" (200). Act 3 (204–6) contains the pivotal scene in which the narrator comes across Vawdrey's private self, writing in the dark in his bedroom. Act 4 (207–14) offers a moment of pause and consideration in which Blanche and the narrator reflect on their findings. Their walk in the valley and their meeting with the previously nonexistent Mellifont—what could be called act 5—neatly mirror the issues raised in act 3. The "play" of the text progresses toward its close with an act that has the narrator and Vawdrey trapped in a hut, waiting out a storm while, in a scene not available to the audience's scrutiny, Blanche ostensibly meets Vawdrey's private self. In the final act, the story ends with a traditional denouement in which the party breaks up and drives away as the curtain falls on the play of the text.

The story thus follows a traditionally realist pattern of beginning, middle, and end and appears to progress in a logical fashion. The reassuring, linear progression of the action defies any notion of the absurd or untoward and is given further support by the equally neat alternation between backdrops—outdoors and indoors—that locate the events firmly within a recognizable and frequently public arena. That the story assumes the appearance of a play is reinforced by the characters' occupations: most of them are involved in the theater in one way or another.

In another context (in his preface to *The Awkward Age*), James exults in the "divine distinction of the act of a play" (*Art of the Novel*, 110). Such a device, he argues, allows for the creation of wholeness and closure in a story that can "remain shut up in its own presence" (*Art of the Novel*, 111). It seems that James would cast a containing network of theatrical allusions and dramatic conventions over his tale in order to assert the self-contained verisimilitude of its subject matter and thereby repress any disconcerting textual waywardness.

Finally, unity and realism are asserted in the text by the apparently harmonious pairing of opposites, what James calls in the preface "the precious element of contrast and antithesis" (*Art of the Novel,* 251). On one level of analysis, James's insistent pairing of antithetical notions, characters, and scenes seems to be a logocentric attempt to defy the play of *différance* and to reinforce the text's apparently "water-tight" unity and mimetic value. The private self of Clare Vawdrey is paralleled with the public self of Lord Mellifont, absences with presences, effacement with assertion, thus creating a set of mirrored concepts that initially seems to bestow upon the text a happy symmetry and to inspire Coleridge's willing suspension of disbelief, which is necessary for the credibility of the narrator's encounter with the artist's inscrutable, creative self.

Although Todorov and Posnock offer widely differing analyses of "The Private Life," they agree on an important point: that the story inspires contradictory readings. Posnock writes:

> Although my insistence on reading the story as a realistic narrative containing an uncanny episode disputes Todorov's interpretation, what is of most generic significance is that the tale is so designed as to permit a mimetic and a non-mimetic reading. This doubleness makes the tale a "piece of ingenuity" as James called it. (59)

Posnock's view might be more correctly summarized by saying that the story offers a mimetic *or* a non-mimetic reading because he has little sympathy with an opposing view. What Todorov proposes (simply put, that the tale is an allegorical fantasy) and what Posnock proposes (that there is only one Vawdrey, no "private life," and that the narrator's perceptions are contaminated by anxieties) are mutually exclusive.

In her book *The Concept of Ambiguity: The Example of James,* Shlomith Rimmon-Kenan offers a detailed definition of ambiguity and its "irresolvability . . . in the hope that [it] will stop the endless debates among critics, debates motivated by a compulsion to choose between mutually exclusive hypotheses, when the very phenomenon of ambiguity makes such a choice impossible and undesirable" (xi–xii). Rimmon-Kenan's definition of ambiguity is appropriate to "The Private Life" in a number of ways, especially as it explains the features and function of singly directed and doubly directed clues in James's writing. Singly directed clues are described by Rimmon-Kenan in this way:

> Every scene, conversation, or verbal expression which supports only one hypothesis is balanced somewhere else in the narrative by another scene, conversation, or verbal expression which supports exclusively the opposite hypothesis. In the linear process of reading, such singly directed evidence momentarily seems to offer the comfort of definitively turning the scale in favor of one of the mutually exclusive possibilities. But they soon recede to the background, and the comfort they seemed to offer is frustrated when other pieces of evidence, supporting with equal definitiveness the other alternative, come to the fore. (52–53)

Doubly directed clues, on the other hand, are "scenes, conversations, or verbal expressions which are open to a double interpretation, supporting simultaneously the two alternatives" (53). Thus, an example of singly directed clues may be found in the various elements in the text that make it a realist construct. On the other hand, there are (as I shall show below) a number of narrative gestures in the text that defy such a reading and that have equal persuasiveness. A doubly directed clue may be found in Lady Mellifont's reaction to the narrator's attempt to see the absent Lord Mellifont, who is supposedly resting in his rooms. On the one hand, it certainly seems that Lady Mellifont has the same suspicions as the narrator as to the nonexistence of her husband's private self. There is something to be said, however, for Ross Posnock's theory that Lord Mellifont is indeed having an affair with Blanche Adney and that his wife is aware of this. Her reluctance to allow the narrator to enter Mellifont's rooms stems from an abhorrence of revealing this fact, as it would dispel the public impression she has created of marital solidity and fidelity. Thus, an ambiguity is created as to whether Lord Mellifont's lack of a private self causes him physically to disappear in that neither this hypothesis nor its contradiction is allowed to acquire a definitive substantiation.

My argument is based upon Rimmon-Kenan's assertion that ambiguity cannot and should not be resolved; moreover, I would suggest that the reader of this tale is required to relinquish a logical sense of the impossible and to dissolve conventional oppositions between the feasible and the fantastic. It certainly seems that there *are* two Vawdreys: not simply in an allegorical sense but in a realistic one as well. The various elements that contribute to the text's mimetic tendencies demand this reading. However, James has written this story in such a way as to offer its central hypothesis as plausible and implausible at the very same time.[5] That is, while insisting on the verity of events and propositions, he simultaneously denies their feasibility; he laces the text with singly and doubly directed clues.

James's contradiction and negation of the very things he has posited as credible are achieved in the very first line of the story: "We talked of London, face to face with a great bristling, primeval glacier" (189). This sentence is remarkable in a number of ways. It introduces the pattern of contrast and antithesis that pervades the story and that, although intended to create a neat harmony between opposing concepts and terms, actually has some distinctly disruptive effects. The civilized, metropolitan ethos of London is pitted against the timeless, raw immensity of the glacier, creating a discordance of scene and conversation, the jarring of which resonates throughout the tale. Although the conversation is ostensibly between the members of the group gathered upon the balcony of the inn, the glacier is incorporated, by the syntax of this sentence, into the conversation as a mute, inscrutable participant whose ominous silence creates a flaw in the tidy symmetry of the group's composition. Interestingly, James uses the same words "face to face" later in the tale when the group sits on a "platform of echoes" confronting the "ghosts of the mountains" (214), thus reinforcing the sense of impasse and futility created by the phrase. The word "echoes" suggests that the characters' words are continually turned back on them without comment and implies conversational stasis; at the same time, an echo, an aural effect that is always at one remove from its source and mocking in its diminishing repetitions, carries with it a same-but-different quality that parodies the mimetic values set up elsewhere in the narrative. Thus, to talk "of London, face to face with a great bristling, primeval glacier" becomes an absurd act, the incongruity of which will infect the events that follow.

Considerable ambiguity is provoked by Vawdrey himself, who seems uncertain as to the character and power of his "private" self:

I said to Clare Vawdrey that his mistake could easily be corrected by his sending for the manuscript. If he would tell me where it was I would immediately fetch it from his room. To this he replied: "My dear fellow, I'm afraid there *is* no manuscript."

"Then you've not written anything?"

"I'll write it to-morrow."

"Ah, you trifle with us," I said, in much mystification.

Vawdrey hesitated an instant. "If there *is* anything, you'll find it on my table." (201)

The evident lack of control that Vawdrey appears to have over both his private self and his art gives us some clue as to James's concern with aesthetic failure. If art's redemptive power stems from its ability to make "relations [which] stop nowhere . . . happily *appear* to do so" (*Art of the Novel*, 5), then this flawed connection between the artist and his art is one that predicates disjunction and failure. Furthermore, Vawdrey's doubt here, contrasted with the narrator's own conviction that the private self indeed exists, is only one example of the mimetic value of the text being undercut by unsettling contradictions and uncertainties.

Blanche Adney also creates continual doubts by her inscrutability and affectation:

There was a light of inspiration in her face, and she broke out to me in the quietest whisper, which was at the same time the loudest cry, I have ever heard: "I've got my *part!*"

"You went to his room—I was right?"

"Right?" Blanche Adney repeated. "Ah, my dear fellow!" she murmured.

"He was there—you saw him?"

"He saw me. It was the hour of my life!"

"It must have been the hour of his, if you were half as lovely as you are at this moment."

"He's splendid," she pursued, as if she didn't hear me.

"He *is* the one who does it!" I listened, immensely impressed, and she added: "We understood each other."

"By flashes of lightning?"

"Oh, I didn't see the lightning then!"

"How long were you there?" I asked with admiration.

"Long enough to tell him I adore him."

"Ah, that's what I've never been able to tell him!" I exclaimed ruefully.

"I shall have my part—I shall have my part!" she continued, with triumphant indifference; and she flung round the room with the joy of a girl, only checking herself to say: "Go and change your clothes." (226–27)

Blanche's responses to the narrator's eager questions are extraordinarily evasive. Greeting the narrator with a "whisper" that is also, perplexingly, "the loudest cry," at no stage does she answer a question directly but dodges clarity by means of cryptic remarks ("Ah, my dear fellow!" and "Oh, I didn't see the lightning then!"). She assumes the actress's mantle of imperviousness to her audience's desires ("as if she didn't hear me" and "triumphant indifference") and freezes the narrator's inquiries with an imperious and chilling "Go and change your clothes." Blanche brings to bear on this parody of a conversation all of the affectations with which her profession has equipped her, and the intriguing possibility that Blanche has indeed *not* seen the private Vawdrey at all is unsettlingly raised. Her behavior in this passage might be affected to conceal the fact that she has *attempted* to see him but has failed. She is envious of the narrator's privileged experience and will not admit to her failure, playing instead upon his evident sexual jealousy as a form of revenge. This would explain why, at the end of the story, we read that "she is still, nevertheless, in want of the great part" (227). If Blanche is indeed fabricating here, her failure to see the private artist casts doubts upon the credibility of the narrator's vision, doubts that are intensified by his irritation with Vawdrey's refusal to recognize him as a fellow artist as well as by the possibility that his attraction to Blanche might be obscuring his grasp of events. Blanche's inscrutability contributes to the general ambiguity of the text, and this is epitomized by James's early description of her as "beautiful without beauty and complete with a dozen deficiencies." The reader is continually unsettled by the shifting identities and motives of Blanche Adney.

In many ways, what Blanche is really up to is unimportant except in the way in which her behavior contributes to the web of doubts that have formed over the otherwise logical and mimetic values of the text. The reasons I have offered here for Blanche's dissembling undercut the hypothesis that the narrator's vision is to be believed because it is one shared by Blanche Adney. In a fascinating series of doubly directed clues, that which creates certainty in one sense is the very perception that creates uncertainty in another.

Dramatic devices in the story might well contribute to its mimetic credibility, but the theatrical motif also serves to deny the values of "organic form" (*Art of the Novel,* 84) and "continuity" (*Art of the Novel,* 5) it inspires. Frequent references to plays, scenes, actors, and audiences create a sense of illusion and artificiality that runs counter to the apparent verisimilitude of events. Lord Mellifont, in particular, is repeatedly referred to as playing to an audience or "spectators" (195). He is a great public figure whose stage is the world. Like a true performer, he has "a little more art than any conjunction—even the most complicated—could possibly require" (197) and "fills the stage" to such an extent that the narrator and Blanche "could no more have left him than [they] could have left the theater till the play was over" (221). And to lend further credence to the distorting effects of the theatrical motif in the story, the group as a whole is positioned like actors on a stage "on [their] platform of echoes, face to face with the ghosts of the mountains" (214).

There is also a disjunction between the text-as-play and the fact that the narrator—ostensibly the "writer" of the text—is only a would-be playwright who simply has a "beautiful" play in his head (227). Thus, the notion of the text as a theatrical piece is denied by the narrator's inability—in spite of the evidence of the text as a construct of words on a page—to write a play at all. It becomes increasingly evident that the text of "The Private Life" contains some striking metafictional tendencies in that it is a play but not a play, designed by a writer who contains the script only in his head. And there are other aspects of the text that support this argument. As much as Mellifont's disappearances demonstrate that he has only a public life and has had to sacrifice his private life accordingly, such a disappearance also mimics the fact that a character's existence is constituted only inasmuch as he or she is mentioned in the words on the page. Just as Mellifont "disappears," so, in fact, do all the characters disappear at one point or another. For as long as we are concerned, say, with the narrator and Vawdrey in a hut in a storm, Lady Mellifont, Blanche, and Adney cease to exist on the page. As Patricia Waugh notes,

> [a]s linguistic signs, the condition of fictional characters is one of absence: being and not being. Fictional characters do not exist, yet we know who they are. We can refer to them and discuss them. . . . All

statements have "meaning" in relation to the context in which they are uttered, but in fiction the statement is the character is the context. Thus characters in metafiction may explicitly dissolve into statements. They may act in ways totally deviant in terms of the logic of the everyday "commonsense" world, but be perfectly normal within the logic of the fictional world of which they are a part. (92–93)

Although Vawdrey's doubled selves and Mellifont's private nonexistence are "nonsense" and lead many critics to jump to the all-too-easy conclusion that "The Private Life" is an allegorical text, a reading of the text alert to its metafictional dimensions extracts "sense" from "nonsense."

James's presentation of Lord Mellifont can be seen to be one of the most important ways in which "The Private Life" is rendered a metafictional text. And it is interesting to note that, apparently coincidentally, Muriel Spark's avowedly metafictional text *The Comforters* presents a character who disappears in the very same manner as Lord Mellifont. Spark's Georgina Hogg is described as "not all there" (175), "[n]ot a real-life character" (157), and "as pathetic and lumpy as a public response" (207). When visitors approach her room, they are struck by a sense that it is "uninhabited" (158), "that nobody was there" (206), in spite of the fact that she appears when the door is opened. Their suspicions are, it turns out, quite justified: "as soon as Mrs Hogg stepped into her room she disappeared, she simply disappeared. She had no *private life* whatsoever. God knows where she went in her privacy" (177, emphasis added).

In Spark's allusion to the absence of Mrs. Hogg's "private life," there is a strong linguistic echo of James's tale. Although Lord Mellifont cannot be said to be quite as repulsive and objectionable as Mrs. Hogg, the similarities in James's and Spark's treatment of character are startling, so much so that Spark seems to be drawing directly on James's work. By problematizing their characters' ability to exist beyond their textual constitution, James and Spark both disrupt pretensions to truth-value in their texts. One is also tempted to note parallels between the narrator in "The Private Life" and Caroline Rose, another character in *The Comforters:* both are presented as writing the text in which they are rendered as fictional constructs. Two of Caroline's companions discuss her dilemma:

"Caroline is embroiled in a psychic allegory which she is trying to piece together while she lies with her leg in that dreary, dreary ward. I told you of her experience with the voices and the typewriter. Now she has developed the idea that these voices represent the thoughts of a disembodied novelist, if you follow, who is writing a book on his typewrite-r [*sic*]. Caroline is apparently a character in this book and so, my dears, am I."

"Charming notion. She doesn't believe it literally though?"

"Quite literally. In all other respects her reason is unimpaired."

(184)

As is the case with "The Private Life," the reader of *The Comforters* is required to "believe . . . quite literally" in an (im)possible proposition. Caroline is also writing a book called "Form in the Modern Novel" and is "having difficulty with the chapter on realism" (59), a comment that seems pertinent to the difficulty presented by the aporia of James's simultaneous assertion and disruption of realist strategies in "The Private Life."

Ironically, then, James's contrasts and antitheses, designed to invoke those much-desired qualities of unity and continuity, have combined to structure a text that questions the possibilities of its own existence. Posnock and Todorov, in their insistence on proving their respective classifications of the text as accurate and exclusive, fail to see that the linguistic and structural scaffolding of "The Private Life" at once assumes and dictates the shape of the tale's content: the possible and the impossible coexist and conflict. Just as the voices of the visitors to the Alps are thrown back on to that "platform of echoes" in a manner that threatens the contrived harmony and symmetry of the group, so the narrative of "The Private Life" turns back on itself, rendering self-effacing realism into self-revealing metafiction.

The final lines of "The Private Life" are steeped in dissatisfaction and disillusionment. Blanche Adney is "still . . . in want of the great part" (227), and the narrator remains disgruntled, apparently because Blanche continues to dismiss his attentions. Significantly, however, Vawdrey does finish his play, and it is produced. Once again, the positive and negative values of the text are simultaneously presented and endowed with equal persuasiveness. That Vawdrey has completed his play gives support to the evidence in the text that his private self does exist and creates works of art. The play would appear to be mediocre, however, as the narrator makes no mention of its success, and Blanche is still searching for her "great part." And the narrator's petulant tone at the end of the story—"Lady Mellifont always drops me a kind word when we meet, but that doesn't console me" (227)— could also stem from a dissatisfaction and uncertainty concerning his encounter with the artist-Vawdrey. Our final impression of the narrator is of a distinctly piqued figure, one that qualifies the sincerity of his earlier, elated enthusiasm and casts doubt upon the durability of his theory.

The tale's final comments epitomize its central problem: that the artist's role is an (im)possible one. The sustained duality of the text defies unidirectional reasoning, and this ambiguity—established in the story's opening line—serves as a model for James's concern with the risk of aesthetic failure. Vawdrey's position remains unclear. The banality of his conversation when sitting out a storm with the narrator, as well as his inability to recognize and assimilate his two selves and therefore achieve true aesthetic harmony, testify to his failure, in spite of the fact that his play does find itself written. The "precious element of contrast and antithesis" functions on a thematic and on a structural level, setting up and breaking down possibilities at every turn, working against James's aesthetic ideal of completion as perfection. Art promises to be coherent and to offer unity and mimetic value: the text of "The Private Life" promises to do the same. But the ambiguities concerning Vawdrey's identity and the contradictory structure of the story demonstrate the failure of art to fulfill its promise.

I have suggested that James's own description of "The Private Life" as little more than a "conceit" or a "game" indicates that the writer himself was unaware of—or reluctant to acknowledge—the complex and unsettling narrative procedures that inform the tale. His response is not surprising given the extent to which the story resists generic and narrative unity and flies in the face of his stated ideals concerning art as the locus of perfection. Evidence of authorial blindness, however, need not strip the story of the insights it affords into James's problematics of aesthetic failure. These problematics are constituted by the complex relations that exist between the public and the private, between presence and absence, and between realism and metafiction in the tale. In one sense, "The Private Life" demonstrates a failure on the part of the artist to achieve and to maintain a unified existence from which a work of art can emerge as a coherent and controlled, perfect whole. In another sense, however, "The Private Life" *is* a metafictional game in which complex narrative devices play and enact (the theatrical suggestions implicit in these terms seem appropriate) the (im)possibility of its propositions.

Brooke Horvath, in a discussion of James's *Stories of Writers and Artists*, proposes that James's "aesthetics of defeat" informs the tales throughout but that this theory is illusory and would be "more properly described as the spoken misprint, the written stutter" (107). He contests that the art/life dichotomy in James's writings is one of "polarity/mergence" (104) and regards this as an unacceptable contradiction that demonstrates the stories' flimsiness. Dismissing the art-as-life formulation as "nonsensical mimesis," he writes that

> James presents an aesthetics discernible only insofar as it pervades the reader's mind not as a *presence* so much as a *prescience*. James's obsession with the nonreferential reflects always a concern with comprehension beyond what is stated—the reader as the writer's ghost . . . and this is the approach he takes in delineating art's (and criticism's) attempts to redeem life from failure by giving meaning to failure. (94)

"The Private Life," however, provides a concrete example of how polarity and mergence need not signal an unacceptable contradiction but may exist instead within an opposition of dynamic narrative economy. That which is realistic in the story demands its verisimilitude, but that which is ambiguous defies such an imperative. That this opposition is to be found in the text's structure, and that the text becomes a model for itself, makes the aesthetics discernible and concrete rather than only prescient, as Horvath suggests. Even the nonreferential is given a specificity in the structure of the text: the "written stutter" becomes complex and eloquent discourse. Shlomith Rimmon-Kenan draws a similar inference at the end of her study on ambiguity: "The triumph of art, rather than its bankruptcy, is celebrated by the Jamesian ambiguity, showing not simply how the possible is rendered impossible by art, but mainly how the impossible becomes possible in it" (235). A slight shift in Rimmon-Kenan's conclusion is necessary when applied to "The Private Life." The story itself is a triumph, but thanks to James's extraordinary interweaving of assertion and contradiction, construction and deconstruction, its triumph lies in the way it draws attention, in its themes and in its narrative procedures, to the threats and consequences of aesthetic failure.

Notes

1. In his preface to volume 17 of the New York Edition, James refers to this story rather nonchalantly as a "whimsical theory" (*Art of the Novel,* 250) and a "small game" (*Art of the Novel,* 252). In his notebooks, it is described as a "rank fantasy" (60). With a few exceptions (notably Todorov, Posnock, and Bresnick), critics have accorded "The Private Life" scant scholarly consideration. The story seems to have been regarded as mainly of autobiographical interest, drawing upon James's allusions to Robert Browning and to Lord Leighton (see Lind, Bargainnier, and Posnock). Matthiessen does not include the story in his edition of James's *Stories of Writers and Artists* and, in general, it is mentioned only in passing, if at all. A survey of critical writings on James's tales reveals that the trend has been to dispense with the story in a few lines. Vaid, for example, gives a cursory summary of the plot and evades any critical or analytical effort by concluding that "'The Private Life' is . . . all cleverness and sleight of hand insofar as its execution goes. It is a kind of joke as well as a kind of truth. But a brilliant joke or epigram should not be explicated; it should only be heard" (72). Wagenknecht, although admiring the symmetry of the tale, writes that there "is no plot to speak of in 'The Private Life,' nor is there anything that requires elucidation" (68). I hope to show, however, that such a cursory dismissal of the text is unjustified, and that the text of "The Private Life" is complex and central to James's work as a whole and not merely a frivolous fancy.

    Perhaps significantly, James's apparent ignorance of the complex narrative procedures at work in "The Private Life" is remarkably similar to his assessment of "The Turn of the Screw," whose status as a simple fantasy or ghost story is notoriously uncertain. In this case, however, James's readers have not been as easily misled by his rather glib description of the text as a "perfectly independent and irresponsible little fiction" (*Art of the Novel,* 169), a "fairy-tale pure and simple" (*Art of the Novel,* 171). On the contrary, "The Turn of the Screw" has occasioned considerable critical debate in which Freudian readings (for example) have been vigorously supported and rejected. For a survey of the different readings of "The Turn of the Screw," see Willen and Felman.

2. Generally speaking, the term "metafiction" is more commonly used to describe a twentieth-century, postmodernist narrative technique in which devices such as parody and games are frequently and explicitly incorporated (see Hutcheon). The prefix "meta" does, however, suggest the self-referential, and inasmuch as metafiction refers to "fiction that includes within itself a commentary on its own narrative and/or linguistic identity" (Hutcheon, 1), it is applicable to my reading of "The Private Life," particularly to James's treatment of Lord Mellifont.

3. Rimmon-Kenan refers to allegory in the traditional Romantic sense as a rhe-

torical figure of simple, untroubled, one-to-one correspondence. As Paul de Man has suggested, however, in his essay "The Rhetoric of Temporality"(*Blindness,* 187–228), allegory has considerable potential for ambiguity and dissemination (that is, the endless dispersing and regeneration of meaning).

4. See also Lind and Bargainnier. Lind, although recognizing James's preoccupation with Browning, actually considers Vawdrey to be a figure with whom we should identify James himself and describes the story as "disguised autobiography" (321), a claim that Bargainnier disputes (158).

5. Although Bresnick refers neither to the critical debate that has surrounded "The Private Life" nor to Rimmon-Kenan's work on ambiguity, his point about the "disquieting generic undecidability" of "The Private Life" would be in keeping with my application of Rimmon-Kenan's theory.

Works Cited

Bargainnier, Earl F. "Browning, James, and 'The Private Life.'" *Studies in Short Fiction* 14 (1977): 151–58.

Blackmur, R. P. *A Primer of Ignorance.* New York: Harcourt, 1967.

Bresnick, Adam. "The Artist That Was Used Up: Henry James's 'The Private Life.'" *Henry James Review* 14 (1993): 87–98.

Culler, Jonathan. *On Deconstruction: Theory and Criticism and Structuralism.* London: Routledge, 1982.

de Man, Paul. *Allegories of Reading: Figural Language in Rousseau, Nietzsche, Rilke, and Proust.* New Haven: Yale University Press, 1979.

———. *Blindness and Insight: Essays in the Rhetoric of Contemporary Criticism.* 2nd ed. London: Methuen, 1993.

Derrida, Jacques. *Of Grammatology.* Trans. Gayatri Chakravorty Spivak. Baltimore: Johns Hopkins University Press, 1976.

———. *Positions.* Trans. Alan Bass. London: Athlone, 1981.

Edel, Leon, ed. *The Ghostly Tales of Henry James.* New York: Grosset, 1948.

Felman, Shoshana. "Turning the Screw of Interpretation." *Yale French Studies* 55–56 (1977): 94–207.

Horvath, Brooke. "The Life of Art, the Art of Life: The Ascetic Aesthetics of Defeat in James's *Stories of Writers and Artists." Modern Fiction Studies* 28 (1982): 93–107.

Hutcheon, Linda. *Narcissistic Narrative: The Metafictional Paradox.* London: Methuen, 1984.

James, Henry. *The Art of the Novel: Critical Prefaces by Henry James.* Ed. R. P. Blackmur. New York: Scribner's, 1934.

———. *The Complete Notebooks of Henry James.* Ed. Leon Edel and Lyall H. Powers. Oxford: Oxford University Press, 1987. New York: Scribner's, 1934.

James, Henry. "The Private Life." In *The Complete Tales of Henry James,* 8:189–227. Ed. Leon Edel. London: Rupert Hart-Davis, 1963.

Lind, Sidney E. "James's 'The Private Life' and Browning." *American Literature* 33 (1951): 315–22.

Matthiessen, F. O., ed. "Introduction: Henry James's Portrait of the Artist." In *Stories of Writers and Artists by Henry James,* 1–17. New York: New Directions, 1945.

Posnock, Ross. *Henry James and the Problem of Robert Browning.* Athens: University of Georgia Press, 1985.

Rimmon-Kenan, Shlomith. *The Concept of Ambiguity: The Example of James.* Chicago: University of Chicago Press, 1977.

Spark, Muriel. *The Comforters.* London: Macmillan, 1957.

Todorov, Tzvetan. *The Poetics of Prose.* Trans. Richard Howard. Ithaca: Cornell University Press, 1977.

Vaid, Krishna Baldev. *Technique in the Tales of Henry James.* Cambridge: Harvard University Press, 1964.

Wagenknecht, Edward. *The Tales of Henry James.* New York: Ungar, 1985.

Waugh, Patricia. *Metafiction: The Theory and Practice of Self-conscious Fiction.* London: Methuen, 1984.

Willen, Gerard, ed. *A Casebook of Henry James's "The Turn of the Screw."* New York: Crowell, 1960.

Daniel Won-gu Kim

THE SHINING PAGE
"The Altar of the Dead" as Metafiction

> [Stransom] took, in fancy, his composition to pieces, redistrib-
> uting it into other lines, making other juxtapositions and con-
> trasts. He shifted this and that candle; he made the spaces
> different. . . . There were subtle and complex relations, a
> scheme of cross-reference.
>
> — "The Altar of the Dead," 286–87

HENRY JAMES'S "THE ALTAR OF THE DEAD" is a short story about an elderly
man, Stransom, who adorns a church altar with candles in memory of his
dead friends and associates. The altar becomes the context for a relationship
between Stransom and an unnamed woman who also frequents the altar.
The passage quoted above suggests how the altar in "The Altar of the
Dead" is more than a place of worship; throughout the story, the altar is
clothed in terms that indicate it is an aesthetic object. But though it is lik-
ened variously to a musical and to a visual work, the altar is predominantly
presented as a printed text. For Stransom, the altar represents a "record"
and the candles, "lettered milestones" (262); the altar becomes a "shining
page" and the visitors of the church, its "vulgar" readers (261). By reading
the altar as a text, it is possible to examine the story as a reflexive discourse
on textuality: the altar itself can be read as a realist text and the story as a
whole as an antirealist metafiction.

"The Altar of the Dead" was published in 1895. Many other short stories
and novels from this "middle" period of James's fiction have been read as containing elements of the negative—or antirealism that emerges in his later

work. John Carlos Rowe notes, for instance, how some critics have located in *Princess Casamassima* the moment at which James swerves away from realism toward the modernist's "deepening internalization ... of perspectival relativism" (188).[1] My purpose in reading "The Altar of the Dead" as an antirealist fiction is not so much to resolve the issue of how James's work should be periodized but to argue that this story has an important place in any consideration of James as a writer who foregrounds metafictional processes.[2] The story further demands that we consider the larger issue of textuality in a manner that avoids the easy binary between "traditional" realism and the metafictional qualities characteristic of much twentieth-century writing. Such a reading of "The Altar of the Dead" may mark James as a closer relative of postmodern rather than modernist writers. Although the story is antirealist on one level, it does not manifest any of the stylistic experimentation of high modernist texts. Instead, it works a deep concern for textuality into what is basically a realist narrative frame, prefiguring the "tempered" postmodern realism we recognize in contemporary authors such as Don DeLillo and Salman Rushdie.

In his work on the antirealist movement in literature, *World-Games,* Cristopher Nash explains that realist writers operate on certain foundational premises: "There is a positively determinable world—which we can call that of actuality ... and this world is ... a complete, integrated system of phenomena governed by some coherent scheme of rules ... whose truthful delineation depends ultimately on the comprehensiveness and rationality of its description" (8). For the realist, then, it is the fundamental responsibility of fiction to represent this guiding extra-textual actuality "as it is" or "has been" (8).[3]

According to Nash's account of realism, the first sentence of the short story might well stand as an example of Stransom's realist aesthetic: "He had a mortal dislike, poor Stransom, to lean anniversaries, and he disliked them still more when they made a pretense of a figure" (252). If we read "lean anniversaries" as a euphemism for "spare and empty celebrations," we understand that Stransom's reason for hating these anniversaries is that they are not "true" to the complete actuality of past events or people; they are not true because they are "lean," not comprehensive enough. Stransom's own memory manifests his realist sense of responsibility to accurate, exhaustive representation. His memory contains a thorough record of the past: "he had done many things in the world—he had done almost all things but one: he had never forgotten" (252). In short, Stransom is someone upon whom "nothing is lost," to recall James's phrase from "The Art of Fiction" (49). When Stransom meets his old friend, Paul Creston, standing in front of a jewelry store with his new wife, he is shocked and disgusted because he sees in Creston's taking on a new wife a failure on his part to remember correctly his first, deceased wife's past "actuality." Not only has Creston's original and "true" wife not been remembered, but her due place in the record of her husband's life has been tampered with. The second half of that first sentence, then, completes the picture of Stransom's referential motive: "he disliked [the anniversaries] still more when they made the pretense of a figure" (252). To Stransom, the actuality of the past must be neither understated nor overstated. The past must be represented—indeed, imitated—truthfully "as it has been."

James undermines Stransom's realist text primarily by challenging its claimed objective status, that is, its autonomy and claim to universal truth. Realism is founded on the belief that there is a rational, unified cosmos that can be accurately recreated in a text. As an objective representation of that cosmos, the realist text tends toward a stable, resolvable meaning. The objective status of Stransom's realist text is destabilized when Stransom and the woman reach an impasse over their conflicting interpretations of the altar's meaning; Stransom is forced to admit that, instead of a "concerted" unified meaning, the text has "multiplied meanings" (276). Contrary to Stransom's intention that his altar-text objectively *imitate* the actuality of the past, the woman interprets the altar in terms of what could be called an *expressive* theory of art. Stransom is shocked to find that, for the woman, his altar is a text that expresses her subjective experience of the death of Acton Hague, her lover and a friend-turned-enemy to Stransom. Instead of being a representative and universal record of all dead, the altar for her is a place where the dead are "gathered . . . together for One" (276). She interprets Stransom's altar as an extension of the intensely personal altar she keeps at home dedicated to Hague, "expressive and articulate with memories and relics" (272). Of course, the presence of competing lines of interpretation does not in itself challenge the realist's claim for his text's unambiguity. Realist texts in fact commonly use schemes of binary opposition. But in the typical realist text the opposition is often merely a phase that precedes final synthesis of meaning. In "The Altar of the Dead," this opposition becomes a source of undecidability. When he is confronted by the woman's request for the inclusion of Hague in the altar, Stransom is forced to acknowledge that the subject of his art has been all along a phenomenological, rather than an extra-textual, universal reality: "Mine are only the dead who died possessed of me. They're mine in death because they were mine in life" (276). Stransom is unable to maintain his text's objective status; he must admit that his text is at bottom always mediated by subjectivity rather than having a stable existence as an external and absolute point of reference.

Realism is obviously problematized in the conflict between a realist and an expressive aesthetic; but James also builds specific connections between Stransom and his altar-text and the realist author and text. These connections include Stransom's handling of the characters in his altar-text and in his symbolic deployment of one of realism's major narrative strategies: third-person omniscient narration. Stransom's handling of the "characters" in his text reveals a realist commitment both to a rational, all-encompassing actuality and to an accurate imitation of that actuality. He would like to believe that the candle-personages in his altar represent the complete scope of death. The dead in his altar-text are the dead of all: "he liked to think that [his dead] might be the dead of others, as well as that the dead of others might be invoked there" (262). More important, Stransom would like the presence of these dead in the altar to reflect the coherent ordering of the realist universe. James describes Stransom as being "intensely conscious of the personal note of each candle and of the distinguishable way it contributed to the concert" (263). Stransom sees each of the candles as participating in a larger orchestration of light. Furthermore, he is especially concerned to preserve the rational coherence of this orchestration by maintaining discrete differences between its constituent elements. Stransom must be sure that each character in the altar-text is a complete individual: "he went over [the altar] head by head, till he felt like the shepherd of a huddled flock, with all a shepherd's vision of differences imperceptible. He knew his candles apart, up to the color of the flame" (262–63). In his handling of his text's candle-characters Stransom would appear to agree with J. P. Stern, who wrote that realism is not "concerned . . . with fragments of consciousness" (120–21).

A kind of transparency, then, is the realist's ultimate goal for his text. If the text could only be transparent, the truth of the cosmos would simply become visible to the reader as it has been faithfully reproduced in the text. In a telling bit of narration, James has Stransom possessed of a similarly valued notion of clarity: "George Stransom was in a mood which made lamps good in themselves. It wasn't that they could show him anything; it was only that they could burn clear" (259). Realist writers deploy particular strategies to create the illusion of a text's transparency, the basic principle being to camouflage discursive mediation in order to encourage "natural" reading. One such strategy that James has Stransom employ is the absenting of the author/narrator's mediating presence. Third-person omniscient narration is one of the most commonly cited characteristics of realist narration. It is intended to create a text supposedly free from the intervention of the teller. We have no literal narration to speak of in terms of the altar, but, allegorically speaking, Stransom's attempt to keep his role as the creator of the altar secret is certainly consistent with the goal of third-person omniscient narration. Though James's slippery narrative never states this directly, it can be safely inferred that Stransom does keep secret his identity as the altar-text's writer. Significant benefactors of a church usually receive some form of public recognition, but James makes it clear that "no one did know in fact" (261) the origin of the altar. How could this be possible unless Stransom had made it so? Stransom certainly takes measures to keep the full nature of his authorial intent invisible from the only person—except for the woman—who does know: the ecclesiastic "whose curiosity and sympathy he had artfully charmed" (261). By keeping his identity as narrator secret, Stransom symbolically deploys a realist narrative strategy that corresponds with Flaubert's stipulation: "No lyricism, no comments, the author's personality [should be] absent" (127).

James constructs Stransom as realist and his altar as realist text for the purpose of questioning realism. As discussed earlier, this problematization of realism works in part through the woman's challenge to the objective status Stransom claims for his altar-text. James further destabilizes the altar-text's objective status by setting it up within a complex of mirrored texts. Newspaper accounts represent competing versions of the identity of Acton Hague (257–58). In addition, the woman's altar, which is also dedicated to death, is a text parallel to Stransom's but opposite in its underlying aesthetic principle—expressive rather than objective. Both the newspapers and the woman's altar undermine the unified objective meaning Stransom claims for his text. These mirror texts represent Hague as a man to be remembered whereas Stransom insists that Hague has no place in his altar-text. Which version of Hague is right? More important, how exhaustively complete could Stransom's altar-text be if someone so important to society—as evidenced by the report of his death in the newspapers—and to Stransom's own past is omitted from its all-encompassing mimetic drive? The realist claims that his text refers directly to the ultimate, unambiguous referent: universal reality. By placing the altar in mirror relationship to the newspapers and the woman's altar, James creates hermeneutic instability that makes it impossible to assert the singularity of the relationship between Stransom's text and the meaning of Death: it is impossible to choose which is the "correct" version. The altar-text's internal integrity gives way to a complete dependency on the dialectic relationship between reader and writer. It becomes "a void; it was his presence, her presence, their common presence, that had made the indispensable medium" (285). Indeed, as a text, the altar may not exist at all when removed from its hermeneutic context. When the woman dissociates herself from his altar, Stransom finds that "all the fires of his shrine seemed to him to have been suddenly quenched" (280); his altar "had ceased to exist; his chapel, in his dreams, was a great dark cavern" (284). Contrary to what the realist would like to believe, Stransom's text is not autonomous; it has no meaning beyond "collective" interpretation.

"The Altar of the Dead" may be considered antirealist for actively failing realism. It shows that no objectively precise representation/imitation of actuality is possible within a text because, in human terms, no such actuality exists. In so doing, the story defeats Stransom's attempt to unify the past according to some larger, external design and insists, instead, that our experience is phenomenological: we live always in mediated versions of reality from which the ultimate referent is never accessible. James's challenge to the realist movement as a whole is accentuated in these antirealist strategies. But the story's most direct address to the realist movement in English literature is suggested in Stransom's selection of an empty dark chapel as the place for his altar. This decision aligns him with perhaps the greatest secret hope of literary realism: the ambition to fill with literature the "void" left in society and in the individual psyche by the fall of the Church as a grand narrative. From this perspective, James's choice of a church as the location for Stransom's "text" suggests James's awareness and critical view of the moral tone of the Victorian—

specifically Arnoldian—aesthetic that proposed to make literature the replacement for the traditional belief structures once provided by the Church.

The story's parodic representation of realism and of its Arnoldian agenda is evidence for a stronger connection between James—at least the James of "Altar"—and postmodernism rather than modernism. James applies to Stransom and his altar-text a strategy that is said to be characteristic of postmodernism: the blurring or dismantling of the boundary between mass and elite culture. One of the requirements of the Arnoldian mission to which James implicitly links Stransom was the elevation of literary texts to special status. To justify its taking on the mantle of the Church, literature was granted autonomy from supposedly decaying social and cultural realities. This conferral of authority not only made possible the didactic turn in traditional realism, but it also planted the seed of the theory of aesthetic autonomy that modernism would later declare as its own. This claimed autonomy has been linked, in particular, to the anti–mass culture elitism that postmodernism is said to debunk.[4] Postmodernism challenges the opposition of high culture against low culture, elite against mass, by arguing that such cultural categories are part of a hegemonic struggle. Social elites attempt to defend and consolidate their cultural capital by constructing systems of aesthetic evaluation that reinforce the systems of social and economic difference in which those elites have privileged status.[5] As discussed earlier, the challenge to the autonomy of Stransom's realist altar-text is contained mainly in the unnamed woman's counterreading of his altar and in the opposed mirror-texts—the newspapers and the woman's private altar. James's decision to construct these factors as elements of mass culture implies an awareness of the impossibility of aesthetic autonomy from mass culture. Whereas the newspapers are most undeniably "mass," the woman and her altar also suggest a connection to mass culture. The woman's altar, composed of "simple things" (272), stands in bathetic contrast to Stransom's oeuvre. "Photographs and watercolors, scraps of writing framed and ghosts of flowers embalmed"—to Stransom's bourgeois sense of art, these indicate "a common meaning" (272) where "common" has the double sense of suggesting both thematic unification around the memory of Hague and the supposedly undiscriminating tastes of the masses. The woman herself suggests a figure for the "mass" reader in the fact that she is unnamed. Furthermore, the woman's gender points toward the correspondence between the lack of moral or interpretive authority historically attributed—along with "undis-criminating," "uneducated" tastes—to both mass and female readers. By granting a "mass" reader and "mass" texts the power to subvert Stransom's altar-text, James prefigures postmodernism's dismantling of the boundary between high and low art.[6]

But an interpretation of James in this postmodern context would be incomplete if it were left at an argument for James's critical position on the division between high and low culture. A writer taking on such a position would be assuming authority located beyond or above either elite or mass culture—a position from which it would be possible to apply an "objective" critique. Postmodern writers, on the other hand, are aware that the im-possibility of aesthetic autonomy extends not only to other writers but to themselves. Unlike modernists, who attempt to assert their separateness, postmodern writers are intensely conscious of their implication in and com-plicity with the very social, political, and cultural realities they represented in their texts. As Linda Hutcheon writes, "gone now is the modernist belief that art can really be autonomous or separate from the world. Postmodern literature situates itself squarely in the context of its own reading and writ-ing as social and ideological actualities" (*Canadian,* 10). In his story, James incorporates neither the moral didacticism of a realist position "above" nor the highly experimental style of a modernist fiction marking itself as "be-yond" or "different." By refusing aesthetic autonomy, James can be seen to implicate himself in his mass market context. Indeed, from what we know from his personal documents, James was a writer painfully aware of his sit-uation inside the fiction industry of the nineteenth century. And though he seems at times to find the pressure of market demands on his writing un-pleasant, he does not make the Arnoldian or modernist choice and attempt at all costs to climb or to soar above industrial society's supposed mass torpor. As Michael Anesko argues, "James was continually engaged in an active . . . dialogue with the 'world,' and . . . his finished works were shaped not merely by the imagination alone, but by a constant and lively 'friction with the market'" (vii).[7]

But James does not limit his extension of complicity to mass culture; he extends it to both halves of the high/low cultural divide. His short story pa-rodically subverts Stransom's realism even as it constructs itself problemati-cally in the same vein and, by doing so, indicates a further connection with postmodernism. Postmodern parody does not merely ridicule its sources. Instead, as Hutcheon argues, postmodern parody establishes its source and subjects it to an irony that subverts it without demolishing it (*Poetics*, 26, 39). In similar fashion, James makes us aware of realism's artifice by weakening Stransom's realist project, but he maintains the potency of realism's illusion on the level of the story as a whole. As is the case for the altar-text it contains, "The Altar of the Dead" is told in third-person omniscient narration that encourages its own readers to engage in realist reading. As readers, we know Stransom's inner thoughts and have access to a breadth of information about events and the characters that neither Stransom nor the woman could individually possess. The story would lead us into thinking we can see behind the scenes—that we have the script of which the characters are unaware. The textual mirrors discussed earlier—the newspapers, the woman's altar, Stransom's altar—must also be seen in this light. This array of texts is offered to the *story's* rather than the *altar-text's* readers for resolution of its meaning. The woman does not read newspapers and is therefore not even aware of one of the mirror texts. Further, Stransom, mostly blind to his own partiality, dismisses all but his own text. The narration puts us in the situation of realist readers: the identities of the narrative elements and the relationships underlying them are spread before us—we should be able to achieve a stable, objective interpretation of their significance.

And yet at the end of the story we are denied the interpretive closure that befits our omniscient perspective. The final resolution of ultimate meaning disappears behind a haze of questions. Can we be absolutely certain that Stransom has died? How has Stransom resolved the problem of the altar? Why has the woman changed her mind and returned? As it derails, the ending forces us to recognize that, as readers, we have been drawn into realism's hermeneutics of closure where such activity was not justified (is arguably never justified) by the limited data in the text. "The Altar of the Dead" can be compared, then, with postmodern fiction for its denial of closure, which is what Jean-François Lyotard relates to the foe of postmodernism: the essentializing, totalizing tendency of traditional rationalism (72–74). The more powerful connection of James's story with postmodernism, however, may reside not so much in its denial of such closure per se but in the manner in which it goes about that denial. In "The Altar of the Dead," as in other tales such as "The Turn of the Screw," James manipulates our realist reading tendencies in such a way as to "catch" us. In his New York Edition prefaces, he speaks of "the 'fun' of the capture" when he describes "The Turn of the Screw" as "an *amusette* to catch those not easily caught" (*Art of the Novel*, 172). In his preface to *The American*, James also writes: "The art of the romancer is, 'for the fun of it,' insidiously to cut the cable, to cut it without our detecting him" (*Art of the Novel*, 34). By phrasing his writing intention in terms of an attempt to "catch" his reader, James locates his own writing (and the satisfaction he derives from it) not in the aloof domain of "high"Art—as Stransom would—but in the transacted domain of gamesmanship. "Catching" implies a postmodern aesthetics of play that would pleasurably engage both reader and writer.[8] This aesthetic is the antithesis of modernism, which, as Andreas Huyssen argues in "Mass Culture as Woman: Modernism's Other," struggles constantly to resist contamination by mass culture, to abstain from trying to please a wider audience, to remain always separate, pure (197–98). One might argue that the recognition of ultimate indeterminacy and of the consequent inability to achieve absolute closure is not unique to postmodernism. After all, critics such as Rowe link James with modernism's "perspectival relativism" (188). What would distinguish James and the postmodern writers whom he prefigures, then, is their attitude to the impossibility of totalizing closure, to the impossibility of aesthetic autonomy or critical distance. James does not find—as Stransom does or a modernist might—this reality to be apocalyptic or to represent a deadening threat to his "high-seriousness" sensibilities. The fall of the artist as hero is cause for neither alarm nor despair. Rather than a dungeon-cage for modernism's delicate-bird artist or a quicksand pit for the Arnoldian moralist, James finds in contingent reality a postmodern "play" space. In this space his handling of closure in "The Altar of the Dead" reflects the tendency of postmodern fiction, as Ihab Hassan describes it, to "sustain a *playful* plurality of perspectives, and generally shift the ground of meaning on [its] audiences" (73, italics mine).

Notes

1. See also Ermarth, who argues that James's use of multiple points of view shatters realism's engineering of "consensus."
2. Artist and artwork figures have been a subject of James scholarship for quite

some time. Wirth-Nesher and Chapman are two recent examples. Texts that are not explicitly reflexive have been theorized as such (e.g., Wolk), but "The Altar of the Dead" has not yet been read in this way.

3. Generalizations about realism are always made at the expense of failing to recognize those realist texts that do not fit these generalizations. "Realism" is, after all, a critical construct. The use of such generalizations in this paper is heuristic.

4. Docker provides a broad review of the extensive material on this topic. In *After the Great Divide,* Huyssen argues that, in contrast to postmodernism, modernism recoils from mass culture. As part of this argument, Huyssen finds it necessary to separate the avant-garde from modernism, indicating the difficulties inherent in the argument for a polarizing division of modernism and postmodernism. It is worth pointing out that, as with "traditional" realism, modernism and postmodernism are also critical constructs and are deployed heuristically in this paper to demonstrate the relevance of James's story to elements that are central—and possibly continuous with—both modernism and postmodernism.

5. In his chapter "The Drift of Cultural Studies: From Hegemony to Resistance" (12–23), Holbrook provides a useful capsule review of scholarship to date on the politics of popular culture.

6. The connection between James and this aspect of postmodernism is explored more thoroughly in Jacobson and in Tintner.

7. Anesko provides an extensive and convincing argument for James's commercial identity—perhaps even as a forerunner of the postmodern commercial artist. When he argues that "for too long we have taken James at his word, accepted uncritically his idealized (and occasionally melodramatic) portrait of the artist" (vii), he refutes critics such as Daugherty, who have argued for an Arnoldian "Master" James—a James who wished "to remain aloof from the vulgar herd, to observe the world from an intellectual height" (Daugherty, 4).

8. For literary applications of postmodern ludic theory, see Burke or Küchler.

Works Cited

Anesko, Michael. *"Friction with the Market": Henry James and the Profession of Authorship.* New York: Oxford University Press, 1986.

Burke, Ruth. *The Games of Poetics: Ludic Criticism and Postmodern Fiction.* New York: Lang, 1994.

Chapman, Sara S. *Henry James's Portrait of the Writer as Hero.* London: Macmillan, 1990.

Daugherty, Sarah. *The Literary Criticism of Henry James.* Athens: Ohio University Press, 1981.

Docker, John. *Postmodernism and Popular Culture: A Cultural History.* Cambridge: Cambridge University Press, 1994.

Ermarth, Elizabeth. *Realism and Consensus in the English Novel.* Princeton: Princeton University Press, 1983.

Flaubert, Gustave. *The Selected Letters of Gustave Flaubert.* Trans. and ed. Francis Steegmuller. New York: Books for Libraries Press, 1953.

Hassan, Ihab. *The Postmodern Turn: Essays in Postmodern Theory and Culture.* Columbus: Ohio State University Press, 1987.

Holbrook, Morris. *Daytime Television Game Shows and the Celebration of Merchandise: The Price Is Right.* Bowling Green: Bowling Green State University Popular Press, 1993.

Hutcheon, Linda. *The Canadian Postmodern: A Study of English-Canadian Fiction.* Toronto: Oxford University Press, 1988.

———. *A Poetics of Postmodernism: History, Theory, Fiction.* New York: Routledge, 1988.

Huyssen, Andreas. "Mass Culture as Woman: Modernism's Other." In *Studies in Entertainment: Critical Approaches to Mass Culture.* Ed. Tania Modleski, 188–207. Bloomington: Indiana University Press, 1986.

———. *After the Great Divide: Modernism, Mass Culture, Postmodernism.* Bloomington: Indiana University Press, 1986.

Jacobson, Marcia. *Henry James and the Mass Market.* University: University of Alabama Press, 1983.

James, Henry. "The Altar of the Dead." In *"The Turn of the Screw" and Other Short Novels,* 253–90. Signet Classics. Toronto: Penguin, 1962.

———. "The Art of Fiction." In *"Criticism": The Foundations of Modern Literary Judgment.* Ed. Mark Schorer, Josephine Miles, and Gordon McKenzie, 44–55. Rev. ed. New York: Harcourt, 1958.

———. *The Art of the Novel: Critical Prefaces.* New York: Scribner's, 1953.

Küchler, Tilman. *Postmodern Gaming: Heidegger, Duchamp, Derrida.* New York: Lang, 1994.

Lyotard, Jean-François. *The Postmodern Condition: A Report on Knowledge.* Trans. Geoff Bennington and Brian Massumi. Minneapolis: University of Minnesota Press, 1984.

Nash, Cristopher. *World-Games: The Tradition of Anti-Realist Revolt.* London: Methuen, 1987.

Rowe, John Carlos. *The Theoretical Dimensions of Henry James.* Madison: University of Wisconsin Press, 1984.

Stern, Joseph Peter. *On Realism.* London: Routledge, 1973.

Tintner, Adeline. *The Pop World of Henry James.* Ann Arbor: UMI Research Press, 1989.

Wirth-Nesher, Hana. "The Thematics of Interpretation: James's Artist Tales." *Henry James Review* 5 (1984): 117–27.

Wolk, Merla. "The Sweet-Shop Window: The House of Fiction and the Jamesian Artist." *American Imago* 42 (1985): 269–95.

Patricia Laurence

COLLAPSING INSIDE
AND OUTSIDE
Reading "The Friends of the Friends"

A KIND OF DIZZINESS follows a reading of James's baffling story "The Friends of the Friends." Authors and critics liberate themselves through daredevil acts of aesthetic conjuring, leaving solitary readers to wonder whether critics are friends of the friends, the authors and the readers, or are anxious foes of one other. Foregrounding his own telling of the story in "The Friends of the Friends," James collapses the comforting and traditional space between the "outside," the writer of the story, and the "inside," the reader of the story, creating, as it were, a new space of writer/readership. In this new space, one is left with the feeling that it is very, very dangerous to read, write, and live in stories.

Henry James with his liberating imagination takes us into/out of a region of intimacy in "The Friends of the Friends" where we are no longer certain of what is happening inside or outside of the narrator and of the characters—indeed, of ourselves. We know that we are inside or outside something, but we do not know what, and we move in and out and roundabout in this tale until the geometric certainties of the language—what Gaston Bachelard terms "the dialectics of outside and inside" (210)—collapse. We

117

begin by reading a prologue in which a male narrator has copied fragments of a woman's diary into a "thin blank-book" (371): the fragments copied by this narrator as the representation of this woman's tale are recorded in the story that follows the prologue. Here we read the female diarist's (manqué) observations and her preparations to arrange a meeting of a female friend and the man to whom she is engaged. They, however, resist meeting "as meetings are commonly understood" (374). "The extraordinary way it was hindered" (371), she admits, is only half of her tale. If asked to describe the story, one might say that the story is about a non-story, about a non-meeting, which shifts our narrative analysis to the discourse or to the way the non-story is told or, more accurately, not told. The unsaid, perhaps the unsayable, in the story takes us into a new space of reading and of narrative analysis that we are just beginning to articulate as part of a lexicon of silence in modern narration.

The filtering of experience through friends of friends (and the repetition of the word "friends" makes us suspicious) propels us inward/outward to question the nature of relationships, language, writing, "reality." Yet the narrator of the prologue leaves us, he says, a story that is "nearly enough a rounded thing, an intelligible whole" (371).

"The dialectics of outside and inside," as Gaston Bachelard brilliantly asserts, invade the "linguistic tissue of contemporary philosophy" and of this story:

> From the point of view of geometrical expression, the dialectic of outside and inside is supported by a reinforced geometrism, in which limits are barriers. We must be free as regards all *definitive* intuitive—and geometrism records definitive intuitions—if we are to follow the daring of poets. (215)

The female narrator claims that her tale is a "mystery" of her own producing, and commonly defined words—Bachelard's "definitive intuitive"—that locate us inside or outside of certain experiences as readers are inverted by James in his telling of this tale until we no longer know who is "alive" and who is "dead," what is "common" experience and what are "rare extensions of being," or what is life and what is "beyond" it. At the end of this story, one agrees that the tale is "monstrous" because it brings into question the language that we use to describe experience that bears the fossilized "traces" of an experiential or metaphysical dialectics of out-side and inside that no longer holds in this reading space. This language, according to Bachelard, "limits" us or creates "barriers" to experience and to being, and we should follow rather the "daring" writer's explorations. Derrida's confirming insight that "language bears within itself the neces-sity of its own critique" (254) is realized as James demolishes with daring and subtle language the borderline between internal and external expe-riences embodied in the language he uses. He quietly reveals that the friend of the friend "made up" the woman of the story, as we "make up" our friends, as James does his stories, and as we all do, the better part of life, with talk and language.

James and the narrator in this tale, no longer certain or even believing that "the way it was" is knowable or who the "friend" or "the friend of a friend" is, open up a space of exploration for the reader. It is the space of re-lationship or friendship or the creation of human relationship or the percep-tion of friendship or the art of writing about relationship—most broadly, the space of language that we use to describe experience in fiction and life. One is lost in this space as one reads because the sense of who the "friend" is and who the friends are rotates among the three characters in the mind of the reader. James's retitling of this story as "The Friends of the Friends" en-hances the psychological vertigo, replacing as it does his original title, "The Way It Was," given in 1896.

Early in the story, a narrator in a brief prologue describes the "possibil-ity of publication" (371) of the unpublished diaries of a woman we do not know and who is scarcely revealed in the story that follows. The contents of her diaries have been "copied out" by the narrator in a "thin blank-book" (371). Why, though the words fill the "blank" book, is the book described as "blank"? What about the gaps, holes, and blanks that remain after the woman's words have been recorded on the page? "What" has been left out and what does "leaving out" mean in James or in modern narration?

The narrator in the prologue notes that the woman seldom "let a good story pass without catching it on the wing" but complains that she is "fear-fully indiscreet" in her diary (371). He is made uncomfortable by what she has written and reminds us that he has only sent a "fragment" for, dear reader, he says, "these things would be striking, wouldn't they? to any reader; but can you imagine for a moment my placing such a document before the world?" (371). Yet we are told that "*She* herself had desired the world should have the benefit of it, [and] she has given her friends neither name nor initials" (371, emphasis added). The narrator notes that he is sending on a "fragment" of the diaries divided into several small chapters that presumably follow the prologue, for his last line is, "I leave her the floor" (371). Though he creates the fiction that she "has the floor," we must agree with Virginia Woolf that "the future of fiction depends very much upon what extent men can be educated to stand free speech in women" (39–40). The framing (James, the narrator) leaves us wondering about the ability of male narrators to stand women's "indiscretions." We submit to reading the tale as told, but as Judith Fetterley might say, as "resisting readers." "Nearly enough a rounded thing," the story is complete with the missing parts we, as readers, create. But different readers imagine different things in this dangerous space that James creates. He leaves "us" the floor of the story. Gerard Genette captures this intertwining of the writer and the reader:

> The text is that Moebius strip in which the inner and outer sides, the signifying and the signified sides, the side of writing and the side of reading, ceaselessly turn and cross over, in which writing is constantly read, in which reading is constantly written and inscribed. The critic must enter the interplay of this strange reversible circuit and thus become, as Proust says, and like every true reader, "one's own reader." (70)

Women, perhaps, imagine the woman's voice and experience, her jealousy of the absent women or the absent gaze in her fiancé's eyes: they covet her indiscretions, the freer descriptions of relations between friends and between the sexes taking us beyond or behind or inside or outside the "blank" tale.

The Jamesian word that interests me in relation to this woman's story—and other women's—is "blank." Although James and the narrator "leave her the floor," it is acknowledged that the fragment is the "contents of a thin blank-book" (371). Is this James's acknowledgment that she is, on some level, silenced? Or that this space is left blank for the reader to fill and fill? Perhaps she is "blank" socially and historically until she can tell her story in her own words, including just those passages that the narrator of this story—and that Ted Hughes in "recording" Sylvia Plath's diary or that

John Middleton Murray in "selecting" Katherine Mansfield's letters—
"leaves out." James will tell the story of this interesting woman and others
in *The Wings of the Dove* and *The Portrait of a Lady,* but there will still be
holes, gaps, and blanks. To James, the "blanks" may represent what he does
not grasp about women, about life, about narration, and what, therefore,
cannot be contained in this or in any story. To the reader, these "blanks"—
all that is not said about this woman and her non-meeting with the friends
of the friend—may be the space of a woman's unrevealed psychic life. The
"gaps" are there not because the woman is mute or dumb or blinded but because she must submit to being narrated.

The woman who is "left out" of this tale is not only a being of a society
in evolution but also a being imagined by James being left to be imagined by
the reader. In the scene of the extraordinary woman's visit to the man's room
at the very end of the story, the friend of the friend (and who the "friend" is
rotates in the mind of the reader)—the man—notes that when she came into
the room, he sprang up, but "she, with a smile, laid her finger, ever so warn-
ingly, yet with a sort of delicate dignity, to her lips. I knew it meant silence"
(393). Reminding us of Odilon Redon's pastel of female silence, the woman
assumes the shape of a female muse. She, the writing muse, reminds the man
who is housed in an office of "eternal inspectorship" of his "access to forms
of life . . . your command of impressions, appearances, contacts closed—for
our gain or loss—to the rest of us" (399). "Possessed" by her "alive" and yet
now a "ghost," he guiltily reflects her "absence" in his eyes (399). The "real"
woman will jealously attack his preference for the "imagined" and will accuse him of making it all up: the other woman, her, the story. Both the "real"
woman and the "real" reader are left with the same questions: who or what
is real, and to whom? The paradox may be that the male author's idea of
women or of female characters or of the preference for the imagined life
may become more fiercely protected and furtively shrouded in mystery as
women's speech becomes more persistent and freer. In trying to locate these
"blanks" then as inside women or inside men or inside books or inside blank
writing books or outside men and women in society or life, we realize again
the collapse of the dialectic of outside and inside.

James's blanks, as other tropes of the blank in other writers, are not easily
located in an either-or dialectic of the individual or society or metaphysics.
We realize this in comparing Isak Dinesen's notion of blankness in "The

Blank Page" with James's notion of blankness. The elderly woman storyteller in Dinesen's *Last Tales* tells of a princess of a noble family in the country of Portugal who, on the morning after her wedding night, fails to hand over to the town chamberlain her wedding sheet that would proclaim, "Virginem eam tenemus" (We declare her to have been a virgin). Instead, in a long row of framed sheets of royal princesses in a gallery described in this story, there is one plate on which "no name is inscribed, and the linen within the frame is snow-white from corner to corner, a blank page" (104). Inscribed on this white sheet, this blank page, is a rich story, not emptiness, for according to this elderly woman,

> Who then . . . tells a finer tale than any of us? Silence does. And where does one read a deeper tale than upon the most perfectly printed page of the most precious book? Upon the blank page. When a royal and gallant pen, in the moment of its highest inspiration, has written down its tale with the rarest ink of all—where, then, may one read a still deeper, sweeter, merrier and more cruel tale than that? Upon the blank page. (100)

Considering this story, we may speculate that James with his "royal and gallant pen" presents a woman's "blank-book," shrouded female characters, which a woman author may yet reveal with her pen. Or both Dinesen and James enlarge the meaning of blankness that includes ghosts and absence and the unnameable or the untellable in order to subvert as writers the traditional notion of the "story." James includes but goes beyond/within the social, suggesting the mystery of naming experiences and making up stories about anything as well as "making up" women or friends.

We note in other stories of women represented by men other (w)holes: Samuel Richardson in the eighteenth century describes Clarissa's rape by Lovelace as a "black transaction" (242), a rape unnamed in the novel and marked by silence; Kleist's "The Marquise von O," whose mysterious pregnancy (she does not know how and by whom she has become pregnant) is marked by a dash or blank, which, according to Dorrit Cohn, is "surely the most pregnant graphic sign in German literature" (129); George Meredith in 1859 writes in *The Egoist* of the conforming society surrounding Clara Middleton, who when resisting her father's pressure—indeed society's—to marry an "egoist," tries to think of ways to resist yet "she thought in *blanks* as girls do, and some women. A shadow of the male egoist is in the chamber of their brain overawing them" (114, emphasis added). The notion of a male presence, a male author, male perceptions, male sexuality, or male traditions shutting out the view or language of women—marked or drawn blanks on the white page: dashes, blanks, ellipses, spaces—has a long tradition, as noted by Gilbert and Gubar in their examination of nineteenth-century literature.

To return to the "blank" then, we must acknowledge that in the history of the narration of women's lives, blanks are socially encoded. But blanks are also about the limitations of language to express life and, therefore, are also rhetorical and metaphysical markers. Harold Bloom, in his work on Emily Dickinson, explores her blanks, darkness, and transports in her cryptic lines:

> From Blank to Blank—
> A Threadless Way
> I pushed Mechanic feet—
> To stop—or perish—or advance—
> Alike indifferent—

The blanks are not only the words a poet fits to mechanic rhyme or the blank spaces on the page that create poetry, but the whiteness or darkness of the "threadless" way of a woman poet. Like James, Dickinson collapses the dialectic of outside and inside, and we as readers are "threadless," no longer able to locate the difference between outside and inside in psychological or metaphysical space. Dickinson stands in a void, in the white space of a Kazimir Malevich figure or square with little relation to the "real" world. Harold Bloom, struggling with her "beyond," fails to participate in the collapse of her contraries—darkness and light, bliss and bleak, blank and blind, ends and beyond, dark and transports, outside and inside. "Blank" is not just Emerson's nature's ruins or Milton's blindness or Ursula Le Guin's unnaming, as Bloom maintains in his dialogue of outside and inside (291–309). Having no Theseus to lead her out of the labyrinth of her difficulties, she dreads, among other things, the Minotaur or Milton's bogey "who shuts out the view." Her difficulties are multiple, being human, being a poet, and (what Bloom denies) being a woman and a poet at a particular time and place. Without making her into Bloom's rhetorical female foil, we must note that Bloom shuts out her view in the blink/blank of his critical eye. Brooding on Dickinson's blanks, we can appreciate her "strangeness" and her relation to the universe without denying, as Bloom does, the pain of a woman in the whiteness of her poetic stare.

To return to James and the blankness of relating beyond the "natural" or the "common" as described in Dinesen and Dickinson, we realize what is "monstrous" about his tale. The friend of the friend, describing the way in which the meeting between her friends was hindered, finally concludes that "A mere meeting would be mere flatness" (378). James's breakdown of the distinctions of what happens inside and outside of us; inside and outside of the author and the reader; inside and outside of the characters—and the apparent desire to hinder experience so that relations are preferably not "face to face" but imagined—is "monstrous" to the common perception. The female narrator answers at the end of the story,

> "I'm life, you see . . . what you saw last night was death."
> "It was life—it was life!"
> He spoke with a kind of soft stubbornness, and I disengaged myself. We stood looking at each other hard. (393)

The preference in the art of this story for the death of people and experience in words—words as ghosts—"makes" and "keeps" experience static and beautiful. Yet one wonders why—still—the "key" to keeping the experience is the silencing or death of the female character that then liberates the male's female muse: "Death had made her, had kept her beautiful . . . had kept her silent. It had turned the key on something I was come to know" (387).

Works Cited

Bachelard, Gaston. *The Poetics of Space.* Trans. Maria Jolas. Boston: Beacon, 1964.

Bloom, Harold. "Emily Dickinson: Blanks, Transports, the Dark." In *Western Canon,* 291–309. New York: Harcourt, 1994.

Derrida, Jacques. *Of Grammatology.* Trans. Gayatri Chakravorty Spivak. Baltimore: Johns Hopkins University Press, 1972.

Dinesen, Isak. "The Blank Page." In *Last Tales,* 99–105. New York: Random House, 1957.

Fetterley, Judith. *The Resisting Reader: A Feminist Approach to American Fiction.* Bloomington: Indiana University Press, 1978.

Genette, Gerard. *Figures of Literary Discourse.* Trans. Alan Sheridan. New York: Columbia University Press, 1982.

Gilbert, Sandra, and Susan Gubar. *The Madwoman in the Attic: The Woman Writer and the Nineteenth Century Literary Imagination.* New Haven: Yale University Press, 1979.

James, Henry. "The Friends of the Friends." In *The Short Stories of Henry James,* 371–401. New York: Random House, 1945.

Laurence, Patricia. *The Reading of Silence: Virginia Woolf in the English Tradition.* Stanford: Stanford University Press, 1991.

Meredith, George. *The Egoist.* 1797. Ed. George Woodcock. Baltimore: Penguin, 1968.

Richardson, Samuel. *Clarissa.* 1747–48. Boston: Houghton, 1962.

Woolf, Virginia. "Speech before the London National Society for Women's Service, January 21, 1931." In *The Pargiters: The Novel-Essay Portion of The Years.* Ed. Mitchell Leaska. New York: Harcourt, 1977.

Molly Vaux

THE TELEGRAPHIST AS WRITER IN "IN THE CAGE"

At the beginning of Henry James's "In the Cage," the young, nameless telegraphist is enjoying a respite. Although hard at work counting words and transmitting messages, she has been relieved of the presence of Mr. Mudge, her fiancé, who has risen to a "more commanding position" in an outlying telegraph office (*Eight Tales,* 175). "The girl" (177) unabashedly thinks of Mr. Mudge's absence as a luxury. Their familiarity already has the quality of a scraped platter, and she wonders what marriage could possibly "add" (175). All the descriptions of their relations convey the image of worn-down surfaces. The couple's "contracted future" (175) is a sanded floor. Mudge's inability to drop a subject wears upon the girl and his removal opens up a space that relieves the telegraphist from this constant irritation. In giving her access to other stimuli besides the tangible, the frictional, it awakens her senses and enlivens her imagination.

Many schemes offer themselves for describing how the girl makes use of this opening of time and space within her confinement. Critics have pointed out that her reprieve from her union with Mudge only reimprisons her—in a sexual melodrama, for example, or in a losing effort to defy the gravitational pull exerted by class and gender systems.[1] One reading even asserts that the revelation at the end of the novella that Lady Bradeen has "nailed" Everard (265) is equivalent to the nailing of the girl's coffin (Bauer and Lakritz, 69). The various types the girl suggests—a melodramatic heroine, an ambitious public servant—coexist with another type, whose epistemological sophistication is critical to her function: the writer.

A reader of ha'penny novels, the girl hungers for impressions, for "a play of mind" (179), and finds it in "sudden flickers" brought on by select members of her clientele (177). She hoards the words they squander in their messages, recording and interpreting them. "The knowledge she believes she possesses," as Priscilla Walton observes, "leads the telegraphist to create her own novel through the gaps or absences within the telegrams" (96). But if the telegraphist is writing a novel, she is also noting and examining—as James himself did in his notebooks and prefaces—her own development as a writer. Besides observing the comings and goings of her characters, she is recording her perceptual experiences and the discoveries about consciousness and language that those experiences inspire. In this dimension the novella treats the common Jamesian theme that Millicent Bell calls "the ordeal of a witnessing consciousness":

> Observing, deciphering appearances, it dramatizes the effort which is not only the character's but the author's and . . . the reader's, to create a history. The labors of the Jamesian consciousness are narratological. They aim, often with only partial success, at a putting-together of events to make a story and at the discovery of meaning in this story. (33)

"In the Cage" is an instance where the collaboration of character, author, and reader is only partially successful. Once the girl begins leaving the cage to look for Everard, the discourse on writing and perception ceases. Her consciousness no longer witnesses. Up to this point author and character have been merged. But when the girl begins to search for a place for herself in the story she has been writing, when she seeks to become part of its meaning, James steps back from his heroine. We continue to view the story through the girl's eyes. But for the remainder of the novella author speaks to reader over his heroine's head, as he does in *What Maisie Knew,* "shedding a light far beyond any reach of her comprehension" (*Literary Criticism,* 1162). While the girl continues to weave her story, James comments indirectly on her narration, faulting the efforts at omniscient control of the action that slowly deprive the girl of her visual power and leave her sightless at the end of the novella.

Mrs. Jordan accuses the telegraphist of having no imagination and no sympathy. But it is Mrs. Jordan, the girl decides, who lacks imaginative power. In comparing their talents after Mrs. Jordan has invited her to join her in "doing flowers," the girl expresses a disdain for an occupation so involved with the insubstantial: "Combinations of flowers and greenstuff forsooth! What *she* could handle freely, she said to herself, was combinations of men and women" (178). The girl's work inside the cage is mental work. The talent she applies there, as she sees it, is a creative receptiveness: "[T]here were long stretches in which inspiration, divination and interest quite dropped. The great thing was the flashes, the quick revivals, absolute accidents all, and neither to be counted on nor to be resisted. Some one had only sometimes to put in a penny for a stamp and the whole thing was upon her" (178). The telegraphist views the penny, which we see first put in by Lady Bradeen, as license to read her customers along with their telegrams. In "the waft" that Lady Bradeen "blew through and left behind her" (182), and in the color and light of her eyes, the girl reads her client's birth, family, ancestors, and present situation, which, she deduces, is "a bad moment," despite her possession of "all the conditions for happiness" (181). The girl pronounces Lady Bradeen a goddess, admiring her "magnificent habit" (180) and her insolence. The figure she settles on is Juno, not Venus; the signs of Lady Bradeen's rank and authority have more resonance with the telegraphist than any sexual signifiers. Her presence and her gift are those of a muse and at the same time those of a double. Two of her telegrams are fictions— pretexts for sending the desperate message "Only understand and believe" to Everard ("and that was doubtless not *his* true name either") (181). Through recognizing and interpreting Lady Bradeen's messages, the telegraphist is inspired to begin her own fictional composition: "If our young lady had never taken such jumps before it was simply that she had never before been so affected. She went all the way" (181).

Lady Bradeen's presence, in conjunction with her telegrams, instructs the telegraphist in the relationship between the literal and the figurative and in the art of manipulating the symbolic. In reflecting on the telegrams, the girl begins on the literal level, visualizing Lady Bradeen in the pearls and Spanish lace mentioned in the message to the dressmaker. She then passes from contemplation of this tableau into an interpretive mode in which she self-consciously and exultantly plays with symbols that Lady Bradeen has given her—the string of names mentioned in the telegrams:

> However, neither Marguerite nor Lady Agnes nor Haddon nor Fritz nor Gussy was what the wearer of this garment had really come in for. She had come in for Everard. . . . Mary and Cissy had been round together, in their single superb person, to see him. . . . [T]hey had found that, in consequence of something they had come, precisely, to make up for or to have another scene about, he had gone off. (181)

After this first adventure in the symbolic realm, the telegraphist's writing accelerates. Her "divinations" surface more quickly and are more daring. She exploits the "prodigious view" (186) afforded by the London social season. Appalled by the amount of money her clients squander on telegrams, she nonetheless revels in a sudden sense of being at the center, a sense fostered by her two metiers: "There were times when all the wires in the country seemed to start from the little hole-and-corner where she plied for a livelihood" (187). At this phase in the story there is the illusion that James is at one with his heroine in her authorial perceptions and experiments. The passages in this section have the same exuberant tone that James himself conveys in "The Art of Fiction" in his depiction of the writer as a sensibility that possesses "[t]he power to guess the unseen from the seen, to trace the implication of things, to judge the whole piece by the pattern, the condition of feeling life in general so completely that you are well on your way to knowing any particular corner of it" (*Selected Literary Criticism,* 57). Just as James celebrated in 1884 the knowledge that "there is no limit to what [the writer] may attempt" (*Selected Literary Criticism,* 54), his writer heroine of 1898 exults in the experience of going "all the way."

Whereas Lady Bradeen functions as the telegraphist's muse and model, Everard provides her with an object for her "witnessing consciousness." Through her study of the messages that pass between women and men, the telegraphist makes the general determination that "the men cut the best figure" (189). Their fortunes are more like hers, she finds. They are as likely to have bad luck as good, and hence she can envy them without the animus she bears toward her women clientele. Through identifying with them she escapes the limitations of her sex. Unlike Lady Bradeen, who captures the girl's interest because of her haughtiness, Everard appeals to her through his kindness and forbearance as he waits patiently in line behind "pottering old ladies" and "gaping slaveys" (185). She is fascinated by the range of qualities she thinks she can see in Everard: "He was somehow all at once very bright and very grave, very young and immensely complete" (186). Everard is immediately and simply "all." His warmth suggests to the telegraphist that he is accessible and knowable. The telegraphist builds a world out of every banality they exchange. Commonplace remarks about the weather appear to her "transcendent and distilled" (204). She strives to record every observation, and she begins to write in his voice:

> Every time he handed in a telegram it was an addition to her knowledge: what did his constant smile mean to mark if it didn't mean to mark that? He never came into the place without saying to her in this manner: "Oh yes, you have me by this time so completely at your mercy that it doesn't in the least matter what I give you now." (205)

Like the novelist in "The Art of Fiction," the telegraphist seeks to trace "the implication of things" and gains an exhilarating sense of fluidity and limitlessness in doing so. In Everard's smile she hears a voice acknowledging a relation, acknowledging not only her presence but also the centrality she has imagined for herself. Every sign from Everard seems to open to her "the margin of the universe" (205).

Besides providing the telegraphist with a central character for her novel, a focus for her imaginative powers, Everard's presence offers her a lesson in the slipperiness of language—a lesson she only partly understands. The full message conveyed in her relations with Everard deepens and complicates the conception of the novelist's tasks as set forth by James in "The Art of Fiction" and anticipates James's expansive discussions of that task in the prefaces to the New York Edition. Schooled by Lady Bradeen in looking for "the whole piece" in the pattern, as James describes fiction writing in his early essay, the telegraphist seeks to apply that practice to Everard's words and actions, operating on the principle that

> [e]verything so far as they chose to consider it so, might mean almost anything. . . . What could people mean moreover—cheaply sarcastic people—by not feeling all that could be got out of the weather? *She* felt

it all, and seemed literally to feel it most when she went quite wrong, speaking of the stuffy days as cold, of the cold ones as stuffy, and betraying how little she knew, in her cage, of whether it was foul or fair. It was for that matter always stuffy at Cocker's, and she finally settled down to the safe proposition that the outside element was "changeable." Anything seemed true that made him so radiantly assent. (205–6)

Just as she learns through her work at Cocker's that there is an "immense disparity" between social classes (186), the telegraphist comes to recognize through her imaginative experiments that there is also a wide disparity between language and meaning. She marvels at the fact that, however she describes the weather, her observations seem to evoke a warm, assenting response from Everard. She exults in what she sees as language's fluidity and in the pleasure of manipulating it. But she fails to see the pitfalls that her vision of language presents. If the signs she uses in communicating with Everard evoke the response she desires, then she and her client must both read language in the same way, must share the same intentions. Although she recognizes that language does not have absolute meaning, she believes that the language and facial expressions that she and Everard use with each other do. As a lover, the telegraphist is striving, in the way lovers do, to transcend the limits of her individual consciousness in order to discover her beloved's thoughts and feelings. Her communication with Everard is a "web of revelation . . . woven between them" (207). But the web is attached only at one end— the telegraphist's. It is woven out into space, as innumerable other webs, or possible interpretations of her encounters with Everard, might be spun.

The telegraphist can imagine, or fabricate, only one reading of their exchanges: Everard is gradually submitting to her power. But this interpretation prevents Everard from becoming anything more than a cipher to the reader. As a "centering consciousness" caught up with her object, the telegraphist compulsively weaves a single web of meaning, and in seeking to bind Everard to that meaning, she transgresses the role of the witnessing consciousness. As a "perceiving *character*"—Millicent Bell's term for James's narrators (14)—the telegraphist may be someone on whom nothing is lost, but as Bell points out, this kind of narrator is still a character. She is an interested party and cannot narrate omnisciently. "The very source of interest for the restricted narrative had to be," Bell goes on, "its surrender to the condition of bewilderment" (15). Indeed, James refers to "the muddled state" in his preface to *What Maisie Knew* and "In the Cage" as "one of the very sharpest of the realities" (*Literary Criticism,* 1164). As a writer, then, the telegraphist seeks to operate within the confines of a paradox. Although she can embrace the plurality of linguistic experience, she denies the plurality in experience as a whole. She can acknowledge her own ability to manipulate words. Fair can be foul and foul can be fair when *she* speaks of the weather. But she can't recognize a similar capacity in Everard and thereby apprehend the resonances and ambiguities that all communication generates. Striving to reach beyond the natural bewilderment a lover feels toward her beloved and a writer feels toward her subject, the telegraphist concocts a false intelligence upon which to act. Her presumption that she knows more than she can know leads eventually to the collapse of her fictional world and the closing in of blindness.

Considering the paucity of lower-class characters in James's fiction, it seems important to ask here why James might choose to explore this problem of consciousness through the figure of a woman whose family has recently fallen "down the steep slope" (176) into the working class. In "The Art of Fiction" he argues for the capacity of women from small villages to write about subjects as foreign to them as the military so long as these writers be people "upon whom nothing is lost" (*Selected Literary Criticism,* 57). Clearly, in 1884 he felt that the freedom available in authentic artistic endeavor could be discovered by people outside his own class. But although he celebrates in 1884 the exhilaration of limitlessness in artistic potential, by 1898 he sees the dangers in the limitlessness of creative work. In his preface to "In the Cage" James speaks of the telegraphist's "moral vibrations, well-nigh unrestricted" and her "winged" intelligence and wit (*Literary Criticism,* 1170), yet his project in the novella is clearly to demonstrate that such an intelligence is doomed to failure. In the preface to the novella, he describes his representation of the "brooding telegraphist" as an admonishment to the working class, "even though obscurely enough, of neglected interests and undivined occasions" (1170). Behind this admonishment there seems to be a different kind of warning, one offered to writers. "The action of the drama," James says, "is simply the girl's 'subjective' adventure" (1170). And the events of the novella argue that one can exercise too much subjectivity in the adventure of writing. The telegraphist's wish to rise socially, to "count" (one of the key puns in the novella) in the "high reality" of the class she serves, provides

James with a means for representing excessive subjectivity in writing. A writer cannot understand or write meaningfully, the novella suggests, without a precise and contained, albeit limited, identity. In his preface to the novella, James groups the telegraphist with three other disenfranchised characters—Maisie Farange, Morgan Moreen, and Hyacinth Robinson— all figures who, he says, speculate too far. Each risks the fate that befalls "poor Hyacinth": "He collapses . . . like a thief at night, overcharged with treasures of reflexion and spoils of passion of which he can give, in his poverty and obscurity, no honest account" (*Literary Criticism,* 1170).

From the outset the telegraphist entertains the hope of gaining with Everard "a personal identity that might in a particular way appeal" (185). She forms this aspiration almost in defiance of the knowledge that there will be no daisy for her in the bouquets her clients parade in front of her, no "gleam of gold" in the shower of coins they drop (186, 188). But Everard's warmth and his aura of knowability suggest to her that the "immense disparity" between classes might be traversable, that she might be able to build a relation, if she could at least "touch with him" on some shared fact (205). This fantasy drives her to go looking for him outside the cage and, once she finds him, to try to determine her value in his eyes:

> Could people of his sort [invite girls up to their rooms] without what people of *her* sort would call being "false to their love"? She had already a vision of how the true answer was that people of her sort didn't, in such cases, matter—didn't count as infidelity, counted only as something else: she might have been curious, since it came to that, to see exactly as what. (218)

The uncertainty, the not knowing "exactly as what" she counts for with Everard outside the cage, leads the telegraphist into the temptation of narrating *for* Everard in their exchanges. Here the narrating consciousness becomes a cage containing a cage. The telegraphist seeks to contain Everard's consciousness inside her own. As they sit together in the park, she reads both pleasure and excitement in his manner: "What, in it all, was visibly clear for him, none the less, was that he was tremendously glad he had met her." After he places his hand on hers she decides that "[h]is agitation was even greater on the whole than she had at first allowed for. 'I say, you know, you mustn't think of leaving!' he at last broke out" (223). When he vows to drop by the telegraph office every day and she questions the wisdom of it, "[i]t was as if then for a minute they sat and saw it all in each other's eyes, saw so much that there was no need of a pretext for sounding it at last. 'Your danger, your danger—!'" (227). The girl's presumption becomes ever bolder as she progresses from simply reading Everard's demeanor to creating shared climactic moments. Later, back inside the cage, her illusion of shared experience sustains her as it gains grandiose proportions:

> It had all at last even put on the air of their not needing now clumsily to manoeuvre to converse: their former little postal make-believes, the intense implications of questions and answers and change, had become in the light of the personal fact, of their having had their moment, a possibility comparatively poor. It was as if they had met for all time— it exerted on their being in presence again an influence so prodigious. When she watched herself, in the memory of that night, walk away from him as if she were making an end, she found something too piti- ful in the primness of such a gait. Hadn't she precisely established on the part of each a consciousness that could end only with death? (236)

Everard, as he reveals himself in their conversations, remains a cipher. His initial statements are polite, if mildly condescending to the girl. After she tells him that anything he may have thought "is perfectly true" (220) he be- gins to flirt with her. But he seems then confounded by the intensity of her responses. He blushes when she tells him she has only stayed at Cocker's for him. When she tells him she would do anything for him, he takes her hand but draws back verbally. Instead of addressing her offer, he says, "I say, you know, you mustn't think of leaving!" (223). When she tries to press further with "Then you *have* quite recognised what I've tried to do?" he seems to try to close the issue: "Why, wasn't that exactly what I dashed over from my door just now to thank you for?" She presses her offer again, and he replies, "Oh see here!" (223-24) as if to call her down to his level of reality, to his greater conventionality. But, whereas James and his reader may be able to "see here," to see Everard's ambivalence and the impossibility of their tra- versing the immense social disparity in a way that isn't "horrid and vulgar" (223), the telegraphist is lost in her own need to see otherwise. She resists to the end. Even after Everard's last, long absence and the girl's decision to go to Mr. Mudge at Chalk Farm, she cannot relinquish her fantasy of power:

"She had framed the whole picture with a squareness that included also the image of how again she would decline to 'see there,' decline, as she might say, to see anywhere, see anything. Yet it befell that just in the fury of the escape she saw more than ever" (245).

If James had ended the novella at this point, the telegraphist's illusions of social and narrative mobility would seem harmless to the reader. The ultimate effect would be satirical. But the final section of the work, in which Mrs. Jordan removes all basis for the girl's illusions, casts a tragic shadow over the telegraphist's experience and also darkens James's critique of omniscient writing. Mrs. Jordan is an illusionist by trade. She practices the "fairy" arts of floral decoration and verbal embellishment, playing on her friend's ignorance of the ways of the rich, persuading her "that a single step more would transform her social position" (177). The illusions she creates rest on a vagueness of expression, on verbal indeterminacy. In this her function parallels Everard's. She toys with the telegraphist in a way that convinces the suggestible girl of immense possibilities. She persuades the girl of the existence of a "door of the great world" and reduces that door before her eyes, through her accounts of her relations with the rich, to a "thin partition" (177). The girl concludes that Mrs. Jordan has prospects with Lord Rye and soberly awaits Mrs. Jordan's announcement of their engagement. The ensuing conversation is a parody of the girl's conversation with Everard in the park. The two women speak on the basis of different narratives—Mrs. Jordan attempting to describe her betrothal to Mr. Drake, who has recently left service with Lord Rye and been "engaged" by Lady Bradeen, and the telegraphist assuming that Mrs. Jordan has become engaged to Lord Rye and then assuming that her actual intended, Mr. Drake, must be a close friend of Lord Rye's. "And awfully rich?" she asks. "[H]e *has* put by," Mrs. Jordan replies (256). The revelation that Mr. Drake, a symbol to the girl of an open door into society, "verily *was* a person who opened the door" (258), prompts a collapse of the figurative into the literal: "[A]nd what our heroine saw and felt for in the whole business was the vivid reflection of her own dreams and delusions and her own return to reality. Reality, for the poor things they both were, would only be ugliness and obscurity, could never be the escape, the rise" (260-61). This collapse gains a tragic quality when Mrs. Jordan reveals Everard's true status as the debt-ridden compromiser of Lady Bradeen. The telegraphist strives to prolong the fiction of her romantic figure with a statement in which she merges herself with Lady Bradeen: "His debts are nothing—when she so adores him" (263). But that effort is foiled when Mrs. Jordan announces that it was Lady Bradeen who saved the couple from scandal by locating the lost telegram rather than the efficient telegraphist who remembered the telegram number. The telegraphist is forced to recognize that not only has her narrative been untrue to life; the role she created for herself—that of saving Everard—has been written out of the story.

When actual events supersede the telegraphist's fictions, her writing enterprise turns in on itself, like her vision. Priscilla Walton observes that the "[t]elegraphist ceases writing when she thinks that she 'knows'" (160). But this would suggest that she stops writing when she steps out of the cage to look for Everard. In effect, she begins writing badly, with false confidence. Her fictional enterprise continues to the end, but it is flawed. James's critique of her writing shows the same distaste for excessive subjectivity that Virginia Woolf would express thirty years later in *A Room of One's Own*. Woolf's description of the flaws she sees in Charlotte Bronte's writing are applicable to the telegraphist's difficulties: "She will write in a rage where she should write calmly. She will write foolishly where she should write wisely. She will write of herself where she should write of her characters. She is at war with her lot. How could she help but die young, cramped and thwarted?" (69–70). James would never consign a witnessing consciousness to the kind of tragic end that Woolf observes in the lives of women writers of the past. He allows the telegraphist her life and her experience—the kind of margin that Lambert Strether alludes to when he says to little Bilham in Gloriani's garden, "Still we have the illusion of freedom; therefore don't, like me to-day, be without the memory of that illusion" (*The Ambassadors*, 213).

This story of a young writer's failed experiments provides a link between James's celebration of the power of creative adventuring in 1884 in "The Art of Fiction" and his more cautionary and technical discussions of fiction writing in the prefaces to the New York Edition of 1907–9. There is "no limit to what [the writer] may attempt," James asserts in 1884 (*Selected Literary Criticism,* 54). But his novella of 1898 demonstrates—and his discussions of 1907–9 confirm—that the writer and his "deputy," the "centering consciousness," fall into trouble when they strive to operate omnisciently. As James advises in his preface to *The Princess Casamassima,* "[T]he wary reader for the most part warns the novelist against making his characters too *interpretative* of the muddle of fate, or in other words too divinely, too priggishly clever" (*Literary Criticism,* 1090). Art renders meaning through containment. Thus, while creative free associations—like the telegraphist's "jumps"—may "lead on and on," as James describes imaginative work in the preface to *Roderick Hudson,* the writer must establish, through the centering consciousness, a "stopping-place," must devise by "a geometry of his own" a circle that contains the subject even while it gives the appearance of continuing possibility (*Literary Criticism,* 1041). When the telegraphist steps out of her cage, she becomes too "interpretative," too "clever." As she presses "on and on," without bounds, her creative enterprise loses its defining form and collapses.

The bleak sense of creative failure in the final moments of "In the Cage" recalls James's expressions of despair after the poor reception of his play *Guy Domville* in 1895. In his notebook he laments the "wasted passion" and "squandered time" given to the theater (*Complete Notebooks,* 115), and he reports in a letter, "As I walked home, alone, after that first night, I swore to myself an oath never again to have anything to do with a business which lets one into such traps, abysses and heart-break. . . . I have practically renounced my deluded dreams" (*Letters,* 521). James consoles himself for his failure with the prospect that "the divine principle of the Scenario" might be applied effectively in narrative writing. Indeed, through the practice of the scenic method in his later novels and in "In the Cage," he converted his "infinite little loss" into "an almost infinite little gain" (*Complete Notebooks,* 115). Unlike her creator, the telegraphist reaps no tangible reward from her failure. She has lost consciousness of herself as a writer. A perpetual reminder of the inescapability of aesthetic limits, she walks the London streets sightlessly, her thoughts "too numerous to find a place" in the final sentences of the story (266).

Note

1. For a critique of readings of the novella as melodrama, see Carren Kaston, who argues that the telegraphist rescues herself from the melodramatic plot through her acceptance of Mudge as an alternative suitor (112). For a discussion of the

telegraphist's fantasies as a response to the service-class experience, see Bauer and Lakritz.

Works Cited

Bauer, Dale M., and Andrew Lakritz. "Language, Class, and Sexuality in Henry James' 'In the Cage.'" *New Orleans Review* 14 (Fall 1987): 61–69.

Bell, Millicent. *Meaning in Henry James.* Cambridge: Harvard University Press, 1991.

James, Henry. *The Ambassadors.* 1903. London: Penguin, 1986.

———. *The Complete Notebooks of Henry James.* Ed. Leon Edel and Lyall H. Powers. New York: Oxford University Press, 1987.

———. *Letters.* Ed. Leon Edel. Vol. 4. Cambridge: Belknap-Harvard University Press, 1980.

———. *Literary Criticism: French Writers, Other European Writers, The Prefaces to the New York Edition.* Library of America. New York: Literary Classics, 1984.

———. *Eight Tales from the Major Phase.* New York: Norton, 1969.

———. *Selected Literary Criticism.* Ed. Morris Shapiro. Cambridge: Cambridge University Press, 1978.

Kaston, Carren. *Imagination and Desire in the Novels of Henry James.* New Brunswick: Rutgers University Press, 1984.

Walton, Priscilla. *The Disruption of the Feminine in Henry James.* Toronto: University of Toronto Press, 1992.

Woolf, Virginia. *A Room of One's Own.* 1929. San Diego: Harcourt, 1981.

Lomeda Montgomery

THE LADY IS THE TIGER
Looking at May Bartram in "The Beast in the Jungle" from the "*Other*" Side

Virtually all readers and critics agree that John Marcher is obtuse, ego-tistical, selfish, and most of all, exceedingly unfair in his treatment of May Bartram. Traditionally, May Bartram is seen as a saintly woman who waits patiently for Marcher to realize that her love is "the thing" that he is waiting for. She is seen as a woman who unselfishly subjugates herself to Marcher's destiny and is exploited by him. The exact nature of the metaphoric beast that lurks in the jungle waiting to spring forth has been interpreted more diversely than the nature of the protagonist and the *ficelle* character. Freudian readings interpret the beast as fear of sexuality, whereas more recent criticism has argued that the beast is Marcher's homophobia.[1] Marcher's own interpre-tation concludes that the spring of the beast is the recognition that, in waiting for the beast, he has lived an empty life—that "no passion had ever touched him" (310). There is, however, an alternative way to read both May's charac-ter and the nature of the beast, a reading that necessitates a very different reading of Marcher's character.

In the final meeting between May and Marcher, when they speak of "the thing" that was to have happened to Marcher, May points out that they are speaking from the "*other* side," that "the thing" has already happened and is behind them (304). Because she has seen the "beast" and Marcher has not, the "*other* side" then becomes May's side, *her* perspective. I suggest that looking at May and at the nature of her relationship with Marcher from her side, "the *other* side," reveals something quite different from traditional readings of both her and the beast waiting to spring. A close reading of the text—with careful attention to the precise language of the prose, echoing metaphors, linguistic parallels, and patterns of imagery—suggests a very different story: one in which May is not a selfless character but *is* the beast, a lamia figure who does not subjugate herself to Marcher's destiny or his ego but rather defines his destiny, possesses his ego, and devours his identity.

From the beginning, the language of the text establishes a parallel between May and the beast. The first time that the narrator uses the beast metaphor he says, "Something or other lay in wait for [Marcher] . . . like a crouching beast in the jungle. . . . The definite point was the inevitable *spring* of the *creature*" (287, italics added). This is not the first time the words "spring" and "creature" have been used in the text. Before the introduction of this metaphor, both words have been used in connection with May Bartram. When she asks Marcher if he has taken others into his confidence, he responds, "I've taken nobody. Not a *creature* since then [since he supposedly shared his secret with May]" (282, italics added). Later the narrator notes that Marcher "took the intercourse [between himself and May] for granted. . . . It simply existed; had *sprung* into being with her first penetrating question to him" (286, italics added). These subtle linguistic parallels call for a closer look at May.

Ruth Yeazell, among others, asserts that the beast springs three times: "when May makes her humble gesture of love . . . when the self absorbed Marcher fails to comprehend her gesture . . . and once more, most horrifyingly, at his final moment of full awareness" (39). I suggest that the beast springs for the first time when their intercourse springs into existence and remains in close proximity to Marcher, intermittently leaping, until that final scene. Marcher senses the presence of the beast early on, commenting to May: "I can't name it. I only know I'm exposed." She answers: "Yes, but exposed—how shall I say?—so directly. So intimately" (292). The only "thing" he is really intimately exposed to is May Bartram herself. The first time Marcher senses that May knows something he does not know, he questions the presence of the beast, "asking himself if he were, by any chance, of a truth, within sight or sound, within touch or reach, within the immediate jurisdiction of the thing that waited" (294). He feels the presence of the beast but fails to recognize it as May, even though he has excluded all society but hers. Because the narrative is filtered through Marcher's consciousness, the reader misreads May because Marcher misreads (or fails to read) her character and the subtext of what she says to him.

What is it in May's nature and behavior that supports the conclusion that she is the beast? I used the term "lamia figure" at the outset, but I do not intend the term in the literal, supernatural sense but rather in the same metaphorical sense that James uses the term "beast." In Greek and Roman mythology and in other literature, the figure of the lamia is varied, but the essence is that she is a witch-like creature who appears in the form of a beautiful woman, enticing and devouring men and/or children. The descriptions of May's appearance and behavior suggest a quality about her that is, if not literally beastly, at least metaphorically lamia-like.

Most significantly, from the very beginning, May "knows" something about Marcher that he has told no one else. After they meet and have passed "all trivial information," the narrator says that Marcher "would have liked to invent something, get her to make-believe with him that some passage of a romantic or critical kind *had* originally occurred. He was really almost reaching out in imagination—as against time—for something that would do" (280). May seems to read his thoughts: "she herself decided to take up the case and, as it were, save the situation . . . what she brought out, at any rate, quite cleared the air and supplied the link" (282). The narrator explains that Marcher had "strangely enough lost the consciousness of having taken [May] so far into [his] confidence" (282). In fact, there is no textual evidence that he ever remembers the incident of the revelation of his secret. She simply "knows" in much the same way the intercourse simply "springs."

Although "it was not in him to tell anyone," he considers her knowing his secret "exquisite luck" and "would doubtless have devoted more time to the odd accident of his lapse of memory if he had not been moved to devote so much to the sweetness, the comfort, as he felt, or the future, that this accident itself had helped to keep fresh" (285). The lamia has cast her spell and created a "sensitive bond" (284). Marcher never questions "the mysterious fate [that] had opened his mouth in youth" and is certain "that the right person *should* know . . . and that May Bartram was clearly right, because—well, because there she was" (285–86). Later when Marcher thinks May knows something he does not know, he attributes her knowledge to her "finer nerves," saying "that was what women had where they were interested, they made out things. . . . Their nerves, their sensibility, their imagination, were conductors and revealers, and the beauty of May Bartram was in particular that she had given herself so to his case" (294). Marcher realizes that there is something unusual about May but refuses to see her "finer nerves" as anything less than positive, as essentially female, certainly not mysterious or unique among women.

He comes closer to realizing the mysterious uniqueness of May's character when he finally describes her physical appearance in the crucial hearth scene, when all readers and critics agree that the beast springs. Up to that point, May is described only as "distinctly handsome" (278), but in this description, there is an air of "other worldliness" about her. She is

> as white as wax . . . she was the picture of a serene, exquisite, but impenetrable sphinx, whose head, or indeed all whose person, might have been powdered with silver. She was a sphinx, yet with her white petals and green fronds she might have been a lily too—only an artificial, wonderfully imitated and constantly kept, without dust or stain, though not exempt from a slight droop and a complexity of faint creases, under some glass bell. (297)

After this, she is described as beautiful "with a strange, cold light" and as having a "cold charm in her eyes" (298–99). Later the narrator says her "wasted face delicately shone . . . and it glittered, almost as with the white lustre of silver" (301). The language of these descriptions suggests that there is something mystical, even unnatural, about May, and there are no contradictory physical descriptions to refute this conclusion. Once again Marcher sees May and describes what he sees without understanding, on a conscious level, the meaning of his own vision.

This approach to the text requires us to scrutinize May's words as carefully as we have Marcher's. In doing so, we find that one of the strongest arguments for the reading of May as a lamia figure is her own rhetoric. Marcher has described her as a "sphinx," and she certainly speaks in riddles. Martha Banta observes that May's "words are controlled, limited and numbered by her secret's demands" (207). There is a pervasive sense that something besides social decorum governs what she can and cannot say. There always seems to be a "right" answer to questions posed to Marcher by May. At the beginning of the hearth scene, Marcher explicitly expresses a concern that he might say the "wrong word" (297), but the focus on exact answers is seen from the beginning when May agrees to watch with Marcher. She asks him three times if he is afraid, seeming not to be satisfied or even able to agree to watch until he gives her precisely the right answer. Rachel Salmon points out that "he never shows that he hears her, but counters with the thrice-repeated non-sequitur: 'watch with me.' Only when he admits that he does not know whether he is afraid, that he 'should *like* to know' and that he wants her to help him find out, does she agree to the vigil" (310).[2] We see the same desperate need to adhere to the rules of the riddle in the hearth scene. May wants Marcher to give the right answer as much as he wants her to name "the thing," and yet for some reason neither can say the right words, even though both their lives seem to depend on it. This is an ironic and complex variation of the sphinx myth. In the original myth, if the man doesn't answer the sphinx's riddle correctly, the sphinx kills him, but in May's case, if Marcher doesn't answer the riddle, she is the one who dies. At the same time, she has, like a lamia, stolen or devoured his life, so that when she (the sphinx) dies, he dies too.

In discussing May, a few critics do what Marcher does—they stalk around the edges of the jungle but at the last minute back away. Martha Banta says that May "is no angelic woman whose good love has no ambition but to save a man if it could. She is the passionate virgin who completely possessed another's consciousness and thus gave him all the being he has" (211). I agree with Banta's observation, but if we look at her conclusion from the "*other* side," we see that in completely possessing Marcher's consciousness May is *taking* rather than *giving*. She takes possession of his identity, his consciousness, and makes it her own. First she creates a bond of secrecy, then she keeps the secret front and center of their lives. We are told that Marcher "didn't expect, that he in fact didn't care always to be talking about it" and suggests to May that maybe "the great thing he had so long felt as in the lap of the gods was no more than this circumstance, which touched him so nearly, of her acquiring a house in London" (287). But we are told that May "was by no means satisfied with such a trifle, as the climax to so special a suspense, she almost set him wondering if she hadn't even a larger conception of singularity for him than he had for himself" (287). Several times the narrator notes that May seems even more obsessed with Marcher's destiny than he is: "she had a wonderful way of making it seem . . . the secret of her own life too. . . . She traced his unhappy perversion through portions of its own course into which he could scarce follow" (288). He says that "while they grew older together, she did watch with him, and so she let this association give shape and colour to her own existence" (288) and that "her original adoption of his own curiosity had quite become the basis of her life" (294). From Marcher's perspective, she has given over her identity to his, but viewed from the "*other*" side" she has made his identity her own.

Lamias devour their prey, and in a metaphoric sense May accomplishes this when she takes possession of Marcher's identity and gains almost complete control over his life. Again, we must avoid being as obtuse as Marcher and examine the precise language of the text. We are told that by sharing his secret, "[May] took his gaiety from him—since it had to pass with them for gaiety—as she took everything else" (288). The narrator says that May "was dying, and [Marcher's] life would end" (302). May denies Marcher his secret by dying without sharing her knowledge of it, and, in doing so, she maintains control over him: "she had forbidden him, so far as he might, to know, and she had even in a sort denied the power in him to learn" (307). By declaring that what was to happen has happened without Marcher's being aware of it, she has stolen his vision of himself, his identity. He calls it "the lost stuff of consciousness," but the language of the text suggests it is not lost but stolen. The narrator likens Marcher and his "lost stuff of consciousness" to "a strayed or *stolen* child" and "an unappeasable father" (307, italics added). This is consistent with the classic vision of the lamia who devoured children. One of the last things May says to Marcher before she dies is "It has touched you. It has done its office. It has made you all its own" (303). She could have easily substituted "I" for "it," and the statement would have been equally consistent within the context of the story. By not telling Marcher the nature of "the thing," May has made him all her own; she has devoured his identity and taken it to the grave with her. The text confirms this conclusion when the narrator says that as Marcher stood before her grave, "his point of orientation," imagining her eyes watching him, he "settled to live—feeding only on the sense that he once *had* lived, and dependent on it not only for a support but for an *identity*" (309, second italics added).

In addition to the physical images of May as "other worldly" discussed earlier, during the scene at the hearth, when all readers agree that the beast springs, May's physical movements embody the springing motion of the metaphoric beast. She rises from her chair "as if to make it more vivid for him" and "hovered before him," then "with her gliding step, diminished the distance between them, and stood near to him, close to him, a minute, as if still full of the unspoken" (299–300). When he fails to recognize her as "the thing" (the beast), she gives way to "a slow, fine shudder" and "regained her chair" (301). This moment is recalled by Marcher in the final scene when he realizes that "the beast had lurked indeed, and the beast, at its hour, had sprung; it had sprung in that twilight of the cold April when, pale, ill, wasted, but all beautiful, and perhaps even then recoverable, she had risen from her chair to stand before him and let him imaginably guess. It has sprung as he didn't guess" (311). After May's death, Marcher senses that "the Beast had stolen away" (306), and he again refers to her as a "creature" when he visits her grave: "The creature beneath the sod *knew* of his rare experience" (308).

At the final meeting between May and Marcher, he asks, "You mean it [the beast] has come as a positive, definite occurrence, with a *name* and a *date?*" (303, italics added). She replies: "Positive. Definite. I don't know about the *'name,'* but, oh, with a *date!*" (303, italics added). This language is echoed when Marcher visits May's grave: "He stood for an hour, powerless to turn away and yet powerless to penetrate the darkness of death; fixing with his eyes her inscribed *name* and *date,* beating his forehead against the fact of the secret they kept" (307, italics added). Collectively, these images suggest that May *is* the beast and that what Marcher feels in the end, in the "stir of air [that] rise[s], huge and hideous, for the leap that was to settle him" is actually May, the lamia figure, finally claiming her prey.

As we look at the story from the "*other* side," we are faced with the question of May's motivation. Traditional readings center Marcher's motivation around his inflated ego and essential selfishness. The motives of the lamia figure are more sinister. She is not human but appears to be while she entices and devours her prey. We have already seen that within this metaphor May entices and devours, but what of her "humanness"? Donna Przybylowicz suggests that May is "dehumanized at Marcher's hands" (104). But from the "*other* side," May's own rhetoric suggests that she gets what she wants. When Marcher asks, "How shall I ever repay you?" May answers, "By going on as you are" (293). According to May's own words, their relationship is a fair trade: "If you've had your woman, I've had, my man . . . I don't know why it [their relationship] shouldn't make me—*humanly, which is what we're speaking of*—as right as it makes you" (293, italics added). This is the desire of the lamia, to appear human in order to devour her prey. May's needs as a lamia figure are satisfied, and she expresses that satisfaction explicitly, assuring Marcher that what he calls her curiosity "will be but too well repaid" (290).

This reading of May as a lamia figure, as the metaphoric beast, necessitates a new reading of Marcher. He remains extremely obtuse, hearing but not understanding May's own words and speaking without understanding what he himself is saying. However, if May is a lamia figure, then Marcher is not nearly as egotistical or selfish as traditional readings assert. We have already seen in our examination of May's motives that Marcher is quite conflicted about May's dedication to "the watch" and over the toll it may be taking on her life. Just before the hearth scene, Marcher "recognized how long he had waited, or how long, at least, his companion had. That she, at all events, might be recorded as having waited in vain—this affected him sharply, and all the more because of his at first having done little more than amuse himself with the idea" (295). What he doesn't recognize, until the end, is that it is *she* who has made "the thing" the center of their lives. If May is the metaphoric beast, then Marcher becomes a victim, and his anxiety about his own safety is justified, as is his seemingly selfish behavior. Many critics discuss his pursuit of the beast, but only once does the language of the text actually suggest any form of active pursuit: "a man of feeling didn't cause himself to be accompanied by a lady on a tiger-hunt" (287). Ruth Yeazell points out that "Marcher the tiger-hunter is in reality Marcher the terrified . . . while he pursues his beast, Marcher flees in terror from ordinary human contact and from love" (37). I agree that he is terrified, not because he is fleeing from human contact, but because he is always in the presence of the beast, without recognizing, of course, that this is why he is afraid. On some level, he realizes that with May's death, the beast disappears: "now that the Jungle had been threshed to vacancy and that the Beast had stolen away . . . Marcher waded through his beaten grass, where no life stirred, where no breath sounded, where no evil eye seemed to gleam from a possible lair, very much as if vaguely looking for the Beast, and still more as if missing it" (306).

A close reading of the final paragraphs indicates that Marcher comes to recognize that May has, in fact, been the metaphoric beast. Banta says that Marcher "did not know that his lady's love was the tiger" (212). I suggest that he did not know that the lady was herself the tiger, until the final moments of his life. As he stares at May's grave, he once again refers to her as a "creature," and, as he stares at her name on the stone table, "he rested without power to move, as if some spring in him, some spell vouchsafed, had suddenly been broken forever" (310). Although he recognizes that "no passion had ever touched him," he also realizes that "*she* had lived—who could say now with what passion?" (311). As he remembers the hearth scene and recognizes that it was then that the beast had sprung, he also remembers the physical image of May rising from her chair and springing. The final lines of the text tell us that Marcher "saw the Jungle of his life and saw the lurking Beast," but we know also that at that moment he is physically looking at May's tomb. He is, in fact, totally consumed with her tomb at that moment of recognition, suggesting a merging of literal and mental images. His desperate reaction to the final leap when the air stirs and the beast rises "huge and hideous" indicates that his knowledge of the nature of the beast has become conscious. The shock of realizing that he has lived most of his adult life in the presence of the beast (in the person of May Bartram), in the lair of her London home, that she limited his life, that she enabled and encouraged him to withdraw from society, and that she consumed his identity accounts for his final, desperate reaction, which is, if not literally death, equivalent in its effect: "his eyes darkened . . . and, instinctively turning, in his hallucination, to avoid it, he flung himself, on his face, on the tomb" (312).

The ambiguity of the ending of "The Beast in the Jungle" is James's genius, and for this reason I do not suggest that reading the text from the "*other* side" is the only valid perspective. I do suggest that reading May as a lamia figure, as the metaphoric beast, is a textually sound reading, based on close examination of the language and images from a different perspective, that it adds another dimension to an already complex short story, and that it may prompt a closer look at other seemingly passive Jamesian *ficelle* characters.[3]

Notes

1. See particularly Sedgwick.
2. Although Salmon's observation is made to further a slightly different point, it also supports the notion that May communicates in riddles.
3. Solomon takes a similar approach in evaluating the character of Mrs. Grose in "The Turn of the Screw." Reading the language of the text closely and precisely, as I have done in this essay, he concludes that the governess "never realizes, as the thoughtful reader must, that she, and Miles, and indeed, Miss Jessell and Peter Quint, have all been the victims of that most clever and desperate of Victorian villainesses, the evil Mrs. Grose" (211).

Works Cited

Banta, Martha. *Henry James and the Occult: The Great Extension.* Bloomington: Indiana University Press, 1972.

James, Henry. "The Beast in the Jungle." In *Tales of Henry James,* 277–312. Ed. Christof Wegelin. New York: Norton, 1984.

Przybylowicz, Donna. "'The Lost Stuff of Consciousness': The Priority of Futurity and the Deferral of Desire in 'The Beast in the Jungle.'" In *Henry James's "Daisy Miller," "The Turn of the Screw," and Other Tales.* Ed. Harold Bloom, 93–116. New York: Chelsea House, 1987.

Salmon, Rachel. "Naming and Knowing in Henry James's 'Beast in the Jungle': The Hermeneutics of a Sacred Text." *Orbis Litteratum* 36 (1981): 302–22.

Sedgwick, Eve Kosofsky. "The Beast in the Corner." In *Sex, Politics, and the Nineteenth Century Novel.* Ed. Ruth Bernard Yeazell, 148–86. Baltimore: Johns Hopkins University Press, 1986.

Solomon, Eric. "The Return of the Screw." *The University Review* (Kansas City) 30 (1964): 205–11.

Yeazell, Ruth Bernard. *Language and Knowledge in the Late Novels of Henry James.* Chicago: University of Chicago Press, 1976.

Annette Gilson

"SOME PANTOMIMIC RAVISHMENT"
"Broken Wings" and the Performance of Success

ALTHOUGH JAMES STATES in his preface that he cannot remember "the buried germ" (ix) that inspired "Broken Wings" (1900), he attests to the story's importance to him when he adds that this does not matter,

> for when had I been, as a fellow scribbler, closed to the general admonition of such adventures as poor Mrs. Harvey's, the elegant representative of literature at Mundham?—to such predicaments as Stuart Straith's, gallant victim of the same hospitality and with the same confirmed ache beneath his white waistcoat? The appeal of mature purveyors obliged, in the very interest of their presumed, their marketable, freshness, to dissimulate the grim realities of shrunken "custom," the felt chill of a lower professional temperature—any old note-book would show *that* laid away as a tragic "value" not much less tenderly than some small plucked flower of association left between the leaves for pressing. (ix)

James attests quite candidly to the relevance of this story to his own experience with the problem of marketability, a problem that is especially felt by a "mature purveyor" like himself. In the nineties, James had attempted to establish himself once more in the popular market (perhaps, as F. O. Matthiessen has suggested, remembering the success he had tasted with *Daisy Miller*).[1] His efforts went unrewarded, and a number of stories during and after this time treat unhappy authors in relation to unappreciative marketplaces. After the failure of *Guy Domville* in 1895 James's sense of being unpopular only increased, and his response to this was to distance himself from the market, as he has Ray Limbert do in "The Next Time." Limbert, the narrator remarks, is an author for whom "The voice of the market had suddenly grown faint and far" (*Stories,* 279). But as Marcia Jacobson observes, "Retreat to the purely private is never possible for the author who would publish"; she adds, "For a writer as alert to the concerns of his culture as James was, discovery and acceptance of his place as a minority writer did not lessen his interest in the larger literary marketplace" (98–99). Indeed, as Michael Anesko points out, James eventually recognized that "smaller, more discriminating publics existed in tandem with [the mass market] and might be capable of supporting writers of distinction . . . that quite a few firms were willing to pay for the privilege of publishing one of the better sort" (143).[2] Jonathan Freedman concludes that although James "negotiated brilliantly the demands of [the] market—wheeling and dealing with publishers, editors and agents; courting first one reading public, then another, then another," he was "all the while complaining bitterly about the vulgar demands of the marketplace in which he performed so brilliantly" (178). James's complaints about the marketplace, Freedman argues, were part of a very skillful construction of himself as alienated author whose very alienation from the marketplace was proof of his mystified and exalted status as "disinterested, artistic novelist" (178).

All this helps to put into perspective James's complex relationship to the literary marketplace of the late nineteenth and early twentieth centuries, a marketplace that is part of the focus of the story "Broken Wings." Yet in this story James is not setting up the artist as the pseudoreligious officiator at the altar of the aesthetic. The painter Stuart Straith and the novelist Mrs. Harvey are, much like James himself, self-consciously playing the role of artist to that important audience, members of upper-class society, here represented by the country-house set at Mundham, where Straith and Harvey meet after ten years of estrangement. Like the author, both have experienced success in the past only to face, in the present, as James phrases it, "the grim realities of shrunken 'custom,' the felt chill of a lower professional temperature" (ix): Straith now designs costumes for the stage, and Mrs. Harvey has turned to journalism (in particular the production of "London Letters" on current theatrical productions) to make a living. That the two actively try to "keep up" with the rich does not trouble them until they realize that they are also playing the role of successful artist for one another out of wounded pride. The two had been in love ten years ago, but each thought the other more successful and so restrained his or her emotions, in part so as not to impede the successful career of the other, and in part because neither felt good enough in the eyes of the other. Appropriately, they do not speak at Mundham. They come together only later, at a chance meeting at the theater, where they reveal to one another the truth of their straitened circumstances and lack of "success," as well as their mutual regard for one another.

Though similarities exist between James's position in relation to the marketplace and the situation of Straith and Harvey (for example, James himself published a number of "London letters" in *Harper's Weekly* in 1897), the differences are telling: James defines himself against the market that Straith and Harvey wish they had a place in. But like his characters James deliberately cultivated an upper-class audience so as to secure his position professionally, and it is through "Broken Wings" that we can see the difficulty that this cultivation, much less than the simple desire for a marketplace success, presents to the artist. Leon Edel observes that this story expresses James's growing "antipathy toward the English country-house and large week-end parties that contrasted with the relish he had taken in them fifteen or twenty years before" (339). In fact it is more than antipathy. As I will discuss below, James seems to indicate that there is a real danger to artists in proceeding along this course.

We can better understand the complexity of James's attitude toward the social status of artists and their relationship to upper-class society and the marketplace by further contextualizing this story. David Golumbia points out that we do not know whether Harvey and Straith are supposed to be "true" artists or popular ones. The reason for this ambiguity may lie in what the characters represented to James. Our knowledge of James's own attitude toward his characters can only be provisional, but Adeline Tintner provides a suggestive clue when she points out that the characters of Mrs. Harvey and Stuart Straith are most likely based on Mrs. Oliphant, the prolific Victorian novelist who died in 1897, and her husband, Lawrence. Such a source helps to explain the subtextual tension between popular and artistic success in "Broken Wings," a tension that, as Tintner points out, James felt Mrs. Oliphant to embody. The subtextual status of this tension is itself interesting when we take into consideration Tintner's observation that, by 1899, James was producing an assortment of stories and articles "very much in the manner of Mrs. Oliphant, who worked at any and every literary turn for the money" (3018). While promoting himself as an unpopular and elite author, James was in fact producing a range of literary works, including literary criticism, stories, and travel pieces, much as Jonathan Freedman suggests.[3] But what adds to the interest of "Broken Wings" is the fact that James seems there to be exploring the dangerous conflict of interest that artists face as they attempt to play the market and the rich while at the same time producing their own work.

Because we never know for certain the kinds of artists Straith and Harvey are, James forces us to pay attention instead to their feelings about their straitened circumstances and to the way they handle themselves in relation to the upper-class world they attempt to "keep up" with. We realize that, in dramatic terms, Straith and Harvey do not speak at Mundham because it is Mundham that has kept them apart. In other words, they have accepted the terms of success established by Mundham. As a result they exist in a state of confusion about their own roles in the world of the wealthy, a state that is also one of isolation. And because there is a discrepancy between their "real" economic value in this world and the appearance they project, they feel themselves to be failures, and at the same time, because they have lied, alienated from who they really are. James highlights the opposition between artists and the wealthy by casting their respective worlds as competing subcultures that vie for the authority of defining independent individuality and aesthetic value. But in this case James refuses to resolve that contest by contrasting the quality of the artists' work to the vulgar concerns of philistines. Instead he focuses on the dangers attendant on Straith's and Harvey's conflation of terms, in particular, the dangers of accepting the terms of success established by a culture that is, for all its proximity to them, essentially foreign to the artists.

The story opens with Straith standing alone, looking out over the elaborate terraces and gardens of Mundham, a mundus whose ability to isolate him from any human interaction hints at the role it will play in this story. Straith is isolated even from Mrs. Harvey, who he (mistakenly) believes is a "success" there and whose very way of holding herself is beautiful, he says, because of "the good thing she professionally made of it all" (316). Straith's misunderstanding of Mrs. Harvey's professional relationship to the Mundham set is of a piece with his acceptance of Mundham's definition of aesthetic beauty. The narrator observes: "The air of the place, with the immense house all seated aloft in strength, robed with summer and crowned with success, was such as to contribute something of its own to the poetry of early evening. This visitor at any rate saw and felt it all through one of those fine hazes of August that remind you—at least they reminded *him*—of the artful gauze stretched across the stage of a theatre when an effect of mystery or some particular pantomimic ravishment is desired" (315–16). Straith seems to acquiesce to Mundham's versions of poetic and dramatic effect, in part because Mundham's success seems to give it the right to define these things. As he did with Mrs. Harvey, Straith accepts here that success is defined by social power rather than by aesthetic ability.

Both Straith and Harvey have been ravished by Mundham's performance of success, so much so that they have allowed the notion of this success to eclipse all other ways of valuing themselves. In repudiating his previous compliance with the terms that Mundham had set, Straith muses that Mrs. Harvey

> had really found in the pomp of his early success . . . exactly the ground for her sense of failure with him that he had found in the vision of her gross popularity for his conviction that she judged him as comparatively small. Each had blundered, as sensitive souls of the "artistic temperament" blunder, into a conception not only of the other's attitude, but of the other's material situation at the moment, that had thrown them back on stupid secrecy, where their estrangement had grown like an evil plant in the shade. (327)

The language James uses to describe Straith's and Harvey's blunders is very emphatic: these are not innocent misunderstandings; they are "stupid" and "evil." Straith and Harvey have been guilty of conflating the notion of success, as defined by the wealthy, with their own artistic success. Intent as they are on "keeping up," they attempt to create the appearance of material success for the world and for one another, even though this means that they have less energy to do their real work.

But playing by Mundham's rules does not simply distract the artists. The nature of social interaction in this world is both competitive and hierarchical; the narrator explains that Straith and Harvey "were the only persons present [at Mundham] without some advantage over somebody else" (314). Their lack of advantage is the reason for their presence there: "they could be named for nothing but their cleverness; they were at the bottom of the social ladder. The social ladder had even at Mundham—as they might properly have been told, as indeed practically they *were* told—to end somewhere; which is no more than to say that as he strolled about . . . Stuart Straith had after all a good deal the sense of helping to hold it up" (315). His sense of his own inferiority is part of the reason that Straith has difficulty distinguishing his own sense of individual and artistic success from that put forth by Mundham.

But the danger posed by Mundham is not simply that the artists will question their self-worth. To Mrs. Harvey, the invitation to Mundham is a "crushing"—an inexplicable—blow (319); she can only explain her presence there by observing that London is "wild" (318). It is a blow, she clarifies at the end of the story, because "everything costs that one does for the rich. It's not our poor relations who make us pay" (330). But payment is not simply in the form of the artists' limited financial resources; the rich also take "the imagination" (330). Straith agrees that they have spent their imagination trying to protect themselves from the rich, and at this point the two understand that they can defy the standards for success imposed upon them by the wealthy. They agree not to "keep up," to have instead the courage to live according to their own standards of success. This courage comes from one another: "He took her in his arms, she let herself go, and he held her long and close for the compact. But when they had recovered themselves enought to handle their agreement more responsibly the words in which they confirmed it broke in sweetness as well as sadness from both together: 'And now to work!'" (330).

The key to this curious representation of artists and the wealthy caught up in a bizarre shadow-play—where artists "hold up" the social ladder and provide the rich with imagination, while the rich give to artists (the illusion of) social success—may lie in the theatrical metaphors that structure the story. On the one hand these metaphors emphasize the complicated interpenetration of the two ways of valuing, aesthetic and economic, calling into question which can be termed "performative," which "real." But on a deeper level these metaphors register a profound ambivalence on James's part, one that may be associated with his failure to achieve success in the theater but that also seems tied to his attempts to market himself for the upper class. The theater becomes the site of the conflation of the two subcultures, as well as the stage upon which the competition between the two plays itself out.

This is most evident in the "pantomimic ravishment" that Straith experiences at the story's beginning when he is exposed to the seductions of the wealthy world. This theatrical metaphor initially seems to valorize the values espoused by the country-house set. But Mundham's "strength, robed with summer and crowned with success," is called into question after the two artists unite. In the first place there is, of course, the fact that Straith and Harvey are each forced to sell themselves by mechanically churning out some form of pseudoartistic production linked to the theater, for which they are unappreciated and underpaid. But even more important is the fact that the theater later in the story presents an inverted reflection of the ambiguity surrounding Straith's and Harvey's artistic status.

After seeing each other at Mundham, Straith and Harvey find themselves seated next to each other just as the curtain is about to rise on a popular play. This is a nice dramatic irony: their reduced circumstances bring them together, just as their mistaken belief in one another's "success" kept them apart. The narrator observes:

> The first night of "The New Girl" occurred, as every one remembers, three years ago, and the play is running yet, a fact that may render strange the failure to be deeply conscious of which two persons in the audience were guilty. It was not till afterwards present either to Mrs. Harvey or to Stuart Straith that "The New Girl" was one of the greatest successes of modern times. Indeed if the question had been put to them on the spot they might have appeared at sea. (320)

Golumbia points out that it is impossible to tell from this passage whether

The New Girl is "an artistic 'success,' or a popular one" (155). I would suggest that this is so because in this story theater represents the ambiguous (because performative) nature of success: as soon as a play is declared successful, there is a potential or actual conflation of aesthetic and economic values. And whereas Straith and Harvey are the victims of this performative ambiguity, theater itself becomes, through the association of metaphors, the vehicle for their victimization.[4]

In other words, James's repudiations of the wealthy and of theater are inextricably connected. Preoccupied by one another's presence, Straith and Harvey pay little attention to the production of *The New Girl,* and "one of them" observes that, "whatever the piece might be, the real thing, as they had seen it at Mundham, was more than a match for any piece. For Mundham *was,* theatrically, the real thing; better for scenery, dresses, music, pretty women, bare shoulders, everything—even coherent dialogue; a much bigger and braver show, and got up, as it were, infinitely more 'regardless'" (321). So the phrase "pantomimic ravishment" that had been used earlier in the story to signal Mundham's success becomes unanchored when it becomes evident that, for the theatrical, Mundham beats out theater itself. Mundham borrowed the theater's projective power, its ability to evoke mystery and aesthetic pleasure for an audience, in order to present itself as successful and desirable. However, the story exposes the illusory nature of this borrowed enhancement: the theater is only a weak imitation of Mundham, therefore Mundham cannot base its claims to success on its being like the theater. The implications are that (through an unspecified mechanism) Mundham has constructed the theater as a paean to itself, so that it can seem to imitate what is in fact merely an image of itself; through this imitation it receives valorization, at the same time that it pretends that the two are discrete entities.

By establishing the performative nature of success on a metaphorical level, the story ends the competition between subcultures by annulling it. This is why, at the story's end, when Mrs. Harvey observes that they can choose to have the courage not to keep up, even if they have nothing else, Straith agrees by adding triumphantly, "Let us at least be beaten together!" (330). Clearly the two are not beaten but have finally won by choosing not to play. Of course, the issue of failure has been introduced earlier in the story in another way: through the lack of any "objective" verifications of the quality of the two artists' work. It becomes clear that James in some sense had to leave this question unanswered. If he had claimed for the two artists ability and merit that had gone unacknowledged, he would have been calling on the very mystified and "aesthetic" notion of valuation discussed above, which is simply the inverse of the reductive economic system of value represented in the story by the wealthy. Harvey and Straith must step out of this loop completely in order to be free of it, which they do at the end of the story, embracing one another and their work.

I began this essay with James's own comments on the affinity he felt to Straith and Harvey and his familiarity with the problems with which they had to contend. But perhaps the strongest evidence for James's engagement with these characters is the fact that, unlike most of his stories, "Broken Wings" ends not with renunciation and a gaze directed backward at what has been lost, but with rebirth and happiness.[5] Straith and Harvey look toward the future with a renewed sense of creativity and the promise of meaningful human interactions. They have faced what is, for artists, possibly the most dangerous threat to a sustainable existence (tied as it is to their work): the corruption of their own values. They have faced this and recognized that there still exists for them the possibility of learning from one's mistakes and finding happiness. The metaphorical pun that James makes in this story on theater and on the performative nature of success may indeed provide him with a fleeting vengeful satisfaction, but it is at the same time an elegant symbol both for the story and for his own life.

Notes

1. Matthiessen offers this suggestion in the context of "Broken Wings," remarking on the relevance of this story to James's own experience with the popular market.

2. James, in a letter to William Dean Howells, describes himself in this period as having "fallen upon evil days—every sign or symbol of one's being in the least *wanted,* anywhere or by any one, having so utterly failed" (quoted in Edel, *Henry James: The Treacherous Years,* 94). James's sincerity with regard to the issue of his marketability has been called into question by Jonathan Freedman. Like Marcia Jacobson, Freedman is interested in the ways in which such a stance may have disguised a strategy (or have been a strategy in its own right) for gaining more power in the marketplace. Jacobson observes that James was exaggerating his unpopularity in this letter (86), and indeed James went on to

publish in the *Yellow Book*, though not without becoming associated with the decadent movement, as Freedman points out (177).

3. Edel provides a comprehensive list of James's 1899 publishing frenzy in *Henry James: The Treacherous Years* (338).

4. I do not mean to claim with this reading that James was turning his back entirely on the theater. He affirms his strong attraction to this venue when he writes to William on 6 February 1891, "I feel at last as if I had found my real form, which I am capable of carrying far, and for which the pale little art of fiction, as I have practised it, has been, for me, but a limited and restricted substitute" (*Letters*, 329)—one which, I imagine, he never completely eradicated. But, as Edel notes, James's attitude toward drama and theater had long been one of "ambivalence" (*Henry James: The Middle Years*, 282). Several years after the letter to William, Henry declared to Elizabeth Robins, "I may be made for the Drama (God only knows!) But am not made for the theatre!" (31 December 1894) (*Letters*, 503). This was before the famous "failure" of *Guy Domville*, which James later said caused him to swear "to myself an oath never again to have anything to do with a business which lets one into such traps, abysses and heartbreak" (quoted in Edel, *Henry James: The Treacherous Years*, 83). James wrote in his notebook at this time, "I take up my *own* old pen again—the pen of all my old unforgettable efforts and sacred struggles. To myself—today— I need say no more. Large and full and high the future still opens. It is now indeed that I may do the work of my life. And I will. I have only to *face* my problems. But all that is of the ineffable—too deep and pure for any utterance. Shrouded in sacred silence let it rest" (quoted in Edel, *Henry James: The Treacherous Years*, 95). The language of this passage is reminiscent of the end of "Broken Wings"; perhaps in that story James articulated the struggles he felt with regard to the theater and the problem of marketing himself while honoring the sacred status of the work itself.

5. Critical opinion on how to read the end of "Broken Wings" is divided. Brooke Horvath discusses the story in the context of the aesthetics of defeat that James's artists create to justify their failure both to live and to create art. Horvath includes in this paradigm the artists from "Broken Wings," an assessment that certainly applies to the two before they have made their confessions and turned their backs on Mundham. But Horvath, who does not believe that Straith's and Harvey's resolution will have lasting effects, claims instead that they are simply investing now in "the fiction of the life to come" (106) as a replacement for the fiction of success that they lived by before their communal confessions. The opposite view is presented most emphatically by Edward Wagenknecht, who declares that "Broken Wings" is "one of James's tenderest tales" (127). Edel agrees with him, claiming that after Straith and Harvey confess the truth of their circumstances to one another, "Life together is now pos-

sible; their wings 'broken,' they can face the future and recognize their old love" (*Henry James: The Treacherous Years,* 326). I take on faith (perhaps naively) the transformation Straith and Harvey say they experience, in part because I see this transformation as something that James himself may have wanted to believe in.

Works Cited

Anesko, Michael. *"Friction with the Market": Henry James and the Profession of Authorship.* New York: Oxford University Press, 1986.

Edel, Leon. *Henry James: The Middle Years, 1882–1895.* Philadelphia: Lippincott, 1962.

———. *Henry James: The Treacherous Years, 1895–1901.* Philadelphia: Lippincott, 1969.

Freedman, Jonathan. *Professions of Taste: Henry James, British Aestheticism, and Commodity Culture.* Stanford: Stanford University Press, 1990.

Golumbia, David. "Toward an Ethics of Cultural Acts: The Jamesian Dialectic in 'Broken Wings.'" *Henry James Review* 15 (1994): 152–69.

Horvath, Brooke. "The Life of Art, the Art of Life: The Ascetic Aesthetics of Defeat in James's *Stories of Writers and Artists." Modern Fiction Studies* 28 (1982): 93–107.

Jacobson, Marcia. *Henry James and the Mass Market.* University: University of Alabama Press, 1983.

James, Henry. *Letters.* Ed. Leon Edel. Vol. 3. Cambridge: Belknap-Harvard University Press, 1980.

———. Preface. In *The Novels and Tales of Henry James,* 16:v–xii. The New York Edition. New York: Scribner's, 1909.

———. *Stories of Writers and Artists.* Ed. F. O. Matthiessen. New York: New Directions, 1945.

Matthiessen, F. O. "Introduction: Henry James's Portrait of the Artist." In *Stories of Writers and Artists, by Henry James,* 1–17. New York: New Directions, 1945.

Tintner, Adeline R. "'Broken Wings': Henry James' Tribute to a Victorian Novelist." *AB Bookman's Weekly,* 22 April 1985, 3018–28.

Wagenknecht, Edward. *The Tales of Henry James.* Literature and Life Series. New York: Ungar, 1984.

Earl Rovit

THE LANGUAGE AND IMAGERY OF "THE JOLLY CORNER"

"The Jolly Corner" has a special potency in James's canon, it seems to me, in that it squeezes within its relatively narrow compass many of the major preoccupations and thematic concerns that are treated in a more leisurely fashion in other tales and in much longer fictions. And, further, it does this with a lyrical portentousness leavened by whimsical humor. As though it were a portmanteau compilation charged, however elliptically, to carry all of James's traveling possessions, we can find in it most of the recurrent dialectics of the Jamesian conversation: Europe and America, the past and the present, culture and commerce, sensibility and power, the isolation of consciousness from communal life, the ambivalences of sexual alignments, the illusory promise of a second chance, the ultimate equation of aesthetics and morality. And the tale is told within the atmosphere of the "crepuscular" that James's fictions had become most adroit at realizing. It is, in fact, a masterful rendering in what might be called, in a double sense, "the genre of the interior"—a setting from which nature is ruthlessly banned and in which human beings must cope, both comically and desperately, with their own artificial constructions of themselves. Here are presented the boundary-ambiences of physical and psychological mergings where discrete entities are edged into perilous proximity to that which is most their "other"—forcing a kind of shimmering shudder of incipient redefinition.

"The Jolly Corner" can be and has been viewed as a kind of *You Can't Go Home Again* autobiographical confession; as a middle-aged love story; as a ghost story; as a hunting tale—James's "Big Two-Hearted River," perhaps—as a quest or journey-romance; and/or as an exercise in self-education. To be sure, each of these sometimes-overlapping readings has its own validity, and, collectively, they can provide high-wattage illumination on many of the murky processes of the literary achievement. In this brief essay, my own efforts will be far more modest. I shall try to focus primarily on the extraordinary language and imagery of the tale—language that almost obsessively brings oppositions into apposition and, without resolving the incompatibilities of their mergence, succeeds in framing an oddly satisfying *stasis* of evocative irresolution.

The title itself, which becomes a sustaining leitmotif in the story, is a prime example. The "house on the jolly corner" is the one of the two properties that Spencer Brydon is determined to preserve. It is his childhood home, his ancestral quasi-Egyptian tomb, a house of memory, an inverted crystal bowl containing a "mystical other world," a sportsman's hunting-ground, a seventy-year-old relic of artisanship in the midst of a shoddy sea of "rank money-madness," the claustrophobic prison in which the alter ego of his stifled opportunities has resided in solitary confinement for thirty-three years. But note the peculiar evocativeness of the image of "the jolly corner." "Corner" (derived from "cornu," a horn or tip) is a place where the converging sides or edges of something meet, forming an angular projection, theoretically of infinite extension. With the initial consonant sound of the hard "c," there is an active cutting connotation of the word. A corner essentially defines the space that it aggressively occupies, and it does so with geometric rigor. "Jolly," on the other hand, a soft round word, as it were, suggesting good cheer, merriment, plumpness, signifies in all the directions most alien to "corners." With its double "l's," the very look and the open-mouthed sound of the word imply an excess and childish innocence too overflowing to be constrained within clean-cut angles. Curiously enough, the house per se is never referred to as "the jolly corner," but, through its association with the larger location, it becomes so identified in the reader's mind, even though little of jollity occurs there and the architectural corners of the house themselves become blurrily indistinct as Brydon stalks and is stalked by his alter ego.

It ought also to be noted that there is a surprising paucity of hard-edged physical description in the story—in, that is, what might be called concrete "thinginess." As probably befits a tale in which the acuity of identification and the reliability of perception are consistently exacerbated by the deliberate ambience of light-shade, of objects overlayered by their auras, most of the imagery is disproportionately diffused on what Spencer Brydon's heightened feelings are *like* rather than on a delineation of the actual *things* that furnish his world and that stimulate his responsiveness. Interestingly enough, Brydon and Alice Staverton are never physically described. Thus, if only because of their relative sparseness, the items that do make a concrete appearance take on an importance well beyond their actual signification. A partial list of such items would include—and notice how they tend to fall into natural couplings—Mrs. Muldoon's broomstick, Brydon's steel-pointed cane, the black-and-white marble squares of the downstairs landing, the candles that Brydon uses to illuminate his nocturnal forays, the electric street lamps on the avenue, the "hard silver of the autumn stars" (458), the silver-plated doorknobs, skyscrapers, Brydon's monocle, the alter ego's pince-nez, the impressionistic fragments of his evening dress ("of gleaming silk lappet and white linen, of pearl button and gold watch-guard and polished shoe" [475]), and, finally, the stumps on his right hand where two fingers appear to have been accidentally shot away.

Yet, as is already evident in the pairings implicit in the foregoing list and as may be inevitable in a narrative in which the central conflict is between mirror "doubles," almost every element surrounding that struggle becomes severely polarized—and that on the most basic levels. In a drama enacted in the "cold silvery nimbus" (474) of dusk, in the autumn of the year, and one in which the major players are on the shank-end of middle age—that is to say, when the only suspense in an impending change is whether it will be accepted gracefully or bitterly—the degree of difference between the apparently incongruous contending forces can only be marginal. In fact, part of the consistently ironic tone that pervades the tale ("humorous" might be too extravagant a word) derives from the incongruity between the desperate melodrama with which Brydon imbues his struggle—and he is quite right to do so—and the larger perspective that views a relatively ineffectual middle-aged man coming into a kind of grudgingly resigned possession of himself. In other words, with something of the same delicate balance between the heroic and the mock-heroic that characterizes some other stories of this period ("The Beast in the Jungle," for example), "The Jolly Corner" presents a quixotic narcissist flailing valiantly at the real windmills and giants of his fearful imagination.

But, returning to the curious polarization of the language, it is interesting to see the kinds of consistent oppositions in which the text revels: soft/hard, round/angular, sharp/blurry, bright/dark, cold/warm, passive/active, masculine/feminine, quality/quantity, old/new, open/closed, inside/outside, etc. Obviously, many of the items fall into multiple categories, and those not always predictable (Alice Staverton's last name, for instance); in general, however, these oppositions conform to the recurrent dialectics of the Jamesian discourse previously alluded to (power and sensibility, commerce and culture, etc). And yet, although the development, climax, and denouement of the narrative structure adhere essentially to a melodramatic formula where the forces of goodness and righteousness grapple successfully with falsity, evil, and death, the plethora of antonymous oppositions within the text eludes the easy valuations that melodrama leads us to expect.

Short of a line-by-line exegesis, this is difficult to demonstrate, but let me cite a characteristic Jamesian sentence that occurs early in the story, one referring to Brydon's visits to Alice Staverton's Irving Street house, which he uses as a sort of safe haven in the turmoil of this new Manhattan given over to "the builders and destroyers" of frenetic capitalistic enterprise. We should remember that one of the disturbances with which Brydon is beset after his thirty-three-year absence from New York is the recent adoption of a severe postal system of numbered addresses—including both the numbered east-west streets as well as the north-south avenues:

> If he knew the way to it [Alice's house] now better than to any other ad-
> dress among the dreadful multiplied numberings which seemed to him
> to reduce the whole place to some vast ledger-page, overgrown, fantas-
> tic, of ruled and crisscrossed lines and figures—if he had formed, for his
> consolation, that habit, it was really not a little because of the charm of
> his having encountered and recognised, in the vast wilderness of the

wholesale, breaking through the mere gross generalisation of wealth and force and success, a small still scene where items and shades, all delicate things, kept the sharpness of the notes of a high voice perfectly trained, and where economy hung about like the scent of a garden. (439)

At first glance, this passage seems merely to be repeating the kind of mutually exclusive opposition of images that we have already looked at: the either/or choice between the "pale pressed flower" of an old-fashioned sensibility and "the hard-faced houses" and "great builded voids" of a city intent on obliterating its past in dollar-driven spasms of vulgar "renovation" and "reconstruction."

A closer look, however, suggests that the categories are far less exclusive than it pleases Brydon to believe. The charged imagery of the city as "some vast ledger-page, overgrown" or a "vast wilderness of the wholesale" and the casual ambiguity of the word "figures," which nominally refers to the commercial activities of cash-accounting even as it points to the lurking presence of the "crisscrossed figure" that waits defiantly behind "the hinged halves of the inner door" in the depths of Brydon's house of consciousness—such a sinuous use of language belies Brydon's easy sureties and frames his *mano a mano* confrontation within a much wider and more complex force-field than he has the courage or perspicacity to recognize. For example, the "charm" that Brydon feels in the "small, still scene" that "kept the sharpness of the notes of a high voice perfectly trained" denies even as it seems to affirm Brydon's celebration of delicacy and sensibility in this "gross" world of "wealth and force and success." "Sharpness" and "high" have already been associated in the story with skyscrapers, steel-pointed walking sticks, masculine business practices, etc. A voice "perfectly trained" is, perforce, under the rigorous regulation of mathematical scale and pitch, and the "notes" themselves can refer as easily to the money that rewards the city's commercial dealings as they can to Alice's amateur arias. And likening "economy" to "the scent of a garden" (especially with the buried pun on the word "scent") brings the extended metaphor to a daring climax in which the arrayed oppositions are so thoroughly interpenetrable as to make a clear rational division between them impossible.

What is impossible for the reader, however, is possible on a very different level of perception for Brydon, who, after all, as an agent within the text, must deal short-sightedly with what he sees as his own closed predicament. That is, given his character and emotional circumstances, it would be literally impossible for him to accept the world of merged unlikenesses that awaits him beyond the threshold of the ominously closed door. It is at this point that he "jumps" at the "value of Discretion," and it is also at this point in the narrative that the first-person narrator, hitherto scrupulously absent from the impersonal focalization, takes momentary control of the story:

> Discretion—he jumped at that; and not, verily, at such a pitch, because it saved his nerves or his skin, but because, much more valuably, it saved the situation. When I say he "jumped" at it I feel the consonance of this term with the fact that—at the end indeed of I know not how long—he did move again, he crossed straight to the door. He wouldn't touch it—it seemed now that he might *if* he would: he would only just wait there a little, to show, to prove, that he wouldn't. (468)

James's language, once again, has it brilliantly both ways. Consciously choosing "discretion" or judgment as the better part of valor, Brydon attempts to save his dignity and "the situation." But he is more profoundly committing himself to the choice of the other meaning of "discretion" as an act of separating or making sharp distinctions between. He may tell himself that he is acting out of "pity" and "respect," but what he actually does do— whether because of cowardice or the brute instinct of survival—is to reestablish clear demarcations between "inside" and "outside" by crossing to the other end of the house and by opening the casement "to let in the air of the night" (469). The "situation" he is intent on saving is the narrowly exclusive construction of that personality within which he has led a comfortable, albeit unproductive, thirty-years of denial and rootlessness.

This decision sets the scene for the climactic meeting with the alter ego even as it forecloses any chance of recognition, much less reconciliation. When that apparition does reveal itself "in its great grey glimmering margin" (475) and even drops its masking hands to show unmistakably to Brydon that "the bared identity was too hideous as *his*" (476), Brydon resists, rejects, retreats before the unbridled "rage of personality" (477) and falls into a swoon. With maimed hand and smothered life, the alter ego is permanently "othered." Brydon survives, his "self" restored to its diminished sameness, his "situation" saved in what he will interpret as a miraculous rescue. At the risk of sounding a tone far harsher than would be consonant with the subtleties of James's text, one might suggest that it is as though Francis Macomber had been cuddled in Margot's adoring, welcoming embrace after his humiliated flight from the cornered lion.

In the final section of the story, the text details the extent of Brydon's regressive submissiveness to his fate as a diminished entity even as he declares his defeat to be a stupendous victory. It is difficult to assess precisely the nuances of ironic mockery that modulate his presentation, but it is instructive to note carefully the progression of images that attend Brydon's movement through the action of the story. In his initial and exhilarated discovery of a previously undreamed-of "capacity for business and a sense for construction" (438), he had surprised himself by behaving "almost with a certain authority" (438). In fact, with Alice as admiring onlooker, he "had found himself quite 'standing-up'" (440) to the man in charge of rebuilding his other property into an apartment house. Concomitantly, however, his nightly prowls are characterized as "craping up to thim top storeys in the ayvil hours" (443), but the broad humor of Mrs. Muldoon's dialect should not disguise the fact that the change from "standing-up" to "craping" is a crooked distortion of the angular thrust of the vertical plane. And, further, it is possible that James might have been aware of the Britishism in which a "corner-creeper" was a slangy definition for an underhanded and stealthy person.

Where the final images of the alter ego had emphasized the defiant rigidity of his resolute pride ("as still as some image erect in a niche or as some black-vizored sentinel guarding a treasure" [475]), Brydon's last appearance—his final stage presence, as it were—is marked by everything the alter ego is not. As the one mounts his energies into a last-ditch stand ("his planted stillness" [475]), Brydon welcomes the sense of being "abysmally passive" (478) and becomes almost blissfully supine. He regains consciousness, his head "pillowed in extraordinary softness and faintly refreshing fragrance"— more precisely, in "the ample and perfect cushion" (478) of Alice's lap. In the later conversation when Brydon is back in his own room, that lap is replaced by "a mantle of soft stuff lined with grey fur" (479) and, throughout this final scene, almost entirely in dialogue, he who began his adventure standing up erect, who hunched into a stooping posture as he crept in silent pursuit of his prey, who jumped into strategic withdrawal at the prospect of confrontation, relapses gratefully into prone surrender. The stage directions for his last speeches are indicative of his pathetic acquiescence to his abject state. "'Oh keep me, keep me!' he pleaded," "'Where have I been?' he vaguely wailed." He emits a "mild moan" and "with his long wail" (480–82) denies that the alter ego has any connection to him. Secure once more in the complacencies of his restrictive definitions of *self* and *other,* and, encouraged to this end by an Alice who clearly knows him better than he does himself, Brydon softly collapses as a comic victim of his own futility in a textual world (a "ledger-page ... of ruled and crisscrossed lines and figures" [439]) where aesthetic incongruities and paradoxes demand moral responses of greater courage than Brydon is able or willing to muster.

One is reluctant to overstate the implications suggested by this analysis of James's remarkable use of language and imagery. "The Jolly Corner," it seems clear to me, is dominantly in a mock-heroic mode, but it is also true that much of it—especially in the middle section—attains a lyrical and emotional urgency that the opening section does not fully prepare for and the closing section effectively ignores. It is as though the fortuitous tension inherent in the metaphor of "the jolly corner" generated a proliferating family of similarly incompatible oppositions that the narrative structure of the tale faithfully reflects without being able to reduce or resolve. The disturbing arbitrariness of Alice's clairvoyant dreams and the too-facile transformation of Brydon into compliant infantile dependence throw the story, in my judgment, into an odd and somewhat jarring imbalance. On the other hand, this may indicate an integrity to the uncompromising dissonance of the tale's central imagery—an integrity attained even at the cost of contriving a denouement that disappoints in its improbability and in its glib closure. Perhaps what I am hesitatingly proposing is that the aesthetic transaction of the Jamesian text is synonymous with a moral action and that both must be responsible to a set of principles that transcend both the text and the recalcitrant conflicts of psychological motivations. Were the adamant structural oppositions that drive the narrative to be dissolved or melded in some quasimystical harmony, the story might very well have assumed a more unified and aesthetically shapely form. For this to have happened, however, the text would have had to have been false to its own central dissonance and, by extension, to the brutal implacabilities of the human condition. It is a tribute to James, I believe, that the latter course was neither an option nor even a significant temptation. And it is possible that this is a major reason why "The Jolly Corner" retains its vitality and evocativeness.

Work Cited

James, Henry. "The Jolly Corner." In *The Novels and Tales of Henry James,* 17:435–83. New York Edition. New York: Scribner's, 1908.

Michael Pinker

TOO GOOD TO BE TRUE
"Mora Montravers"

In "Mora Montravers," Henry James's last completed story, James portrays with comic irony a genteel Edwardian couple attending their of-age niece's "coming out." In the cover blurb he wrote for *The Finer Grain,* the collection including "Mora Montravers," James postulates that each story exhibits

> a central consciousness . . . involved . . . in the . . . active play of the victim's or the victor's sensibility. Each situation is . . . a moral drama, *an exposure of . . . the sentient, perceptive, reflective part of the protagonist . . .* wearing for the hero or heroine the quality of the agitating, the challenging, the personal adventure . . . [in which] the hero . . . exhibits the finer grain of accessibility . . . to moving experience . . . by his connection with and interest in the "grain" woman. . . . (Quoted in Wagenknecht, 161–62, emphasis added)[1]

But does this story's aesthetic hero credibly expose a *sentient, perceptive, reflective part* to his character? The premise collapses as James skewers his susceptible protagonist's pretensions by delineating an infatuation owing more to latent, if repressed, lust than to any loftier motives. The gentleman in question lends a comic turn to what is most "moving" in his "experience."

Commentators largely ignore how James counters the effusions of the central intelligence in "Mora Montravers" through his use of language.[2] The plot follows at a discreet distance a clever girl's peculiar entry into society as a vision unfolding before the eyes of her uncle. Mora's abrupt brush-off of her guardians, scandalously leaving their Wimbledon nest to live with a poor young painter who has been giving her lessons, nettles their habitual complacency. But the act also charms Uncle Sidney Traffle. Its novel complications excite him to regard his quest to save her respectability as a "moving experience" beyond anything in his career. Bewitched by Mora's allure, Traffle casts her as the heroine of a romance of his own creation, testament to *his* "finer grain of accessibility." His language defines the allure that surrounds Mora in his imagination, a web of words in which he has become lost.

As he unravels what he imputes as her motives, Traffle delights in embellishing the vision his niece assumes in his consciousness. His wife Jane's horror of disgrace contrasts with her husband's sudden faith in Mora's integrity, brought on by his unavowed recognition of her sexual availability. The wonder of Mora's "coming out" accompanies a gradual awakening of interest, expressed in James's duplicitous language, in this formerly overlooked, if attractive, young woman. Yet in the pursuit of his niece, Traffle's vaunted sophistication proves delusory. As he responds to the conflicting stratagems of his wife, her niece, and Mora's artist-admirer, Walter Puddick, Traffle almost loses his bearings in their greater comedy.

James's irony betrays Traffle's blind devotion to an ideal that Mora's actual "predicament" debases. More intimate acquaintance with her situation persuades Traffle to read Mora's behavior in a way his wife regards as perverse: "It was by his original and independent measure that the whole case had become interesting and been raised above the level of a mere vulgar scandal" (328). At first "odiously stricken" (267) by "the thing he had so often read about in clever stories" (267), Traffle deplores how Jane's charity to her niece has been compromised. He can only "respond distortedly to the grim and monstrous joke" (267) Mora apparently has played on them both. Its potential effect on society is more palpable still. The "treacherous fact of her beauty . . . misled their acquaintance" (268) as well as the Traffles to take

Mora for what they wanted her to be instead of who she was. *Now* how were they to deal with her?

Traffle sets off to locate Mora and to learn what he can. He visits the "little painter-man" (268) to whom she had fled and, against his better judgment, finds him "unexpectedly and absurdly interesting" (268). Puddick's "almost impudent absence of any tone of responsibility" (270) in the affair arrests Traffle. His personal interest is piqued when "the canvas on [Puddick's] easel . . . the cleanness of its appeal" (271) arouses his latent aestheticism. Returning home delighted at the turn events are taking, Traffle considers how "a man of the world [should take] the impartial, the detached, in fact—hang it!—even the amused view" (269). The impression Puddick has made induces Traffle to believe Mora will "reward some independent, some intelligent notice" (269). In James's terms, his connection with and interest in the "'grain' woman" confirms Traffle's resolve that "if any 'fun' . . . was to come of the matter, he'd be blamed if he'd be wholly deprived of it" (270).

The "fun" begins in trying to bring Jane and her niece together. At first Jane is adamant in refusal: "she could have but her own word—Mora was a monster" (278). But her husband persists, appealing to the romance implicit in Mora's name:

> "Well," he laughed—quite brazen about it now—"if she is [a monster] it's because she has paid for it! Why the deuce did her stars, unless to make her worship gods entirely other than Jane Traffle's, rig her out with a name that puts such a premium on adventures? 'Mora Montravers'—it paints the whole career for you. She *is,* one does feel, her name; but how couldn't she be? She'd dishonour it and its grand air if she weren't." (278)

Like Walter Shandy, Traffle weighs the relative value of names as a key to determine the course of a career. Is Puddick's "vulgar name" (279) a bar to Mora's marrying him? Trying to urge Jane toward a *rapprochement* with her niece, Traffle ponders what effect retaining a *good* name may have on the young woman, whether her becoming "Mrs Puddick" might be at issue:

> He didn't believe it could be Mora's reason, and though he had made . . . a brave fight, he had after reflection to allow still for much obscurity

in their question. But he had none the less retained his belief in the visibly uncommon young man. (279)

Puddick's mien and manner seduce Traffle; he *believes* in the painter. His faith in Mora also more fervent as a result, Traffle sounds his own note in conversation with his still-skeptical wife:

> "If we're having the strain and the pain of it let us also have the relief and *the fun.*"
> "Oh, the 'fun'!" Jane wailed; but adding soon after, "If she'll marry him I'll forgive her."
> "Ah, that's not enough!" he pronounced as they went to bed. (279–80, emphasis added)

Yet her husband's new, more tolerant view of the affair begins gradually to mitigate Jane's scornful distress.

When soon after Mora appears alone on his doorstep, unashamed, Traffle is completely won over by her beauty. Ascribing immense significance to her every word and gesture, her very *presence,* Traffle confidently exalts Mora's "remarkable" nature. The young woman's "extraordinary prettiness" (281) disarms her uncle. He finds reasons for Mora's behavior she never has to confirm. Angelic Mora rarely descends from sublime imperturbability to intone more than a few words in his presence. Without betraying the least intelligence of her real motives, Mora's charms encourage Traffle to deny her any impure aim. As Mora herself divines, "You've thought . . . all sorts of horrible things about me, but observe how little my appearance matches them, and in fact keep up coarse views if you can in the light of my loveliness" (281). But when does Mora actually say this? Still, Traffle rebukes his "vulgar" presumption, as if answering what he has imagined her saying:

> he afterward reflected . . . that he must have taken for granted in her, with the life she was leading, so to call it, some visibility of boldness, some significant surface—of which absurd supposition *her presence . . . had disabused him* to the point of making all the awkwardness his and leaving none at all for her. (281, emphasis added)

Beguiling himself, Traffle takes Mora's mere presence as corroboration of his fantasy. The worshipful hero winds himself up to such a pitch, nothing Mora appears to be, says, or does need support any of his claims for her. He regards them as proven, certain, accepting his explanations as her own: "She was in truth exactly the same—*except for her hint* that they might have forgotten how pretty she *could* be" (281). What hint? Mora has said nothing. What is the provenance of this "hint"? "So much was he to feel *she had conveyed,* and that it was *the little person presenting herself . . . on these terms*" (282). What terms? Mora herself is mute. From whence arrive these surmises?

When she finally does speak, Mora seems to be trying to save appearances: "I've come to see you because I don't want to lose sight of you—my being no longer with you is no reason for that" (282). But Traffle's interpretation of her intent and appreciation of her charms lead him to a more profound sympathy:

> She was going to ignore, *he saw . . . It opened out before him . . . to put on emphasis where Mora chose to neglect it. . . .* Mora had put him somehow into the position of having to explain that her aunt wouldn't see her— *precisely that was the mark of the girl's attitude.* (282–83, emphasis added)

Absorbed in a vision of Mora conjured from nothing, Traffle ignores the "vertiginous view of a gulf" (282) separating Mora his niece from Mora the goddess, the "grain" woman of his fantasy. In thrall to her beauty, he has spun a "prodigious" romance around her charms. Yet James explodes this fantasy shortly thereafter, as Traffle ruminates idly,

> However, grave and imperturbable, inimitably armed by charming correctness, as she sat there, it would be her line in life, *he was certain,* to reduce many theories, solemn Wimbledon theories about the scandalous person, to the futility of *so much broken looking-glass.* (283, emphasis added)

The oblique reference to Lewis Carroll's singular "romance"[3] puts Traffle's vision in perspective. After Mora leaves, Traffle considers all he has ascribed to her with his "rolling eye" (284), none of it based on anything Mora ever says or performs in his presence:

> [H]e had only fixed on her a rolling eye . . . which had the air of signifying heaven knew what. *She took it, clearly . . . for the most rather than*

*for the least it might mean; which again made him gape with the certitude
that ever thereafter she would make him seem to have meant what she liked.*
(284, emphasis added)

As "a proved conspirator from that instant on" (284), Traffle accepts
this "subtle" befuddlement as proof of Mora's influence. James presumes
we too will be swept along by his hero's excess of vision:

> For what else in the world did it come to, *his failure of ability to attri-
> bute any other fine sense* to Mora's odd "step" than the weird design of
> just giving them a lead? They were to leave her alone, by her sharp
> prescription, and she would show them once for all how to do it. (284,
> emphasis added)

Lending Mora a provident rationale, Traffle again asks Jane to accept her
niece as *he* would regard her. But his wife's withering reply is instructive:

> "Then you mean . . . that I'm to go and call upon her . . . just as if she
> were the pink of propriety and we had no exception whatever to take
> to her conduct . . . that I'm to grovel before a chit of a creature on whom
> I've lavished every benefit, and to whom I've offered every indulgence,
> and who shows herself, in return for it all, *by what I make out from your
> rigmarole,* a fiend of insolence as well as of vice?" (284–85, emphasis
> added)

Yet Traffle is unabashed at "this freedom of address to him, unprecedented
in their long intercourse" (285). In the throes of his rapture perceiving only
Jane's "dear foolish face" (285), the intent of her response eluding him,
Traffle offers another explanation, "*his truth,* of which it was the insidious
nature to prevail": "What [Mora] wanted, I make out, was but to give us the
best pleasure she could think of . . . our not only recognizing how little we
need worry about her, but of our seeing as well how pleasant it may become
for us to keep in touch with her" (285).

At length Jane capitulates to her husband, in his terms discerning "the
bolt of finest point" (286) in his discourse, perhaps also humoring his stri-
dent enthusiasm. Traffle, nonetheless, is triumphant: "He had rarely
known her to achieve that discrimination before" (286). Still, Jane, "a goose
of geese" (291), remains in need of his passionate instruction: "The pleasure

then, in her view, you 'make out'—since you make out such wonders!—is to be all for us only?" (286). Traffle's "wonders" do prevail. Jane receives Puddick to prove her husband wrong, but a visit by the artist, who also appeals to *her* taste, influences her to hasten what she knows will secure Mora's marriage to him, her "four hundred and fifty" (294). Awaiting Mora's response, Traffle gloats serenely, "We seem to have lived into [the affair] and through it so, and to have suffered and surmounted the worst, that . . . I scarce see what's the matter now, or what, that's so very dreadful" (300). Yet Jane's "conspicuous propriety" (302) leaves her still mildly perturbed while "[she] waited for the proof that she had intervened to advantage—the advantage of Mora's social future" (302).

Relieved now that his "nerves treated him at moments to larger and looser exactions" (303), Traffle visits the National Gallery to enjoy its private freedoms: "One couldn't be a *raffiné* at Wimbledon—no, not with any comfort; but he quite liked to think how he had never been anything less in the great museum" (303). The Old Masters work their usual magic on one who savors his "places of pilgrimage . . . in corners unnoted and cold" (304). But in "one of the Dutch rooms" (304) stands another worshiper, "surprised . . . in her invincibility" (304). His "wonder" at his niece's presence increasing, Traffle renews his homage to Mora's brilliance:

> [W]hat especially did the business for him . . . was again the renewed degree, and . . . the developed kind, of importance that the girl's beauty gave her. Dear Jane . . . was sunk in the conviction that [Mora] was leading a life; but whatever she was doing it was clearly the particular thing she might best be occupied with. (304)

How could a creature so breathtaking stoop to any mean or sordid purpose? Traffle's "sense of the mere tribute" (305) owed his "'grain' woman" invests her with ethereal grandeur, "the rare shade of human felicity, human impunity, human sublimity . . . surely dwelling in such a consciousness. How could a girl have to think long . . . of anything in the world but that her presence was an absolute incomparable value" (305). Her resplendent *tableau vivant* shames Traffle into recognizing that his desultory worship of art—"what I should have tried to go in for" (306)—amounts to little more than mere folly, whereas the language depicting his awe at Mora's person transforms her into a heavenly creature. Herself ignorant of this virulent fancy, Mora says, "You

try to make grabs at some idea, but the simplest never occurs to you" (308).
These words reveal Mora as more "wonderful" for being "plain." Yet her
actual dissimulation wins her uncle's adherence by the value she achieves just
by being herself. No trace of any vulgar stigma assigned by Aunt Jane to
Mora's conduct appears to taint her fetching surface.

Greater wonders await; Mora has married Puddick, silencing criticism. Elated, Traffle hardly blinks at the appearance of "the gentleman in
the doorway, a slightly mature, but strikingly well-dressed, a pleasantly
masterful-looking gentleman, a haunter of the best society . . . waiting for
him to go" (312). O augury of Mora's brilliant future! With this revelation
Traffle departs the museum world, only mildly astonished at how much he
has been taken in while looking the other way. Thankfully, the impression
is momentary and evaporates in a gust of hot air:

> When he had turned his back and begun humbly to shuffle, as it
> seemed to him, through a succession of shining rooms where the walls
> bristled with eyes that watched him for mockery, his sense was of hav-
> ing seen the last of Mora as completely as if she had just seated herself
> in the car of a rising balloon that would never descend again to earth.
> (313)

Ultimately Traffle prefers his conception of Mora to its alternative. Mora is
indeed more than she seems, whereas Jane's independent discovery that
"Walter" improves a tea-table better conveniently soothes her wounded vanity. So Mrs. Traffle's chastened "man of the world" (269) might just as well go
along with the arrangement. In saving appearances, the couple's scruples
attain true sublimity. What Mora might have been matters now not at all as
a new world of "fun" dawns in the Wimbledon drawing room.

Thus James's hero fulfills his creator's stated intentions ironically.
Traffle's "personal adventure," the imaginative metamorphosis his niece
unwittingly "agitates," is to play the fool to her ambition. Mediator of Jane's
moral niceties and Mora's covert liberties, Traffle experiences "wonders" of
imaginative sympathy. Although Mora eludes her uncle's reach, her allure
impels Traffle to compromise his class so that the young woman may pursue her personal romance "wonderfully" free of middle-class constraints.
Her uncle's devotion to Mora's "wonders" limns what James in the jacket
copy for *The Finer Grain* called "the vivacity and the active play of the vic-

tim's or the victor's sensibility" (quoted in Wagenknecht, 161) with devastating irony. Relishing the fortuitous conclusion of this "rum case" (270) to the hilt, Traffle achieves a fatuous exhilaration while musing on "the fun some people did have" (333). His final judgment on this matter, that "Jane . . . was in for such a lot" (333), proves that his desire for "nice and dreadful" (301) amusements has only increased. But by the treatment of his hero James himself more likely regards this penchant for "fun" as resembling an earlier pronouncement on the affair of Mora itself: "Never was a scandal . . . less scandalous" (301).

Notes

1. As Wagenknecht attests, "the 'blurb' seems to have been used only in part on the jacket but was printed in its entirety by E. V. Lucas in *Reading, Writing, and Remembering* (Methuen, 1932)" (257).
2. None of the works consulted for this essay focuses on James's language or rhetoric as its central concern: Bender, Dyson, Lyons, Martin and Ober, Tintner, or Wagenknecht.
3. Such earlier mocking references as "chance reflection . . . in some gloomy glass" (267) and "sounded the depths of slumbering mirrors" (267) similarly describe how Mora's "indecency" has addled his peace of mind.

Works Cited

Bender, Bert. "Henry James's Late Lyric Meditations upon the Mysteries of Fate and Self-Sacrifice." *Genre* 9 (1976): 247–62.

Dyson, J. Peter. "Romance Elements in Three Late Tales by Henry James: 'Mora Montravers,' 'The Velvet Glove,' and 'The Bench of Desolation.'" *English Studies in Canada* 5 (1979): 66–77.

———. "Bartolozzi and Henry James's 'Mora Montravers.'" *Henry James Review* 1 (1979–80): 264–66.

James, Henry. "Mora Montravers." In *The Complete Tales of Henry James,* 12:267–333. Ed. Leon Edel. Philadelphia: Lippincott, 1964.

Lyons, Richard S. "Ironies of Loss in *The Finer Grain.*" *Henry James Review* 11 (1990): 202–12.

Martin, W. R., and Warren U. Ober. "The Shaping Spirit in James's Last Tales." *English Studies in Canada* 9 (1983): 341–49.

———. "'Superior to Oak': The Past of Mora Montravers in James's *The Finer Grain.*" *American Literary Realism* 16 (1983): 121–28.

————. Introduction to *The Finer Grain,* xi–xiii. Delmar: Scholars' Facsimiles and Reprints, 1986.

Tintner, Adeline. "James's Mock Epic: 'The Velvet Glove,' Edith Wharton, and Other Late Tales." *Modern Fiction Studies* 17 (1971–72): 483–99.

————. "The Metamorphoses of Edith Wharton in Henry James's *The Finer Grain.*" *Twentieth Century Literature* 21 (1975): 355–79.

Wagenknecht, Edward. *The Tales of Henry James.* Literature and Life Series. New York: Ungar, 1984.

Part Two: Weaves

Brooke Horvath

"A LANDSCAPE PAINTER"
AND "THE MIDDLE YEARS"

Failures of the Amateur

I

THE SPECIFIC QUESTIONS raised by Henry James's stories of writers and artists are many: what is art's inherent work in the world and how might that work best be done and assessed? What are the limits of authorially sanctioned meaning and to what extent do meaning and worth (aesthetic, social, monetary) depend upon an audience's approval, creative participation, predisposition to use art in one or another way? What potential for personal fulfillment or regret resides in a life devoted to art? Several years ago I suggested that these stories, far from forwarding any direct, unambiguous answers to such questions, in fact offered portraits of failed artists whose defeat stemmed from faulty stands on such matters, specious assumptions. That is, I argued that James's views on art, to the extent they inhabited these stories, must be inferred from what the artists presented were not.[1]

In developing that argument, I was taking James seriously when, in his preface to *The Tragic Muse,* he declared that an artist as fictional character cannot be "the artist *in triumph,*" for such an artist, according to James, lives only in his work and hence, presumably, free from the sort of conflict and requisite character traits needed to drive a plot up one side of Freytag's pyramid and down the other in a manner calculated to elicit reader sympathy. Of this triumphant artist, James wrote,

> His romance is the romance he himself projects: he eats the cake of the
> very rarest privilege, the most luscious baked in the oven of the gods—
> therefore he mayn't "have" it, in the form of the privilege of the hero,
> at the same time. The privilege of the hero—that is of the martyr or of
> the interesting and appealing and comparatively floundering *person*—
> places him in quite a different category, belongs to him only as to the
> artist deluded, diverted, frustrated or vanquished; when the "amateur"
> in him gains, for our admiration or compassion or whatever, all that
> the expert has to do without. (Preface, 96–97)

Given such an understanding of the possibilities of the artist as character, the question I thought at the time to ask was this: what, then, makes even those characters who appear to be artists "in triumph," failures of one or another sort? In what ways are even they "deluded, diverted, frustrated or vanquished"?

Now, one might quarrel with what James wrote in his preface. Mightn't, for instance, a triumphant artist fail in any number of ways as a person, and in a manner capable of provoking "admiration or compassion or whatever"? Or mightn't a true artist nevertheless reach a crisis regarding (among other things) the reception, commodification, or utility of her work? James arguably produced both kinds of artist stories: "The Author of *Beltraffio*" an example of the former, "Broken Wings" of the latter. But however one weighs James's notions, he said what he said. And if one accepts what he said as determining the sort of artist he believed could properly figure in a story, it would seem to follow that only the defeated artist qualifies—the "amateur," whose failure as artist is what earns him this epithet.

To explore this hypothesis further, I would like to consider two stories: "A Landscape Painter" (1866), written during what Leon Edel called James's "untried years," and "The Middle Years," the only story the author published during what Edel describes as the "troubled months" of 1893 (when James, like his fictional author, was longing for a "second chance").[2] The former constitutes James's first fictional statement about art but concentrates so intently on its amateur artist's nonartistic floundering that it may seem, despite its title, not a story about an artist at all. The latter, featuring a triumphantly professional artist riddled by self-doubts concerning his reputation and accomplishment, is a much later look at artistic success and failure.

II

"A Landscape Painter" concerns Locksley, "a short man, dark, and not particularly good-looking" (7) but nonetheless a gentleman worth $100,000 a year with a passion for sketching and painting.[3] When the story opens, he has been dead seven years, and a close friend is reminding us of Locksley's unfortunate engagement, a dozen years earlier, to Miss Josephine Leary, a woman of great outward beauty but "a certain lack of animation" (8) with whom Locksley severed connections upon learning she loved him only for his money. Shortly thereafter, we are further reminded, Locksley took himself into retirement from love, wealth, and society, moving to the small seacoast village of Cragthrope, where he intended to paint away his blues while passing for an indigent artist.

Mentioning that Locksley wrote some "very bad" poetry as well as "a mass" of uninteresting papers "on all subjects"—suggestive, perhaps, of the dilettante's lack of focus—the narrator allows that his friend did produce "a number of remarkable paintings" (10) as well as one text of special merit: a diary, a portion of which comprises the remainder of the story.[4] From the pages "shown" us, we learn that, after his unfortunate affaire de coeur and relocation to Cragthrope, a chance encounter leads Locksley to board with Captain Richard Blunt, a retired skipper, and his attractive daughter, Esther, a piano teacher at a school for young ladies. Falling under Esther's spell, Locksley quickly charts a course through infatuation to courtship and marriage, all copiously detailed before the diary breaks off when, still believing he has successfully hidden his upper-class past, Locksley is disabused of that assumption by Esther, who confesses that she has known otherwise and, indeed, married him for that reason.

The diary is offered for our perusal ostensibly because it will cement our sympathy and admiration for this promising artist who, defeated (twice) in love, died young. But what the diary tells rather is a story of artistic delusion, diversion, frustration, and vanquishment springing from a host of character failures. If we can understand Locksley's defeat in life and love to be connected to his status as artistic dilettante, this is because, as Peter Rabinowitz observes, it is a narrative convention for authors to indicate and readers to understand a character's morals by textual details that bespeak that character's aesthetic taste. "In many texts," Rabinowitz writes, "we are asked to assume . . . that people with the correct aesthetic views are also morally correct, while those with aesthetic failings have moral failings as well" (92). In "A Landscape Painter," Rabinowitz's observation cuts two ways: not only does Locksley's insipid taste suggest character limitations responsible for his grossly inaccurate reading of self and others, especially Esther, but his life failures—his enthrallment to appearances, prejudicial conventionality, snobbery, and lack of self-knowledge—likewise reveal a hackneyed artistic sense. Leo B. Levy, for instance, argues that "Locksley's love of nature is an integral part of his self-deceptions: the way he sees— and paints—landscapes cannot be separated from his limitations. What he loves is an idealized nature, mirroring his pleasant fantasies about himself and about a young woman." Subscribing to a "romantic as opposed to realistic modes of perception," Locksley's love story, Levy concludes, "involves the repudiation of an outworn aesthetic" (407–8).

A trivial romanticism, then, informs Locksley's conventional taste, working itself out in an infatuation with idealized surfaces, charming effects, the cozily picturesque. This can be seen first of all in how he views his art, from the Let's-Paint-with-Locksley bluster of "And now for the victories of the brush!" (12) to his concern that his "artistic odds and ends" be disposed "in as picturesque a fashion as possible" before the Blunts enter his room (21). A similar inclination can be seen in his response to Esther at the piano—"I confess that I was more taken with the picture of the dusky piano, and by the *effect* of Miss Blunt's performance, than with its meaning" (20; James's emphasis)[5]—as well as in his self-indulgently jejune dreams of future glory: "One of these days I mean to paint a picture which in future ages, when my dear native land shall boast a national school of art, will hang in the *Salon Carré* of the great central museum, (located, let us say, in Chicago) and remind folks—or rather make them forget—Giorgione, Bordone, and Veronese" (54).

Despite fantasies of fame, what Locksley most enjoys is the idea of being an artist, presenting himself as artist. Consequently, when the weather turns bad, he paints only "languidly" because what matters most is the pleasantness of the activity; as he writes at one point: "I am thoroughly at my ease; my peace of mind quite passeth understanding. I work diligently; I have none but pleasant thoughts" (23–24). When something more pleasant, more amusing, comes along, art takes a holiday, as the diary's rapid preoccupation with Esther reveals. One can anyway readily imagine the canvases likely to result from a mind that offers the following description of "a noble seaview": "Beyond the broad bay I saw miniature town and country mapped out before me; and on the other hand, I saw the infinite Atlantic,—over which, by the by, all the pretty things are brought from Paris" (13).

Locksley's views of himself and others are similarly unsubtle. Thus, assessing himself, Locksley can observe, "I suppose I am too proud to be successfully rich," feeling his money prevents others from seeing his intrinsic worth. Consequently, he continues, "I have determined to stand upon my own merits" (16). Or marveling at how easy it has proved to conceal his superior breeding, he writes, "I manage more cleverly than I expected to stifle those innumerable tacit illusions which might serve effectually to belie my character" (30–31). Similarly, when this landscape painter considers others, his remarks, although kindly meant, are smugly condescending, clichéd, prescripted. For instance, given the two types he perceives Blunt to be—"an odd union of the gentleman of the old school and the old-fashioned, hotheaded merchant-captain" (16–17)—Locksley cannot but imagine his disguise has deceived Blunt completely: "bless his simple heart!" Locksley concludes (15). Esther, imagined sight unseen as an old maid ("Teacher in a young ladies' school. . . . I suppose she's over thirty. I think I know the type" [18]), proves upon acquaintance charming but consistently déclassé— not only because social inferiority is for Locksley a necessary part of her provincial charm but also because he needs to retain a sense of his own superiority. Indeed, Esther suffers throughout the sophisticate's prejudgment of the rustic: she is "a very commonplace person" whose reaction to his paintings is disappointingly unoriginal (21); "I am afraid she is sadly ignorant. She reads nothing but novels" (22); she is "honest, simple, and ignorant" (25); her father, Locksley perceives with amusement, "is proud of her grace, of her tact, of her good sense, of her wit, such as it is" (27).

Smug, inaccurate stereotypes, Locksley's assessments reveal that he is, among other things, a bad reader. He is in particular a bad reader of women, placing them on pedestals—he was fond of comparing Josephine to the Venus of Milo (7)—from which height he might better ascertain their flaws while sentimentally idealizing them. If Esther is "a woman of character" (20), "a pure and upright soul" (34) "so unlike—certain of [her] sisters" (25), one must ask how unlike Josephine Locksley eventually finds her or how, given that his diary breaks off abruptly, he finally understands why she has done what she's done in marrying him under what he understands to be false pretenses. Not that Esther does not supply clues that ought to trouble both Locksley's assessment of her and his assumptions regarding the sort of impression he is making on her. "I very much dislike teaching the children," she confesses (32), slashing at the mental canvas upon which Locksley has been hard at work; later, she admits an intention "to marry the first rich man who offers," amending that to "the first man who offers," even "if he is poor, ugly, and stupid" (which amounts to a request that Locksley propose), explaining that she is "tired of living alone in this weary old way . . . and turning and patching my dresses" (39–40). That she subsequently rejects the marriage proposal of a young local lawyer ought to alert Locksley that it is he she now counts on for her financial salvation even as he ought to understand that her attraction is not going to turn on his appearance or intelligence (his "intrinsic worth").

Indeed, one should not necessarily see Esther's deception of Locksley as a reason to condemn her: she is, if nothing else, only beating him at his own game.[6] As the foregoing discussion suggests, not only is Locksley almost willfully obtuse in his insistence on misreading Esther and misconceiving himself, but Esther so much as tells him (well before he proposes marriage) that she is onto the game (only verifying her suspicions about this "poor" artist by sneaking a look at the diary). Encouraging Locksley to comprehend her motives and his own, insisting that she never proffered false professions of love and can't accept his injured surprise, asking that he acknowledge both her victory in their game of mutual deception and the conditions of their future union, and urging him to "be a man!" (67), Esther exclaims heatedly at the story's close, "Mercy! didn't you see it? didn't you know it? see that I saw it? know that I knew it? It was diamond cut diamond" (66).

If Locksley suffers from a threadbare romanticism, it is relevant to note that Esther is the story's realist. As Miriam Allott has argued, "A Landscape Painter" can be read as an ironic realist's comment on the naive "sim-plesse" of Tennyson's "The Lord of Burleigh" with Locksley the bemused victim of James's debunking of the poet's sentimental presumptions about men, women, and social class. Under such a reading, Esther speaks for the author, and, within the context of the story, she speaks as the truer artist. With this in mind, her assessment of Locksley is particularly noteworthy.

As one who earns her living from her art, Esther has never been free to indulge illusions or set aside her art when it proves less than pleasant. Thus, when the weather keeps Locksley indoors, "through all [the] pouring and pattering, Miss Blunt sallies forth to her pupils" (24). Again, "For poor Miss Blunt, it is day after day the same story: a wearisome round of visits to the school, and to the houses of the mayor, the parson, the butcher, the baker, whose young ladies, of course, all receive instruction on the piano" (27). But more to the point, she possesses an artist's sensibility, one that takes in, as-sesses, and makes something of her chances.

As aesthetic realist, Esther's critique of Locksley's character (36–39) highlights a host of shortfalls all within Esther's framing observation that "for an artist, you are very inartistic" (36).[7] She proceeds to accuse him of a lack of subtlety and clumsiness in striving for an effect (here, his attempt to extract a compliment). Continuing, Esther charges Locksley with feigned and patronizing sociability, a self-serving cordiality that masks conceit, it-self a defense against the fear that beneath his assumed superiority, his in-nate inferiority awaits exposure (36–37). "If I were a man," she wonders, "a clever man like yourself, who had seen the world, who was not to be charmed and encouraged but to be convinced and refuted, would you be equally amiable?" (37). Esther further paints Locksley as weak, cowardly, lazy, inexperienced, impatient, excessively satirical, overly concerned with others' opinions of him, and self-deluded ("You consider that you are working now, don't you? Many persons would not call it work" [39]). "It *is,*" she bluntly informs him, "your own fault, if people don't care for you. You don't care for them" (39). It is no wonder that, even as amateur artist, Locksley has limited himself to pretty landscapes.

It should also be noted that Locksley's character shortcomings include not only gender- but class-imposed limitations on his aesthetic sensibility, a sensibility already handicapped by an inability to imagine depths, motives, ambiguities, ironies, otherness. These debilities are intertwined.

Thus, when Locksley's stereotyping of women causes him at one point jokingly to tell Esther she lacks sentiment and sweetness, she replies, "Sentiment and loveliness are all very well, when you have time for them. . . . I haven't. I'm not rich enough" (46). Indeed, throughout the story Esther draws Locksley's attention to the class-based differences between them. For instance, complaining that it is "a constant vexation . . . to be poor," Esther reproaches "poor" Locksley for being "too fine a gentleman" and advises him in the interests of overcoming his cowardly conceitedness to "Go and teach school, or open a corner grocery, or sit in a law-office all day, waiting for clients" (38).[8]

In short, "A Landscape Painter" adds to its catalog of traits detrimental to an artist the suggestion that members of Locksley's social set are disadvantaged as artists insofar as their insular society and the protection wealth buys limit their experiential range, consequently making it difficult to imagine those economically beneath them while encouraging a conformist and trivial aesthetics. Additionally, the contrast between Esther's perseverance despite rainy weather and weariness and Locksley's fair-weather pursuit of art as pleasurable activity ("I have none but pleasant thoughts") suggests that affluence and achieved social status remove several of the goads to artistic creation, including the need to work seriously to support oneself and to achieve through one's art a culturally significant self.

Although Locksley gushes throughout his diary about the beauty of sea and shore, and while entries provide evidence of continuous sketching and painting, art for Locksley is, finally, a hobby, therapy, lifestyle prop—which is why "A Landscape Painter" seems finally a love story with a rather unsurprising surprise ending turning on comeuppance. James's title, however, asks us to consider Locksley in his artistic role, and insofar as Esther's long list collects character flaws inimical to the creation of art, this catalog more than accounts for why Locksley is, after all, right to present himself as a poor artist.

III

Unlike "A Landscape Painter," "The Middle Years" presents a mature and ostensibly triumphant if regret-riddled professional artist.[9] As the story opens, Dencombe, seriously ill and recovering at a Bournemouth "health-resort," is about to open a package containing his latest (and last) novel, *The Middle Years*. Although neglected by the general reading public, Dencombe's work, the reader is to understand, is good—perhaps, James (typically) implies, too good to be popular—and his most recent effort is his best, a breakthrough that prefigures for the terminally ill author the shape of still better things to come, should time and health allow. As the story unfolds, Dencombe, with the help of the young Doctor Hugh, at Bournemouth to tend an ailing, eccentric Countess, must reconcile himself to the fact that for him there will be no second chances at art or life, that his middle years, like his future, are behind him.

Locksley and Dencombe seem at first glance to possess very different sensibilities. For instance, whereas the former thrills to "the beauties of wave, rock, and cloud," which fill him "with a sensuous ecstasy" ("A Landscape Painter," 11–12), the latter dismisses the sea as "all surface and twinkle, far shallower than the spirit of man" ("The Middle Years," 53)—indicative of a sensibility captivated by glittering exteriors versus one aware of murky depths. Yet the two are alike in telling respects. Like Locksley, Dencombe is given to instantaneous stereotyping of others. First glimpsing Doctor Hugh, the Countess, and her paid traveling companion Miss Vernham, Dencombe brings his powers as "an approved novelist" to bear erroneously to imagine Doctor Hugh as "the son of the opulent matron" and the object of Miss Vernham's "secret passion," this last personage imagined to be "the humble dependent, the daughter of a clergyman" (55).[10]

Further, whereas whatever posthumous reputation Locksley may enjoy rests on the success of the frame-narrator's efforts (who offers Locksley's diary to "convert [its readers] to my opinion that [Locksley] had in him the stuff of a great painter" [10]), Dencombe is asked to rest his hopes (at least partially) on Doctor Hugh's ardent conviction that *The Middle Years* has given the public a chance finally to appreciate Dencombe, "to pick up the pearl!" (74). Additionally, both men are victims of loss, sorrow, and disappointment: Dencombe's wife died in childbirth, his son of typhoid while away at school [66], and his development as a writer, which seems to bother him most of all, "had been abnormally slow" with the result that "it had taken too much of his life to produce too little of his art" (57).

Again, like Locksley, Dencombe is when we meet him in retreat from the world, dies young ("You're not old," Doctor Hugh tells Dencombe, adding that he means "physiologically" [66]), and seeks redemption ultimately in a sympathetic other (Doctor Hugh) whom he initially attempts to deceive by concealing his identity while Hugh copiously praises Dencombe's work.[11] Doctor Hugh's salvific value to the lonely Dencombe is underscored by the religious language that percolates throughout the text, revealing Dencombe's commitment to a romantic (and self-apotheosizing) religion of art: thus, for example, following an attack of his illness that throws him into depression, Dencombe imagines Doctor Hugh as a "servant of his altar" who has "set him up for connoisseurs to worship," a "clever son of the age" nonetheless possessed of "all the old reverence in faith" who will work for Dencombe the "miracle" captured in Doctor Hugh's deific pronouncement, "'You *shall* live!'" (68).

In short, both Locksley and Dencombe look back upon lives of dissatisfaction at the end of which there is little art to justify the sacrifices made, and both turn for that justification to another for a sympathetic reading or reflection of self.[12] These among other similarities suggest the possibility that, in his own way, Dencombe may be as much of a failure—"an artist deluded, diverted, frustrated or vanquished"—as Locksley clearly is.

It would be callous to insist that Dencombe fails because his health fails (vanquishment), or because he realizes his full powers (or imagines he does) too late to employ them (frustration), or because he turns for comfort in Doctor Hugh's direction (diversion) or must of necessity convince himself that his most recent work is "extraordinarily good" (56) and promissory of future greatness (delusion). Nor would it be correct in the context of James's aesthetic to locate Dencombe's failure in his lack of popular acclaim any more than it would be proper to fault Dencombe for destroying Doctor Hugh's hopes for a fortune, which would suggest an arguably immoral selfishness that could hold severe aesthetic repercussions—for Dencombe in fact does all he can to prevent just such an eventuality. Neither is it entirely accurate to attach Dencombe's failure to his having given up on art, although he more than once seems to be doing just that: "It was not true, what he had tried for renunciation's sake to believe, that all [novelistic] combinations were exhausted. . . . the exhaustion was in the miserable artist" (61).

Feelings such as these, or his depressed conviction that "he had not done what he wanted" (55), might constitute grounds for judging him a failure, but they are understandable under the circumstances and soon fade as he peruses his work, finding forgotten beauty and renewed inspiration in it.

Indeed, Dencombe is so sympathetic a character, his problems so beyond his control, the language of the story's close so persuasive, that he seems ultimately "transcendent," according to Sara S. Chapman, who sees Dencombe redeemed by his eventual understanding "that the value of the artist's life lies in his ability to have 'made somebody care'" (58, 54). This is a reading with which many of the story's critics have concurred and is doubtless largely responsible for the feeling that "The Middle Years" is, in the words of Edward Wagenknecht, "the most beautiful of James's stories about writers" (75).[13]

I do not wish to imply that making one's readers "care" is an unworthy aim. However, a look at the commentary "The Middle Years" has received reveals that even those critics who do not see the story as one of artistic defeat finger aspects of the text that ought to trouble readings of Dencombe as triumphant. Chapman herself reminds us that although Dencombe is not the story's narrator, he is its "central consciousness" through whose "physically and emotionally weakened perceptions . . . he himself and the other characters are presented" (55). If such weakened perceptions call into question the perspicacity of Dencombe's self-assessments (including his admiration for *The Middle Years* and belief that his talent has at last flowered), surely such weakness must cast greatest doubt when most severe: as Dencombe lies dying in the story's final paragraphs. Similarly, although James L. Babin likewise believes that Dencombe finds "the 'value' of his life and work revealed to him" in Doctor Hugh's choice of Dencombe and art over the Countess and fortune, a choice that proves Hugh "cares" about the things that ought most to matter (510–11), he notes Dencombe's anxiety throughout most of the story over "the value of a life that seems to him now to have been largely wasted in false starts and long apprenticeship" (506) and the flimsiness of those hopes on which he has gambled for salvation before his illness's final onslaught: a cure, a second chance free of struggle and false starts and doubt, a suddenly sympathetic public (514). I would suggest that the establishment of such a pattern implies that Dencombe's use of the caring Doctor Hugh to pull victory from the jaws of defeat is just another self-deception.

Not all critics, however, feel that all ends well for Dencombe. Perhaps the most severe overturning of "The Middle Years" is Perry D. Westbrook's reading of the story as satire at the expense of the perfectionist Dencombe's "egotism," which distorts what "actually happened": Doctor Hugh, "in collusion" with Miss Vernham, only pretended to relinquish the Countess's fortune, writing and then stealing off to London to publish the laudatory review that upon his return he flourishes before Dencombe as proof of the author's achievement (134–35).[14] Although this reading is possible, one needn't assume Doctor Hugh has tricked Dencombe—either by authoring the review or pretending to have lost his inheritance—to agree that "The Middle Years" locates Dencombe's failure, his amateurism, in his willingness to believe what is not so, to subscribe to the fiction of worth and accomplishment Doctor Hugh proffers, which encourages him to drop his own (perhaps impossibly) high standards of assessment and to accept the unqualified enthusiasm of an "ardent physiologist" (61) as proof of sufficient accomplishment.

Dencombe has, after all, already formed his (stereotypical) opinions of Doctor Hugh. He thinks of Hugh as "this gushing modern youth" who seems to be his "greatest admirer" but whose acquaintance with Dencombe's work is, as Doctor Hugh admits, a recent infatuation (61–62). "It would," James writes, "shake [Dencombe's] faith a little perhaps to have to take a doctor seriously who could take *him* so seriously" (61), and that faith is shaken later when Dencombe learns that even this ideal reader "had failed to guess" what had been "tried for" in *The Middle Years* (69). If, then, Dencombe's aesthetic equivalent of a deathbed conversion is to be explained, perhaps one need look no further than James's observation early in the story that "It served [Dencombe's] purpose to have a theory which should not be exposed to refutation" (59). What more irrefutable theory— or greater compromise—than an eleventh-hour acceptance of the belief that to have made Doctor Hugh "care" constitutes adequate recompense for "wasted inestimable years" of "hindered and retarded" development and general neglect (67, 57)?

Indeed, a series of substitutions, reversals, revisions, and compromises characterizes "The Middle Years" at all levels. For instance, the story opens with Dencombe thinking that "he liked the feeling of the south, so far as you could have it in the north" (53) and shortly after imagining that "he had never felt before that diligence *vincit omnia*" (56), "diligence" replacing "amor" in the more familiar *amor vincit omnia* ("love conquers all").[15] Again, the Countess, desiring lunch but told there will be none, replies that she will nap instead because *"Qui dort dine!"* (58): to sleep is to dine. Later, when Doctor Hugh tells Dencombe "You *will* live," Dencombe objects ("Don't be superficial") and Hugh replies, "You shall live," to which the author rejoins, "Ah, that's better!" (68). Similarly, the text's religious language reverses and revises itself, leaving Doctor Hugh both the mere worshiper at Dencombe's altar and, a few sentences later, the miracle man capable of saving his god (68).

Dencombe's penchant for revision and substitution is also revealed by the fact that he has not had his new novel in his possession more than a few minutes before he begins amending the text, having always been "a passionate corrector, a fingerer of style" (63). In fact, quite apart from its author's passionate penciling, *The Middle Years* undergoes a series of rapid reversals: it is but the shape of things to come and crowning glory; it initially bores its author, who can remember nothing about it, but quickly becomes the object of enamored fascination; its cover strikes Dencombe as "duly meretricious" (that is, vulgar, tawdry, resembling or evocative of a prostitute) but before the sentence ends exhales "the very odour of sanctity" (55);[16] when Dencombe first notices the book (which he does not recognize as his own) in the hands of Doctor Hugh, its "catchpenny" cover, "alluringly red," provokes condescending thoughts of both "the circulating library" and the book's owner, but when he recognizes the book as his, it serves immediately to elevate Doctor Hugh in Dencombe's estimation (54–55).

Just so, Doctor Hugh himself becomes the beneficiary of Dencombe's revisionary facility, transmogrifying from someone Dencombe first sees as "inflamed" and indiscrete (63) into "an apparition . . . above the law" (68–69) with the power to save and for whom Dencombe is willing to risk his life by attempting to leave Bournemouth at Miss Vernham's request. Doctor Hugh—who can without qualm say that forsaking the Countess is not a serious matter because their agreement involved "no contract but only a free understanding" (69–70) and who, as Christof Wegelin observes, ignores, "almost gaily, Dencombe's approaching end" (642)—becomes the person to whom Dencombe opens up confessionally and whose opinions, literary and otherwise, carry enough weight that, if one believes they sway Dencombe (as James's critics mostly believe they do), they become the pottage for which Dencombe sells his artistic birthright: to know and speak the truth.

Because he cannot write his next, better book, Dencombe allows himself to settle for the next-best thing: Doctor Hugh and his "inflamed" protestations of success, praise of himself in lieu of informed appreciation of his work (Hugh from first to last is mostly an admirer of "fine phrases" [61; see also 73]). "If you've doubted, if you've despaired, you've always 'done' it," Doctor Hugh asseverates (75), but he has been brought to this breathless position by Dencombe, who early on recognized that "This young friend, for a representative of the new psychology, was himself easily hypnotized, and if he became abnormally communicative it was only a sign of his real subjection. Dencombe did accordingly what he wanted with him" (62). Dencombe has, in other words, authored his own deception, a tour-de-force performance perhaps for a dying man, but the work of an amateur. It is this collaboration between "undivined" (61) author and willing acolyte that sets the stage for the story's final substitution, which replaces Dencombe's earlier self-assessments with the profoundly vapid conviction that, in Doctor Hugh's words, "something or other is everything" (75). Or say that Dencombe substitutes solace for success, personality for art, affect for cognition, an infatuated young doctor for both a missing public and future output.

In the first sentence of his story, James introduces us to "poor Dencombe." As Frank Kermode observes, "poor Dencombe" he remains to the end (76; see Kermode, 20). It is as apt an adjective here as it was in "A Landscape Painter." James was clear: "the privilege of the hero . . . belongs to him only as to the artist deluded."

IV

Because James is nothing if not ambiguous, it is of course possible to take both of these stories in other directions. "A Landscape Painter" resides in ambivalence because Esther as realist amounts finally to a rejection of realism as much as of romanticism: exploiting her sense of her own victimhood, Esther's unblinking view of life is a paltry, bitter, and unpleasantly manipulative, mean-spirited one whereas Locksley, whatever may be said against him, finds beauty and joie de vivre almost anywhere he sets up his insipid easel. As for "The Middle Years": if Westbrook's satirical reading is plausible, it is likewise possible that Dencombe is all the while humoring Doctor Hugh, playing a part to sustain the younger man's illusions. "Something or other [may be] everything," but Dencombe's reply—"Comforter!"—is "ironically sighed" (75). Nevertheless, he remains poor in this alternative reading precisely because not taken in, which is to say that he knows that making Hugh care cannot possibly be enough. He is a failure because he so judges himself. But regardless of which reading one chooses, Dencombe lapses into amateurism insofar as he turns from his accomplished work in hopes of catching a glimpse of a more gratifying success, looks away from the one place, if any, where his triumph is recorded.

Triumphant artists may live in their work, but they cannot live only there. Because art is long and life short, and because reach should exceed grasp, to pursue art is sooner or later to fail, the failure harder to accept when, like Dencombe, one deludes oneself into thinking it can be otherwise. Defer it how one may, eventually art brings out the amateur in even the most professional artist. When that happens, the best one can hope for is a splendid failure.

Notes

1. See Horvath, "The Life of Art, the Art of Life." The stories considered were "The Madonna of the Future," "The Author of *Beltraffio*," "The Lesson of the Master," "Greville Fane," "The Real Thing," "The Middle Years," "The Death of the Lion," "The Next Time," "The Figure in the Carpet," "Broken Wings," and "The Story in It."

2. Edel, *Henry James: The Untried Years* and *Henry James: The Middle Years* (314). See, too, Babin.

3. "A Landscape Painter" first appeared in the *Atlantic Monthly,* February 1866. Although excluded from the New York Edition, it was revised by James for inclusion in *Stories Revived* (1885), and this revision is the version included by Leon Edel in *The Complete Tales of Henry James* (vol. 1, 1962). I have elected to quote from the original version as it appears in the 1919 collection *A Landscape Painter* because it presents James's initial critique of a failed artist. Aside from numerous local revisions of wording (e.g., "cultivated" replaces "elegant" in the frame-narrator's description of Locksley; "prodigies" replaces "victories" in Locksley's description of his paintings), the major changes include altering character names (Esther becomes Miriam, Blunt becomes Captain Quarterman, Cragthrope becomes Chowderville) and the conclusion, which in the revision underscores the legitimacy of Esther's actions and removes her challenge that Locksley accept the deception and "be a man," which in context—the two were, after all, on their honeymoon—perhaps had come to seem too salacious.

4. The frame-narrator's assessment of Locksley and his work is not necessarily to be taken at face value. A member of Locksley's social set, the narrator's comments—for instance, his description of Locksley as "a man of what are called elegant tastes" (10)—serves to inform us not that Locksley is an accomplished artist but that his taste is conventional, what society deems elegant or fashionable. It is, after all, the narrator who elaborates Locksley's comparison of Josephine to the Venus of Milo: "indeed, if you can imagine the mutilated goddess with her full complement of limbs, dressed out by Madame de Crinoline, and engaged in small talk beneath the drawing-room chandelier, you may obtain a vague notion of Miss Josephine Leary" (7). Appearing in the story's opening paragraph, this transformation of Miss Leary into both a vapid Belinda or Gibson girl and, grotesquely, a "mutilated goddess" both prepares us for entry into a world of unself-consciously banal taste and causes us to understand that the narrator may be wrong when he presents Locksley as a man "seriously interested in arts and letters" who "had in him the stuff of a great painter" (10).

5. The revised text makes the point more clearly still: "I confess that I was more taken with the picture of the dusky little room, lighted by the single candle on the piano, and by her stately way of sitting at the instrument, than by the quality of her playing, though that is evidently high" (*The Complete Tales*, 1:107).

6. Although I haven't the space to offer a complete defense of Esther, see Rabinowitz, chapter 6, on why readers have conventionally been encouraged, "when a female character is described as a complex combination of contradictory traits . . . [to] give priority to the most negative qualities" (206). Also, it is useful to recall the Rabinowitz passage cited earlier. Insofar as the story is the work of a literary realist, as Levy and Allott believe, "correct aesthetic views" means that as authorial readers—that is, as readers reading as the author wished us to read (cp. Rabinowitz, 21–29)—we are asked to read as aesthetic realists, which means rejecting Locksley's "outworn aesthetic" and pledging at least qualified allegiance to Esther.

7. "For an artist, you are very slap-dash" reads the revised text (*Complete Tales*, 1:118).

8. The revised text underscores class difference at several points. For instance, it includes this additional criticism of Locksley by Esther: "You treat us kindly because you think virtue in a lowly station ought to be encouraged" (*Complete Tales*, 1:118). And at the close of the story, when Locksley tells Esther that her deception was "the act of a false woman," she rejoins, "A false woman? No, it was the act of any woman—placed as I was placed" (1:138).

9. "The Middle Years" was first published in *Scribner's* in May 1893. It was first collected in *Terminations* (1895), from which Leon Edel took the version included in *The Complete Tales*. This text varies only slightly from the version included in the New York Edition.

10. Dencombe's habit of stereotyping others (and the fact that we have this third-person story through his eyes and mind) ought to give pause to those readers

who see Dencombe and Doctor Hugh as two fine sensibilities posed against a crass, indifferent world represented by the Countess and Miss Vernham (cp. Babin and especially Rivkin).

11. It is a question how long Dencombe would have allowed the deception to continue. He justifies it by saying that "if his interlocutor had begun to abuse him he would have confessed on the spot his identity" but saw no harm in "drawing [Doctor Hugh] on a little to praise" (60), but this plan is cut short when Doctor Hugh notices that Dencombe has been amending the text and the flustered Dencombe faints, his identity revealed in the course of getting him safely back to bed.

12. On the homoeroticism that binds Dencombe and Doctor Hugh, see Person.

13. Four other readings—each emphasizing the salvific bond between writer and Doctor Hugh as ideal reader—find Dencombe ultimately triumphant over death and self-doubt. Leland S. Person, exploring James's "homo-aesthetics," locates Dencombe's redemption in "the regenerating power of male desire" (196); Christof Wegelin, less homoerotically, argues that the story charts a positive "change in Dencombe's sense of his career and achievement" (641) with Doctor Hugh liberating Dencombe from despair by teaching him "to assess his achievement properly" (643). Richard Hocks finds the story a "deeply affecting" one in which Dencombe discovers that artistic creation is a mystery beyond "one's designs or regrets" and finds "the true and appropriate 'extension' of [his] art through [Hugh's] appreciation as a reader" (54-55). Julie Rivkin troubles such readings through a meticulous examination of the story that finds James's interest here focused on textual revision as both "the hallmark of literary authority" and "a source of authorial vulnerability" (152). Attending closely to the Countess and Miss Vernham as the sort of potential readers who conjure in Dencombe a "nightmare of unsympathetic reception" (153), Rivkin designates Doctor Hugh the ideally "benign reader" (153), but she likewise finds Dencombe's desire never to have done with his texts—to retain control by never really relinquishing them to any but those who can "echo" and repeat without "deviation" his authorial intentions (162)—a stifling obsession and the source of his anguished sense of failure.

14. See also Krishna Baldev Vaid, who finds the story flawed, calling Dencombe a self-pitier (212) and arguing that James fails to achieve his "desired effect, which obviously is to render the change that comes over Dencombe, the total acceptance with which he meets his end" (207). Similarly, Frank Kermode finds Dencombe only "partly persuaded" by Doctor Hugh and hence at story's end the same "poor Dencombe" he was in the first sentence (20).

15. I have Frank Kermode's notes to thank for drawing my attention to this textual detail.

16. Related to the "alluringly red" "meretricious" cover are other passages that vulgarize the seriously elitist Dencombe by their sexual undertones, for instance, "there could be no complete renewal of the pleasure, dear to young experience,

of seeing one's self 'just out.' Dencombe, who had a reputation, had come out too often and knew too well in advance how he should look" (54).

Works Cited

Allott, Miriam. "'The Lord of Burleigh' and Henry James's 'A Landscape Painter.'" *Notes and Queries*, n.s., 2 (1955): 220–21.

Babin, James L. "Henry James's 'Middle Years' in Fiction and Autobiography." *Southern Review*, n.s., 13 (1977): 505–17.

Chapman, Sara S. *Henry James's Portrait of the Writer as Hero*. New York: St. Martin's, 1989.

Edel, Leon. *Henry James: The Middle Years, 1882–1895*. Philadelphia: Lippincott, 1962.

———. *Henry James: The Untried Years, 1843–1870*. Philadelphia: Lippincott, 1953.

Hocks, Richard A. *Henry James: A Study of the Short Fiction*. Twayne's Studies in Short Fiction Series. Boston: Twayne, 1990.

Horvath, Brooke. "The Life of Art, the Art of Life: The Ascetic Aesthetics of Defeat in James's *Stories of Writers and Artists*." *Modern Fiction Studies* 28 (1982): 93–107.

James, Henry. *The Complete Tales of Henry James*. Ed. Leon Edel. Vol. 1. Philadelphia: Lippincott, 1962.

———. "A Landscape Painter." 1866. In *Henry James, A Landscape Painter*, 7–67. New York: Scott and Seltzer, 1919.

———. "The Middle Years." In *The Complete Tales of Henry James*, 9:53–76. Ed. Leon Edel. Philadelphia: Lippincott, 1964.

———. Preface to *The Tragic Muse* (vol. 5 of the New York Edition). In *The Art of the Novel: Critical Prefaces*, 79–97. New York: Scribner's, 1934.

Kermode, Frank. Introduction and Notes to *"The Figure in the Carpet" and Other Stories*, 7–30, 450–51. New York: Viking Penguin, 1986.

Levy, Leo B. "Consciousness in Three Early Tales of Henry James." *Studies in Short Fiction* 18 (1981): 407–12.

Person, Leland S., Jr. "James's Homo-Aesthetics: Deploying Desire in the *Tales of Writers and Artists*." *Henry James Review* 14 (1993): 188–203.

Rabinowitz, Peter J. *Before Reading: Narrative Conventions and the Politics of Interpretation*. Ithaca: Cornell University Press, 1987.

Rivkin, Julie. "Doctoring the Text: Henry James and Revision." *Henry James's New York Edition: The Construction of Authorship*. Ed. David McWhirter, 142–63. Stanford: Stanford University Press, 1995.

Vaid, Krishna Baldev. *Technique in the Tales of Henry James*. Cambridge: Harvard University Press, 1964.

Wagenknecht, Edward. *The Tales of Henry James.* Literature and Life Series. New York: Ungar, 1984.

Wegelin, Christof. "Art and Life in James's 'The Middle Years.'" *Modern Fiction Studies* 33 (1987): 639–46.

Westbrook, Perry D. "The Supersubtle Fry." *Nineteenth-Century Fiction* 8 (1953): 134–40.

Kristin Boudreau

A CONNECTION MORE
CHARMING THAN IN LIFE

The Refusal of Consolation in
"The Altar of the Dead"

As MANY CRITICS HAVE NOTED, Henry James's 1895 tale "The Altar of the Dead" was written after a series of painful losses that the author suffered in the 1890s. James composed the original notebook entry, describing his conception for this story of a much-bereaved middle-aged man, at the last English residence of Constance Fenimore Woolson, whose suicide in 1894 had suffused him with horror and pity. (In an 1894 letter to William, he attributed her suicide to "an essentially tragic & insane *difficulty in living*" [*Correspondence*, 2:304].) The equally complicated death of his sister, Alice, left the novelist feeling more ambivalent about his loss. In a letter to Francis Boot, James wrote that "even with everything that made life an unspeakable weariness to her, she contributed constantly, infinitely to the interest, the consolation, as it were, in disappointment and depression, of my own existence" (*Letters,* 3:81). Alice had died in 1892, but the pang of her death returned for her brother in 1894, when he learned that his sister had kept a diary during her final years. James received his copy of the diary in Venice, where he had gone to help attend to Woolson's literary remains. 1894 was also the year that James lost another dear friend, Robert Louis Stevenson.

When he learned of Stevenson's death in the South Seas, he is said to have run to their mutual friend, Mrs. Sitwell, crying, "It isn't true, it isn't true, say it isn't true" (cited in Clarke, 3:202).

Small wonder, then, that James, bowed low with the weight of his many griefs, should turn out a tale about a man whose dominant passion is his "sense of being bereft" ("The Altar of the Dead," 450). Writing his 1909 preface to the tale, James claimed "to have lost every trace of 'how I came to think'" of the subject precisely because it had always been with him. "The idea embodied in this composition must... never have been so absent from my view as to call for an organised search. It was 'there'—it had always, or from ever so far back, been there . . . and it naturally found expression at the first hour something more urgently undertaken happened not to stop the way" (v). For James, then, this tale, first appearing in a volume called *Terminations,* had clear origins in his life, origins that his critics have not neglected.

To this biographical reading I would like to add another layer: that of James's understanding of suffering as part of an impressive literary and intellectual tradition, one that had claimed him in his youth and only tightened its grip on the novelist as his own bereavements multiplied. As a young man learning the news of the death of his cousin Minny Temple at age twenty-four from tuberculosis, James revisited his memories of her, hoping to preserve not merely the girl herself but also the ache she had left in his life. Perhaps he was thinking of Emerson, for whom the cataclysmic death of his son Waldo had faded—too soon—into a poor, dim shadow of the grief he'd expected would always remain: "Grief too," wrote Emerson,

> will make us idealists. In the death of my son, now more than two years ago, I seem to have lost a beautiful estate,—no more. I cannot get it nearer to me. . . . [S]omething which I fancied was a part of me, which could not be torn away without tearing me nor enlarged without enriching me, falls off from me and leaves no scar. (344)

I suppose that what Emerson meant in lamenting his idealism was that even our sorest griefs are merely subjective phenomena, destined to fade along with our best thoughts, impulses, and inspirations.[1] Perhaps also he was thinking of Hawthorne's Wakefield (whom he'd later reshape into John Marcher): a lesson in the transience of affective relations. Hawthorne's narrator seems to shake his head as he exhorts his character to "get thee home to good Mrs. Wakefield. . . . It is perilous to make a chasm in human affections; not that they gape so long and wide—but so quickly close again!" (66).

In any case, his return to the subject of Minny Temple in his letters to his parents and to his brother William seems less an attempt to nurse his aching consciousness than to probe the wound, keeping it tender, as if to disprove the romantic contention of his countrymen that, as Emerson put it, "souls never touch" (315). He probed that wound relentlessly in his letters of 1870. "There is . . . something so appealing in the pathos of her final weakness and decline," he wrote to William, "that my heart keeps returning again & again to the scene, regardless of its pain" (*Correspondence,* 1:155). He returned to the subject much later in his autobiography of 1914, where he wrote that Minny's "faint echo from too far off . . . should be tenderly saved" (*Notes,* 252). James's many revisitations of his grief seem analogous to Emerson's effort, a year after the death of his wife, Ellen, to recover his grief by disinterring the body for contemplation.[2]

James also understood the limits of grief. In a 31 July 1888 letter to Robert Louis Stevenson, who had relocated to the South Seas, he warned his friend that too long an absence would effectively obliterate Stevenson from James's consciousness. "You are too far away—" begins one despondent letter,

> you are too absent—too invisible, inaudible, inconceivable. Life is too short a business and friendship too delicate a matter for such tricks— for cutting great gory masses out of 'em by the year at a time. Therefore come back. Hang it all—sink it all and come back. A little more and I shall cease to believe in you: I don't mean (in the usual implied phrase) in your veracity, but literally and more fatally in your relevancy—your objective reality. You become a beautiful myth—a kind of unnatural uncomfortable unburied *mort.*

This letter suggests that James feared what Emerson and Hawthorne had to say about the fleetingness of longing. Were he to cease believing in his friend's "objective reality," James might become like Emerson himself, learning that "grief too will make us idealists."

That, for James, seemed the American way: self-reliant and stoical, the American Romantic lived in isolation from the social world, including even the world of his affections. When the American heroine of *Portrait of a Lady* steps into the English world of Gardencourt, she embodies all of Emerson's values and represents perfect self-reliance: she does not fear inconsistency and she finds it "unnecessary to cultivate doubt of one's self" (104). Self-consciousness poses no problem for Isabel Archer: "she would be what she appeared, and she would appear what she was" (105). Perhaps these very qualities induce her cousin Ralph to predict that Isabel will never suffer, was "not made to suffer" (101). The connection between independence and insensibility is more explicit in Ralph's mother, the representative of manly self-reliance, who, like Emerson, loses a son without gaining a scar. Isabel reflects with pity that "there seemed something so dreary in the condition of a person whose nature had, as it were, so little surface—offered so limited a face to the accretions of human contact. Nothing tender, nothing sympathetic, had ever had a chance to fasten upon it—no wind-sown blossom, no familiar softening moss" (272).

By this point Isabel has learned to pity her aunt, because she has learned to see the world not as an American but as an English Romantic, for whom suffering leaves a gash, touches a life. By the time Isabel returns to Gardencourt for Ralph's death, her attitude to pain has changed. No longer confident of her self-reliance, she now believes in the power of grief to mark people of fine sensibilities. Like Keats, wistfully gazing at unreflective or inanimate things (a nightingale, the figures on an urn), Isabel comes to envy "the security of valuable 'pieces' which change by no hair's breadth, only grow in value, while their owners lose inch by inch youth, happiness, beauty" (614). She envies them, but at the same time she's glad not to be them.

Like his heroine, James understood that while we are not made to suffer, our griefs, when they come, can help us. So in a letter dated 28 February 1902, he advised Hendrick Andersen to open his heart to the gashes of pain left by his beloved brother's death, a feeling he claimed to share:

> I respond to every throb of it, I participate in every pang. I've gone through Death, and Death, enough in my long life, to know how all that we *are,* all that we *have,* all that is best of us within, our genius, our imagination, our passion, our whole personal being, become then but aides and channels and open gates to suffering, to being flooded. But, it is better so. Let yourself go and *live,* even as a lacerated, mutilated lover, with your grief, your loss, your sore, unforgettable consciousness.

James here is borrowing Emerson's metaphor, while encouraging Andersen to rejoice that his loved one has not fallen off without leaving a scar.

Again and again in his ruminations on death, James returns to that scar—or, more frequently, to the unhealed wound. Writing after learning of his cousin's death, he muses to William, "I have been hearing all my life of the sense of loss wh[ich] death leaves behind it:—now for the first time I have a chance to learn what it amounts to" (*Correspondence,* 1:154). In the same letter he observes that a sense of loss should perhaps remain with the bereaved rather than healing over: "We may suppose [Minny's departed spirit] much better pleased by our perfect acceptance of the void it has left than by our quarreling with it and wishing it filled up again" (155).

"The Altar of the Dead" explores the passion of bereavement in a man who is appalled by what he observes as a widespread desire to fill that void left by his departed friends. In his pious wish to accept the void, Stransom "is struck with the way they are forgotten, are unhallowed—unhonored, neglected, shoved out of sight. . . . He is struck with the rudeness, the coldness, that surrounds their memory—the want of a place made for them in the life of the survivors" (*Notebooks,* 98). James's notebook entry suggests that this will be a tale of gaps, the empty spaces once inhabited by loved ones, and in many ways it is. And yet, in the Romantic tradition of compensatory grief, Stransom's voids assume substance, his absent figures reshape themselves into present ground, as James introduces his tale with reversal after reversal.

"He had a mortal dislike, poor Stransom, to lean anniversaries, and he disliked them still more when they made a pretense of a figure" (450). The occasion that Stransom commemorates, no "lean anniversary" but instead a "feast of memory," holds him because it is presided over not by a figure but by mere ground, by the space once occupied by the shape of Mary Antrim.

Antrim's death initiates a loss that, before the end of the first page, has already become a gain:

> She had died of a malignant fever after the wedding-day had been fixed, and he had lost, before fairly tasting it, an affection that promised to fill his life to the brim.
>
> Of that benediction, however, it would have been false to say this life could really be emptied; it was still ruled by a pale ghost, it was still ordered by a sovereign presence. (450)

That presence, or pale ghost, is a mere place-holder, filling Stransom's life with a consummate emptiness. "He had not been a man of numerous passions, and even in all these years no sense had grown stronger with him than the sense of being bereft." Though this "sense" is a positive presence, it is also a sign of negation, and in this tale, negations are the dominant facts. Stransom's primary accomplishment (one of the few that the narrator names) is itself a negation. "He had done many things in the world—he had done almost all things but one—he had never forgotten." Thus whatever Stransom has done (accomplishments and employments too insignificant to be specified), he knows himself primarily for what he has neglected, and that very neglect becomes his defining act. "He had tried to put into his existence whatever else might take up room in it, but he had never made it anything but a house of which the mistress was eternally absent." Though his failure to forget is later materialized in the congregation of candles he assembles to commemorate his griefs, Stransom does not need this reification to demonstrate the presence of his losses; his metaphors all suggest the spatial properties of his bereavements. An empty cup, an empty house, an empty bridal embrace: these are the signs that Stransom's "immense escape from the actual" (451) brings him face to face with a world that—while it is characterized by nothingness—offers him more substance than the world's realities.

Those realities are most glaringly represented by Paul Creston and his new wife, whom Stransom encounters against the "mercenary grin" of a shop-front (452). The context of the shop, crowded with people, highlights the crass insistence of the actual world. "It was the window of a jeweller whose diamonds and sapphires seemed to laugh, in flashes like high notes of sound, with the mere joy of knowing how much more they were 'worth' than most of the dingy pedestrians staring at them from the other side of the pane." Stransom's revenge is to appropriate those jewels for his imaginary world, as he lingers "long enough to suspend, in a vision, a string of pearls about the white neck of Mary Antrim." But his vision is interrupted by another high note, that of Paul Creston's new wife. The meeting, placed in stark relief against Stransom's last encounter with Creston, reminds him of the vulgarity of the actual world. The last time he'd seen Creston, the man had been grieving for his first wife; he had shown Stransom a "wholly other face. . . , the blurred, ravaged mask bent over the open grave by which they had stood together. Creston was not in mourning now" (453).

Stransom is horrified by the reach of the actual, social world, by its alarming capacity to blot out a more ideal world, a world represented not only by Mary Antrim but also by Creston's first wife. The late Kate Creston "had made the passions about her as regular as the moon makes the tides" (454). Her replacement, in contrast, strikes Stransom as a "hired performer" (453) whose presence prompts him to play the social game, to pass over his observation that the two Mrs. Crestons have nothing in common but their name:

> Creston had blushed and stammered over it, but in half a minute, at the rate we live in polite society, it had practically become, for Stransom, the mere memory of a shock. They stood there and laughed and talked; Stransom had instantly whisked the shock out of the way, to keep it for private consumption. He felt himself grimacing, he heard himself exaggerating the usual, but he was conscious that he had turned slightly faint. (453)

Though he can adopt the grimace of polite society, Stransom understands that the affront of social behavior is derived from the incommensurability between its expressions and the actual sentiments behind them. Those who "exaggerat[e] the usual" inflate sentimental values, whereas Stransom understands that true shock and grief can only be experienced privately. Kate Creston, whose passions were regular and natural as the tide, lived her real life in the heart; for Kate, the social sphere was only a means of keeping the passions inviolate. "She had been also of course far too good for her husband, but he never suspected it, and in nothing had she been more admirable than in the exquisite art with which she tried to keep every one else (keeping Creston was no trouble) from finding it out" (454). Unlike Kate, Paul Creston and his new wife are implicated in the overinflated value of the shopfront jewels: "This lady had a face that shone as publicly as the jeweller's window, and in the happy candour with which she wore her monstrous character there was an effect of gross immodesty" (453).

James highlights the distinctions between private and public, sentimental and commercial values in his repetition of economic metaphors. The "cost" of remembering his dead falls upon Stransom's "liberal heart"; meanwhile, the Crestons venture into the grinning, laughing, mercenary shop in order to "decide," as Mrs. Creston says, on a purchase (452). When Stransom approaches the bishops about erecting an altar for his dead, he makes them "assent to his eccentric munificence" because he offers "concessions in exchange for indulgences" (458). Here James urges us to see Stransom's liberal heart contrasted with his liberal pocket, the only kind of munificence the clerics understand. While they grant him his whim, the priests are really selling him a privilege they don't care to understand; the historic term, "indulgences," reminds us of longstanding corruption in the Catholic church. Still, these exchanges constitute for Stransom a kind of social grimace, a public behavior that both enables his private piety and highlights (by means of contrast) the superiority of his own sentiments. His reflection on Creston's speedy remarriage can be taken as a comment on other forms of public behavior as well: "The frivolity, the indecency of it made Stransom's eyes fill; and he had that evening a rich, almost happy sense that he alone, in a world without delicacy, had a right to hold up his head" (454–55).

In contrast to the exaggerated usual, Stransom's passions occupy a very different terrain from these social forms. To be sure, his passions seem to operate according to an economic model, and hence are liable to inflation: "by the time George Stransom was fifty-five such memories had greatly multiplied. . . . He had perhaps not had more losses than most men, but he had counted his losses more; he had not seen death more closely, but he had, in a manner, felt it more deeply" (451).

When he translates his bereavement into quantifiable terms, however, Stransom's economy of pain differs from the economy that motivates his neighbors precisely because he is not driven by the laws of supply and demand. Rather, Stransom expresses his grief in symbols that are legible and meaningful to himself alone, whatever their apparent resemblance to acceptable social forms. For this reason he manages to receive church approval for a nearly blasphemous rite of worship—regardless of the price he pays for the privilege. His rites do not depend upon consensus for their power. The altar he establishes merely imitates, in its material form, the ideal temple in his mind. Though James's narrator intimates that the original of Stransom's altar can be found in the history of Catholicism ("the great original type, set up in a myriad temples, of the unapproachable shrine he had erected in his mind"), actually Stransom's pious reflections on his dead seem to invert this order, converting the material, historical original into the shadowy derivative and elevating Stransom's conception to a kind of Platonic ideal.

Thus when Stransom expresses his homage to the dead in "some outward worship" wherein he might "find his real comfort," he is seeking "some material act" to convey outwardly his inner passion (457). This material utterance of his feelings differs from his social "grimace" in that the candles remain, for Stransom, entirely compatible with his private sentiment; indeed, they offer him a "rich . . . assurance at all times, but especially in the indifferent world" (458).

Though material rather than invisible, then, Stransom's waxen enactment of his bereavements are of an entirely different order from his conduct in the social realm. Even though he erects an altar for others to use, he sees that altar primarily as a private demonstration of his own interiority—which, as we have seen, he has defined as privation. Only in its power to signify that invisible presence in his life does the altar acquire importance for its founder:

> [H]alf the satisfaction of the spot for this mysterious and fitful worshipper was that he found the years of his life there, and the ties, the affections, the struggles, the submissions, the conquests, if there had been such, a record of that adventurous journey in which the beginnings and endings of human relations are the lettered mile-stones. (459)

These milestones, as Karen Smythe has pointed out, are necessarily lettered and legible only to Stransom. Smythe distinguishes between the writing and the reading of Stransom's elegiac altar. The "elegist," she writes, "uses writing to produce a structure that is ultimately designed for the 'living, knowing memory' of the reader, who will both adapt and adopt the content" (319). I will have more to say about Stransom's altar as a text to be read and adapted. For now it will suffice to note that Stransom's "record," though installed in a public place and meant for public appreciation, is legible *as record* only to its author.

Thus the altar is essentially private, essentially different from Stransom's public, professional, and social relations, even though some of those relations might be recorded there. Given the fundamentally private meaning encoded in the altar, it should not be remarkable that the one human relation to spring from Stransom's altar—or, I should say, his one relation with a *living* human—should also appear to Stransom as beyond social norms. The woman he meets at the altar is never given a name, as if her

identity for Stransom transcends such rituals of public recognition as naming. Stransom himself only learns her name eventually. "For long ages he
never knew her name, any more than she had ever pronounced his own; but
it was not their names that mattered, it was only their perfect practice and
their common need" (464). When he does finally learn her name, he learns
that there are other things about her he will never know or care to know.
"He had learned after a long time that she earned money by her pen, writing
under a designation that she never told him in magazines that he never saw"
(466). Like Stransom's unspecified public life, the woman's profession does
not count in their peculiar friendship. Nor do other public matters. They
both "knew the world of London, [but] from an undiscussed instinct of privacy they haunted the regions not mapped on the social chart" (464).

Instead, they flaunt their indifference to conventions, finding in their
unconventional friendship the very absence that has made each of their
lives meaningful:

> These things made their whole relation so impersonal that they had
> not the rules or reasons people found in ordinary friendships. They
> didn't care for the things it was supposed necessary to care for in the in-
> tercourse of the world. They ended one day (they never knew which of
> them expressed it first) by throwing out the idea that they didn't care
> for each other. Over this idea they grew quite intimate. (464)

Growing intimate over what they lack, this couple replicates Stransom's
own conviction that his life is marked by absence. Significantly, when he
first notes the woman, he primarily marks what she lacks: "She had no colour, no sound, no fault, and another of the things about which he had
made up his mind was that she had no fortune" (461). Like his other losses,
his companion's nothingness in the visible, social realm soon mutates into a
significance in the ideal world: "People were not poor, after all, whom so
many losses could overtake; they were positively rich when they had so
much to give up" (461).

Her own richness soon becomes *their* richness: again, an accumulation
of absences. Like the woman's unuttered name, significant communication
between the two is wordless: "not a word had been exchanged about the
place in which they frequently met. . . . It was odd that when nothing had
really ever brought them together he should have been able successfully to

assume that they were in a manner old friends—that this negative quantity was somehow more than they could express" (462). Their coming together over "nothing" is precisely the point: there is "nothing particular between them" (468) because their nothing is everything.

The irony, of course, is that there *is* something between them, and has been all along, only in failing to utter it they have failed to recognize it. The woman's lover, the one she has been mourning, was none other than Acton Hague, the "nearest of [Stransom's] friends" ten years before, "the only man with whom he had ever been intimate" (455), the man whose public quarrel had left Stransom nearly friendless. Both of these mourners have suffered intensely from the "insult" that Hague had exchanged for their passionate loyalty to him. In the instant that Stransom sees the woman's shrine ("a museum in [Hague's] honor") he understands that the meaning of *his* shrine, for her, has been an ironic inversion of his own intent. "It was all for Acton Hague that she had kneeled every day at his altar" (469), even while the architect of the altar had willfully omitted any reference to Hague: "The greatest blank in the shining page was the memory of Acton Hague, of which he inveterately tried to rid himself. For Acton Hague no flame could ever rise on any altar of his" (460).

For the woman, meanwhile, *all* the flames have been for Hague. When confronting Hague's presence in both their lives, then, they must acknowledge that all human relations (not just those of "polite society") are governed by arbitrary signs. Though in their conversation they avoid specific references to the losses of their lives, they have expressed their intimacy in an elaborate language of candles, a language not transcendent but arbitrary, like all languages. Stransom had hoped that his altar would provide comfort for others, but he never expected that comfort to collide with his own: "Whoever bent a knee on the carpet he had laid down appeared to him to act in the spirit of his intention" (459). But having failed to communicate his intention, Stransom has preserved it as a cipher, even for his most intimate friend.[3]

Committing themselves to gaps and voids, they have hoped to transcend language altogether, not realizing that these very gaps are themselves linguistic references. Thus the nothingness that had initially marked the woman for Stransom becomes a glaring sign of presence, the specific presence of Acton Hague, with whose image she is "ineffaceably stamped"

(475). In their presumption of sympathy, they have missed one of the most significant points of contact between themselves, the fact that they are both victims of the same man.

It could hardly be otherwise. After seeking to carry out their friendship (essentially a social exchange) without the help of social implements, this bereaved couple discover the impossibility of transcendent human relations. Although eyes may meet and words may speak, "souls," as Emerson discovered, "never touch their objects." The realm of grief is essentially private and noumenal, unless it can be translated into a language meant to be shared. Stransom's altar is indeed a language, but a language meant for himself alone: he never makes the code for its translation available to others.

Both James and his creation thought of death in terms that transformed the social and phenomenal—that which can be shared, perceived and communicated—into the noumenal and transcendent, into an essentially private realm. For James, the death of his cousin Minny was primarily a translation of a fact into an idea. As he wrote to William in 1870, "The more I think of her the more perfectly satisfied I am to have her translated from this changing realm of fact to the steady realm of thought. There she may bloom into a beauty more radiant than our dull eyes will avail to contemplate" (*Correspondence,* 1:155). Likewise, Stransom identifies the "sovereign presence" (450) that survives Mary Antrim's death as an "immense escape from the actual" (451). In both cases, while death does not utterly destroy an existence (for those who mourn the loss), it does effect a change that is clearly extreme in many senses. I am interested primarily in the epistemological change for the survivors, in this case James and Stransom. Prior to death, the living person (as a visible presence who could communicate her desires and thoughts to others) occupied—for those others—the sphere of perceptions: she was visible and knowable to more than one spectator. The *idea* of the dead person, on the other hand, inhabits a private, nonsensory realm: it can be known intuitively only to the person who conceives of it but never apprehended through the senses and never perfectly shared. Though it can, of course, be translated into language and communicated, no description of this idea can fully capture it, and thus it is essentially and permanently private.[4]

In this regard the idea of the departed soul resembles Emerson's description of the process of inspiration through reading. However inspired an idea may have been at its inception, the moment of inspiration is fleeting and cannot be contained in the written record. Language is an inadequate medium for conveying ideas, which transcend language. Words on a page, then, are only "dead fact." They can recover their original life only by entering the mind of a reader and inspiring a new thought. Emerson refers to that moment of inspiration as "creative reading," when "the page of whatever book we read becomes luminous with manifold allusion. Every sentence is doubly significant." Transcendence occurs during that moment when the scholar contemplates the world, thereby transforming it from a physical to a metaphysical event. "It was dead fact; now, it is quick thought." But these transcendent moments are by their very nature incommunicable, essentially and nonnegotiably private. When Henry James describes the process of loss, grief and consolation both in his letters and in "The Altar of the Dead," he is explaining an emotional phenomenon that has, I am arguing, a precise counterpart in Emerson's account of an intellectual event.

If we consider, for instance, James's argument for life after death, we can see it in terms very similar to those that Emerson uses in "The American Scholar." James's essay "Is There Life after Death," written in 1910 for *Bazaar* magazine, considers the possibility of the immortality of souls, a topic that he designates as "the most interesting question in the world" (602). The condition of being alive, James complains, relegates us to the realm of the physical, thereby arresting our sallies of spirit. "It brings itself home to us thus in all sorts of ways," James writes,

> that we are even at our highest flights of personality, our furthest reachings out of the mind, of the very stuff of the abject actual, and that the sublimest idea we can form and the noblest hope and affection we can cherish are but flowers sprouting in that eminently and infinitely diggable soil (604–5).

James's "stuff of the abject actual," the "soil" of material existence, resembles nothing so much as Emerson's "dead fact" (though for James the actual only hampers; it does not entirely deaden). At transcendent moments we are allowed to glimpse what might be our lot could we be liberated from the abject actual:

> [I]n proportion as we . . . enjoy the greater number of our most char-

acteristic inward reactions, in proportion as we do curiously and lovingly, yearningly and irrepressibly, interrogate and liberate, try and test and explore, our general productive and, as we like conveniently to say, creative awareness of things . . . in that proportion does our function strike us as establishing sublime relations. (612)

These sublime relations, emanating as they do from our "inward reactions," constitute James's counterpart to Emerson's "quick thought": they are ineffable, they rise above the practice of conventions, and most significantly they can be experienced privately but never communicated, never recorded in signs of the "abject actual." When we experience death, in other words (whether our own or that of someone we love) we can only experience it in solitude. Because Stransom's deep mourning is a transcendent event, one that transforms his experience of the dead from social, linguistic and phenomenal relations into spiritual, internal relations, he is profoundly unable to share his experiences of mourning. When his loved ones pass from the status of fact into that of thought, they move beyond the reach of description and communication. Conventional elegies only approximate and thus misrepresent this most private feeling of loss; Stransom's unconventional elegy does not even try to translate his grief into any communicable form.

I take this (very Emersonian) lesson to be the central message of "The Altar of the Dead." Even their shared and compatible grief finally only drives Stransom and his companion apart. We might have guessed as much because Stransom's apparently elegiac temple to his dead fails to reach beyond his own idiosyncratic expression of bereavement. The classic elegy offers consolation to all mourners, a consolation that announces itself as timeless and larger than a specific death or friendship. But Stransom's altar is no elegy at all. When he first entertains the idea he is not thinking of consolation but of something very different, something approaching pleasure or excitement. He is "brought . . . to his feet in the sudden excitement of a plan" (457). Meditating further on that plan, he "reserve[s] to himself . . . the free enjoyment of his intention, an enjoyment that becomes "even greater than he had ventured to hope" (458).

Excitement and enjoyment, of course, need not be incompatible with consolation, though they do seem odd companions. But Stransom's altar is unelegiac in several more important ways. For one thing, its architect does not pretend to offer consolation to the living; his care is all for the dead, the unremembered, who "died again, died every day, of the hard usage of life. They had no organized service, no reserved place, no honour, no shelter, no safety" (451). In erecting his altar, Stransom hopes to comfort the dead. "Now they had really, his Dead, something that was indefeasibly theirs" (459). Though he hopes that others will invoke their Dead at his altar, he's hardly interested in consoling the living.

Even with regard to his own bereavements, Stransom's candles offer less in the way of consolation than of reminder. Finding among his candles a record of "the years of his life," he accepts his history

> with something of that positive gladness with which one adjusts one's self to an ache that is beginning to succumb to treatment. To the treatment of time the malady of life begins at a given moment to succumb; and these were doubtless the hours at which that truth most came home to him. The day was written for him there on which he had first become acquainted with death, and the successive phases of the acquaintance were each marked with a flame. (459)

It might be tempting to understand this analogy as evidence that Stransom has accepted the consolation of philosophy, but the past he accepts and rejoices in is paired off with the ache, not with its (inevitable) treatment. In other words, his flames mark not his eventual triumph over grief, but the many manifestations of grief itself; Stransom records "the successive phases of [his] acquaintance" with death. Although he must acknowledge that suffering does eventually yield to the dulling effects of time, his shrine chronicles particular episodes of suffering, as if thereby to resist consolation, as if to commemorate bereavement rather than overcome it.

The point is more difficult to miss later in the chapter, where Stransom's eagerness to embrace pain nearly incapacitates him for consolation. "There were hours at which he almost caught himself wishing that certain of his friends would now die, that he might establish with them in this manner a connection more charming than, as it happened, it was possible to enjoy with them in life" (460). In meaning and in cadence, this startling sentence neatly echoes one of Emerson's most famous lines, where he grieves that grief has taught him nothing: "There are moods in which we court suffering, in the hope that here at least we shall find reality, sharp peaks and edges of truth" (340). But while Emerson sought pain in order to make his life seem more real, in order to experience in suffering both the burden and the birthright of human beings, Stransom longs for the death of friends because his human relations are all paltry. He finds that his real life is located not with his living acquaintances but with his dead ones, and for the sake of an ever fuller existence he's "almost" willing to consent to more deaths. In his preface, James pronounced it "brutal" that "to be caught in any rueful glance at [the dead] was to be branded at once as 'morbid'" (ix). The narrator's confession, however, indicates that Stransom's rueful glance is not one we typically cast toward the dead: he seems not to regret his losses but to love his regrets. Courting suffering as he does, he is not really capable of offering consolation to the living.

Notes

While writing this essay, I was encouraged by Margaret Dickie, whose help, both personal and intellectual, was a constant support. Margaret was a fount of consolation herself, and I dedicate this essay to her memory.

1. For a reading of Emersonian subjectivity as a "site of constitutional scarcity, . . . the site of vigilant proprietorship" (91), see Dimock. Because "one is entitled to feel pain," then "not to feel it—a suitable amount of it—is to be deprived of something that is rightfully one's own. What we see in Emerson, in short, is what we might call the internalization of property" (92). As I shall argue, James's economy of pain does not correspond to market-driven values like the valuation of property.

2. Richardson offers a moving account of this episode (3–5).

3. Warminski argues that these characters operate as zeugmas, coordinated but opposed: "radically disjunct while indissoluably bound together" (271). "Thus one could say that the altar *both* signifies *every one but* Hague *and* signifies (by negation) *no one but* Hague" (273).

4. Because the idea is not constrained by the linguistic and visual implements of the material world, moreover, survivors are free to imagine a more perfect existence for the departed, a more perfect union with the departed: hence, Minny Temple's "beauty more radiant than our dull eyes will avail to contemplate."

Works Cited

Clarke, Graham. *Henry James: Critical Assessments,* 3: 202. Mountfield: Helm Information, 1991.

Dimock, Wai-Chi. "Scarcity, Subjectivity, and Emerson." *boundary 2* 17.1 (1990): 83–99.

Emerson, Ralph Waldo. "Experience." 1844. In *The Complete Essays and Other Writings of Ralph Waldo Emerson,* 342–64. Ed. Brooks Atkinson. New York: Random House, 1940.

Hawthorne, Nathaniel. "Wakefield." 1835. In *Hawthorne's Short Stories,* 63–71. Ed. Newton Arvin. New York: Knopf, 1946.

James, Henry. "The Altar of the Dead." 1895. In *Henry James: Complete Stories, 1892–1898.* New York: Library of America, 1996.

———. *The Complete Notebooks of Henry James.* Ed. Leon Edel and Lyall Powers. New York: Oxford University Press, 1987.

———. "Is There Life after Death?" 1910. Rpt. in *The James Family,* 602–14. Ed. F. O. Matthiessen. New York: Knopf, 1947.

———. *Letters.* Ed. Leon Edel. Vol. 3. Cambridge: Belknap Press of Harvard University Press, 1974.

———. "Preface." In *The Novels and Tales of Henry James.* Vol. 17. New York: Scribner's, 1909.

———. "Notes of a Son and Brother." 1914. Rpt. in Henry James, *Autobiography.* Ed. Frederick W. Dupee. 1956. Princeton: Princeton University Press, 1983.

James, William. *The Correspondence of William James.* 3 vols. Ed. Ignas K. Skrupskelis and Elizabeth M. Berkeley. Charlottesville: University Press of Virginia, 1992–94.

Richardson, Robert D., Jr. *Emerson: The Mind on Fire.* Berkeley: University of California Press, 1995.

Smythe, Karen. "'The Altar of the Dead': James's Grammar of Grieving." *English Studies in Canada* 16.3 (1990): 315–24.

Warminski, Andrzej. "Reading over Endless Histories: Henry James's 'The Altar of the Dead.'" *Yale French Studies* 74 (1988): 261–84.

Phyllis van Slyck

TRAPPING THE GAZE
Objects of Desire in James's
Early and Late Fiction

"This picture is simply what any picture is, a trap for the gaze."

—Jacques Lacan, *Four Fundamental Concepts*

If the belief that one understands what one sees is one of the powerful illusions that shapes human knowledge and commitment, James understood that this illusion was worth challenging. Throughout his fiction, the visual and plastic arts offer a projective space through which a character's belief in something or commitment to someone is explored.[1] From their first appearance, art objects in James's fiction are objects of desire: they embody or represent an emotional ideal, and they are the subject of a character's obsessive gaze. However, James's characters gradually discover that they desire something they cannot truly have (either because the object is unavailable or because it is not the object they thought it was), raising important questions about a character's commitment to an ideal and forcing him (or her) to examine the knowledge or emotional satisfaction that the object provides. When a character's commitment is thus challenged, not only is the object itself deconstructed but the character's own wholeness, the capacity to create meaning, is also tacitly called into question.

The object of desire in James's fiction is an ironic construct designed to expose the inevitable deformations of the gaze. Jacques Lacan's concept of the gaze may be used to elucidate James's fiction as a study of desire. What we long for—to be seen (understood) from our own perspective or, conversely, to understand another from his own perspective—is impossible. Instead, there is always a gap, an abyss, between what we see and what we imagine or wish to be true about the Other. For Lacan, the gaze is, simply, "the subject sustaining itself in the function of desire" (*Four Fundamental Concepts*, 84). In James's fiction, the powerful impulse to create an "ideal" and to believe that one's ideal is "real" or "true" is undermined as a character confronts the deeper truth of his (or her) subjective shaping of reality.

As the narrators of the early stories evolve into the finely honed central intelligence that dominates novels of the major phase, literal art objects (sculptures, paintings) become portraits characters "create" of each other. Even in the early stories, however, these portraits appear, and, through them, fundamental ideas about the nature of perception and about the structure of desire are explored. It becomes apparent, for example, that desire comes into being and is most often sustained when the object is unavailable or forbidden. Moreover, the composed object or image is defined primarily, even wholly, by the perceiver, hence the illusion that there is an "objective" truth or "reality" that can be known is exploded. In other words, James understood, like Lacan, that "nothing in the world appears to me except in my representations" (*Four Fundamental Concepts*, 81). From the early to late fiction James's characters discover the deeply subjective nature of their knowledge of others and the inaccessibility of all genuine objects of desire.[2]

I

In the early stories, the object identifies a character's longing for aesthetic perfection and, simultaneously, the lack of that ideal in conventional "reality"; however, the object of desire also functions in a more ambiguous and powerful way in the narrative: it is not only a projective illusion but also a necessary ideal. Perhaps the best known early example of an object of art that is an object of desire appears in "The Madonna of the Future" (1873). In this story, a painting, imagined but not yet realized, has given an artist his life project. The artist tells everyone about his "Madonna" and introduces the narrator to the woman who will be its model. When the narrator tells the artist that his subject is too old for a Madonna, the artist's illusion is destroyed, and so is he. Despite the efforts of the narrator to console his "dejected pretender" (218), the artist quietly withdraws from the world and dies. However, the story hints at the notion, developed much more fully in James's later fiction, that a naive faith in the object of one's desire is not exclusive to a poor eccentric artist, that it is, perhaps, a fundamental human tendency necessary for one's emotional survival.[3] In the end, the story's narrator is "sad and vexed and bitter" (220), for something important has been lost when the artist dies: his naive idealism seems infinitely superior to the cynicism of the other characters who populate the story, in particular, another artist who satirizes human life with small sculptures of cats and monkeys made of a "peculiar plastic compound" (214) he has invented. Would it not be better, the narrator suggests, to hold onto one's ideals even if they are illusions?

In "The Last of the Valerii" (1874), another story in which an object of desire threatens to destroy a character's relationship to conventional reality, a young Italian husband begins to lose interest in his American wife after a statue of Juno is unearthed in his garden. His commitment to the statue, like the artist's commitment to his Madonna, is all consuming. She so distracts the young man that he secretly worships her late at night, gradually ceasing to love his wife, whom he had previously adored. As Dorothy Berkson has argued, "He wanders around like a man in a trance, caught in the grip of a 'fabulous passion' that cannot possibly render satisfaction" (84).[4] When the wife realizes that Juno is the source of her husband's disaffection, she orders that the statue be interred once again. As a result, the fantasy space of the young husband is successfully repressed, and he can return to "reality." On the surface, "The Last of the Valerii" ends more happily than "The Madonna of the Future." The husband, far from being angry at his loss, is profoundly grateful to his wife and begins to love her as before. A silent moment at the end of the story in which the two exchange gazes enacts this renewal of commitment: "At last she raised her eyes and sustained the gaze in which all his returning faith seemed concentrated. He hesitated a moment, as if her very forgiveness kept the gulf open between them, and then he strode forward, fell on his two knees, and buried his head in her lap" (252).[5] However, an intriguing moment of ambiguity is inserted at the end that suggests the husband never wholly relinquishes his desire. Many years after the statue of

Juno has been buried, a visitor discovers a marble hand suspended in the gentleman's cabinet: "It is the hand of a beautiful creature . . . whom I once greatly admired," the husband confesses (253). He has retained a vestige of his desire, and perhaps, in some way, its presence has sustained him in a bourgeois existence in which such desire is forbidden.[6]

Nowhere in James is it suggested that one's commitment to one's desire or one's private construction of that desire is merely solipsistic. Rather, something larger is at stake. In both "The Madonna of the Future" and "The Last of the Valerii," the object, real or imagined, sets up a tension between the character's relationship to the traditional order that surrounds him and the private space of his fantasy, a fact emphasized by the narrator's and other characters' clearer, more "objective" understanding of what is real. Initially, the character's obsession with the object makes the other characters see him as deluded or deranged, as a poor soul in need of being brought back to "reality." But, gradually, the narrators in these stories are drawn to the purity and sincerity of the gaze that finds such ideal meaning and fulfillment in the object, for the character has refused to cede his desire. Thus the statue of Juno, like the Madonna, calls into question the ordinariness of other people's lives and endeavors. As the young wife in "The Last of the Valerii" explains to the narrator, "His Juno's the reality: I'm the fiction" (248). The character's obsessive gaze is both frightening and fascinating because he challenges the complacency of those who maintain that such desire must be repressed, a theme James explores in depth in later works through characters such as Mrs. Newsome *The Ambassadors*.

Two stories written in 1868, "The Story of a Masterpiece" and "Osborne's Revenge," explore the complications that ensue when characters enter into relationships with others based on their own illusions about the subjects of their desire, illusions that are fostered and then challenged by a series of images or portraits. In "The Story of a Masterpiece," the narrator, Lennox, comes upon a portrait whose subject bears an uncanny resemblance to his fiancée, Marian Everett. Lennox asks to buy the painting, and, when he finds out it has already been sold, he commissions the artist to paint another just like it. Baxter, the artist, agrees to do so, but the portrait he now paints is not like the first one. Instead of capturing Marian's beauty as the first one did, this portrait reveals something mysterious and unpleasant, something that undermines the main character's faith in his beloved: "As

Lennox looked, the roseate circle of Marian's face blazed into remorseless distinctness, and her careless blue eyes looked with cynical familiarity into his own" (119).

Lennox now understands that the artist was once also in love with Marian. The first portrait, we learn, was painted when Baxter was under the spell of Marian's charms; the second is painted when he has "seen through" his illusion. She is no longer invested with the ideal content through which his love was defined; thus he paints her as she "really" is: "Deep . . . in the unfathomed recesses of his strong and sensitive nature, his genius had held communion with his heart and had transferred to canvas the burden of its disenchantment and its resignation" (112). Although the reader can see that both the first and second portrait are "illusions," that is, they are both symbolic constructions that enable the artist to describe the nature of his relationship with the subject, Lennox resents what Baxter has done. He accuses the artist of having gotten over his love and therefore of painting "too hard, too strong, too frank a reality." "You can't be real," Lennox tells him, "without being brutal" (108). What Lennox resents even more, but cannot openly acknowledge, is that the new portrait forces him to experience the emotional change that the artist himself went through some time before. It is more than a case of Lennox seeing through his "illusions," however. He knew that Marian was superficial before ("Marian, where *is* your heart?" [110] he had once asked her), but something has been made visible in the portrait that challenges Lennox's understanding of Marian in a way that his own insights thus far have not: "Was she a creature without faith and without conscience? What else was the meaning of that horrible blankness and deadness that quenched the light in her eyes and stole away the smile from her lips?" (110–11).

Like the artist in "The Madonna of the Future," Lennox becomes a man without a purpose, for his object of desire has been robbed of meaning. Although he still marries Marian, he does so with the knowledge that her identity includes something that shatters his romantic illusion: "there were moments when Lennox felt as if death were preferable to the heartless union which now stared him in the face, and as the only possible course was to transfer his property to Marian and to put an end to his existence" (119). In the last scene of the story, he deliberately and violently destroys the portrait that bears the painful knowledge of her "deadness," the visible empty core exposed by the artist, which has divested her of the symbolic meaning necessary to sustain his love. Lennox's decision to go through with the marriage, despite this knowledge, describes the inevitable necessity of returning to conventional reality: to continue to live as if one's "image" of another is the "real thing." However, as in "The Madonna of the Future" and in "The Last of the Valerii," the narrator's subtle fascination with the idealism of the main character in contrast to the cynicism of those who surround him suggests that individuals lose something important when they are forced to abandon their illusions.

In "Osborne's Revenge," as in "The Story of a Masterpiece," a woman is also misunderstood, but, happily, the error is in the eye of the beholder. Out of loyalty to a friend who has committed suicide, ostensibly because a young woman has jilted him, the narrator, Philip Osborne, seeks out his friend's lover, determined to find her corrupt, only to discover that she is noble. Osborne's ideas about the young woman are based entirely on information he receives secondhand, first from his friend, Graham, before the latter commits suicide, and then from a female confidant, who we later learn is far from objective. Deciding to avenge his friend's death, Osborne deliberately establishes a relationship with Miss Congreve; however, in each encounter with her, he composes a portrait that contradicts his assumptions, and he finds himself increasingly charmed: "it was something of a problem to reconcile the heroine of his vengeful longings, with the heroine of the little scene on the beach, and to accomodate this inoffensive figure, in turn, to the color of his retribution" (26). The contradiction between the image of Henrietta Congreve supplied by his friend, Graham, and his own impressions generates a split in Osborne's consciousness: "he began to be sadly, woefully puzzled by the idea that a woman could unite so much loveliness with so much treachery, so much light with so much darkness" (45). Naturally, in the course of Osborne's efforts to discredit and to punish Henrietta, he finds himself in love with her. When he declares himself, Henrietta tells him that she is betrothed to someone else and has been for some time. In the end, Osborne learns that his friend's passion for Henrietta was also one-sided. He is informed by an outsider that Henrietta "is the sweetest girl in the world," that "she never became engaged to Graham" nor solicited his attention. The entire romance was Graham's private invention, his "fixed idea," and the young man was "as mad as a March hare" (58–59). In following his friend's footsteps, Osborne discovers that his own desire is based on the impossibility of its realization. Both young men, it is suggested, have fallen in love with Henrietta primarily because she is beautifully indifferent to them.

Osborne's dilemma anticipates the more complex and multilayered struggle for meaning, based on a conflict between the perceiver and the object of desire, developed in James's later fiction. If, in the early stories, there is still a belief that the "truth" about an individual can ultimately be known, those stories in which misreadings play a significant role suggest that James is working toward a more radical, less essentialist conception of knowledge, one that takes into account the individual's role in shaping an image of another. In 1874, the same year James wrote "The Last of the Valerii," he published a much longer study of frustrated desire, "Madame de Mauves," in which a young man thoroughly idealizes an unavailable woman. The heroine of the story's title is a pretty and wealthy American who has married a poor and unfaithful but pedigreed Frenchman. The young Euphemia de Mauves, like Isabel Archer, is idealistic and overly confident about her choices, and she marries an Osmond despite warnings from her family and friends.[7] Disappointed in love, her ideal image of her husband destroyed, Madame de Mauves lives a sad and lonely life until Longmore, a young American, discovers her and makes her the object of his desire.

Anticipating the gentle voyeuristic style of Lambert Strether, Longmore constructs a series of idealized portraits of his subject from a respectful distance, but Madame de Mauves, like Madame de Vionnet, is a woman whose emotions and true character remain somewhat obscure to him.[8] The young man is a perfect match for this reserved and unhappy beauty, for he also is idealistic and noble, rejecting suggestions on the part of her sister-in-law and even the husband himself that he enter into a relationship with Madame de Mauves. What makes the story an intriguing study of desire is not Madame de Mauves herself, who, until the end, is a rather one-dimensional figure, but the psychological evolution of the young man whose own desire, like Strether's, is engendered by what he believes to be his subject's purity and suffering. "He began to regard his hostess as a figure haunted by a shadow which was somehow her intenser and more authentic self. This lurking duality in her put on for him an extraordinary charm" (145).

In an effort to come to terms with his feelings, Longmore makes a trip to the country, and the scene James composes anticipates Lambert Strether's journey to the French countryside where he discovers the "truth" about Chad and Madame de Vionnet. Like Strether, what Longmore discovers is a truth about himself. Reflecting on the sadness of women's fate, Longmore takes a walk in the forest, lies down, and slips into a dream. Standing at the bank of a river, he recognizes Madame de Mauves on the opposite bank, looking at him "very gravely and pityingly" (191). He wishes to stand by her side, but the water is deep. An oarsman appears (who turns out to be M. de Mauves) with a boat and conveys him to the opposite shore, but Madame de Mauves is not there: "He turned with a kind of agony and saw that now she was on the other bank,—the one he had left" (191). The "waters" that might lead to fulfillment are treacherous; it is safer for Longmore to remain on the "opposite bank," where his desire, constructed from the beginning around Madame de Mauves's unavailability, remains intact. The obvious symbolism of the dream is consistent with other details of Longmore's response to Madame de Mauves. Shortly before this dream, Longmore describes Euphemia as "being somehow beyond him, unattainable, immeasurable by his own fretful spirit," and this perception evokes in him "a kind of aching impotence" (173). And when he is told that Madame de Mauves's husband has urged her to have an affair with him, he is exultant not because he imagines his love will be fulfilled but because "circumstance . . . was to force the beauty of her character into more perfect relief" (182–83). He knows that she will not submit to him. Aware that her husband has suggested to Longmore that he seduce her, Madame de Mauves tells Longmore that she will respect him only if he leaves her. At each stage, Longmore's and Madame de Mauves's attitude toward their desire is identical: renunciation is preferable to fulfillment.

Longmore goes home, and several years later he hears the rest of Madame de Mauves's story from the mutual friend who introduced them:

> He [the husband] had repented and asked her forgiveness, which she had inexorably refused . . . whether or no her husband had been in love with her before, he fell madly in love with her now. He was the proudest man in France, but he had begged her on his knees to be readmitted to favor. All in vain! She was stone, she was ice, she was outraged virtue . . . he gave up society, ceased to care for anything. . . . One fine day they learned that he had blown out his brains. (209)

Longmore, on hearing this story, does not return to France but remains, once again, "on the opposite bank," "conscious of a singular feeling,—a feeling for which awe would be hardly too strong a name" (209).

Although Longmore remains blind to the darker side of his beloved, the story suggests that Madame de Mauves is someone other than the idealized figure of his fantasy. References to her rather narrow puritanism offered by the heroine herself ("I have nothing on earth but a conscience . . . nothing but a dogged, clinging, inexpugnable conscience" [171]) are wildly romanticized by Longmore, and the reader is offered consistent evidence that she fears emotion, that, in some real sense, she is "ice." Even as a child, "She was profoundly incorruptible, and she cherished this pernicious conceit as if it had been dogma revealed by a white-winged angel" (129), and, in the moment that she turns Longmore away, Madame de Mauves resembles Mrs. Newsome more than Madame de Vionnet: "her impatience had become a cold sternness. She stood before him again, looking at him from head to foot, in deep reproachfulness, almost in scorn" (196). Madame de Mauves's utter consistency in rejecting both Longmore and her husband and her refusal to deviate from her original values and vision ("she has loved once . . . if she loved again she would be *common*" [199]) make her an impossible object of desire for both Longmore and her husband, ironically bringing together, in a state of permanent longing and loss parallel to her own suffering, men of opposite temperament and values.

Although their desire is based on a misreading and the desired object (or subject) is chosen because it is inaccessible or forbidden, James's characters, without exception, adopt a consistent ethical position; that is, they refuse to cede their desire.[9] Their quest suggests a kind of integrity that leads the narrator in the "The Madonna of the Future," for example, to admire the artist in his delusion. The reader's sympathy is also with the character who is so committed and so often disappointed. Although the characters in "The Madonna of the Future" and in "The Last of the Valerii" are literally forced to relinquish the objects of their desire, on another level, neither gives up completely: in dying, the artist makes the claim that it is better not to live than to abandon his ideal; in retaining the "hand" of the statue, the young husband retains an important symbol of his desire, one that may well have sustained him, reminding him that there is something important about one's most personal desire, something that cannot be destroyed. And if Lennox in "The Story of a Masterpiece" deeply laments the loss of his desired object, the collapse of his illusion, whereas Longmore in "Madame de Mauves" clings to his illusion, both positions suggest that absolute commitment is central to all desire.

In tracing the construction of desire, James exposes more than the naivete or blindness of some of his characters and more than the tragic awareness of others. Although Lennox's despair at the loss of his illusion suggests that such knowledge can never again be denied; although Osborne's humiliation as he finds himself in the same position as his friend reflects the capricious one-sidedness of desire; and although Longmore's staunch loyalty to Madame de Mauves's vision of herself is clearly a screen for his own repression, other characters, narrators, and the reader are consistently forced to admire the tenacity of the character's commitment. To abandon one's desire, James suggests, is to abandon one's "self," one's subjectivity.

From the artist in "The Madonna of the Future" to Madame de Mauves, James's desiring subjects anticipate the position of emotional consistency, which is the hallmark of many of the major novelistic characters, including Isabel Archer in *The Portrait of a Lady,* Lambert Strether in *The Ambassadors,* Maggie Verver in *The Golden Bowl,* and even Milly Theale in *The Wings of the Dove.* It becomes the task of the later novels to examine the deeper implications of this quest, to explore its ethical and epistemological consequences for James's characters. They also insist on their vision, and, in their commitment, they demand that their subjects of desire match their personal ideals. However, as in the early stories, despite their profound commitment to the desired object, something inevitably undermines the image the character has created, something that eludes definition, and this mysterious element challenges the individual's belief that knowledge of another is possible, initiating a more complex analysis of subjectivity and desire.

II

The characters in James's late novels come to see that their portraits reveal, most of all, their authors' capacity to represent what they wish to see and to conceal that which lies behind or stands in opposition to their desire. Yet, at critical moments, these idealized portraits betray their composers by exposing something that does not fit, a contradictory element that undermines the integrity of the image. As their subjects gaze back at them, they shatter their perceivers' belief in the wholeness, authority, and power of the gaze. In other words, James's novelistic characters glimpse the lack not only in the subjects they study, the individuals to whom they have made commitments; they also glimpse, briefly, a lack in themselves.

In *The Ambassadors* and in *The Golden Bowl,* for example, characters put all of their faith in their representations of others.[10] Lambert Strether and Maggie Verver, like the characters in the early stories, believe blindly in the virtue and perfection of their subjects, Madame de Vionnet and Prince Amerigo. Eventually, though, they are forced to contemplate the psychological illusions that have shaped their quest for an ideal love object, and the portraits they create reflect the complexity, the ambiguity, and ultimately the inherent limitations of their quest. Unlike those of the early stories, the characters in the late novels, however, move beyond despair, resignation, or renunciation; instead they move to embrace that aspect of their subject that they have denied or that has eluded definition. In *The Wings of the Dove,* for example, Merton Densher, like Longmore, commits himself wholly to Milly Theale when she becomes supremely inaccessible, in death, but unlike Longmore, he is aware of the nature of his desire.

In *The Ambassadors,* Lambert Strether, like the artist in "The Madonna of the Future," confronts that aspect of Madame de Vionnet he has repressed in his elaborate portraits of Chad's *femme du monde.*[11] Late in the novel, his subject suddenly comes into view as if he has called her to enter his final picture, his personal "Lambinet" of the French countryside: "It was suddenly as if these figures, or something like them, had been wanted in the picture" (461). As the boat carrying Chad and Madame de Vionnet floats into view, Madame de Vionnet's pink parasol shifts a little, and, for a brief moment, Strether sees her for the first time, that is, he sees the piece of her that does not conform to the way he has represented her to himself thus far: she is clearly involved with Chad Newsome in a way Strether has been at pains to deny. This moment of exposure brings about Strether's recognition; he sees that he is responsible for his idealized image of Madame de Vionnet, and, some have argued, this leads to his renunciation of the world he has shaped since his arrival in Europe.[12]

However, as Strether reflects on the failure of his vision, he is gradually able to embrace that aspect of Madame de Vionnet he has previously denied in his elaborate portraits. He recognizes that she is not only his *femme du monde* but simultaneously a "simple maidservant crying for her young man" (483). In this moment, he recognizes her as a subject in her own right. That is, unlike the artist in "The Madonna of the Future" and unlike Lennox in "The Story of a Masterpiece," Strether does not allow his knowledge of Madame de Vionnet's frailty, her failure to be his ideal, to destroy his portrait. Instead, her vulnerability enables him to enlarge his image of her: "She was older for him to-night, visibly less exempt from the touch of time; but she was as much as ever the finest and subtlest creature, the happiest apparition, it had been given him, in all his years, to meet" (483). Strether's conception of Madame de Vionnet is expanded as he acknowledges that aspect of her that stands outside his naive, idealized image, and he is able, for a brief moment, to glimpse the mysterious otherness of Madame de Vionnet.

Another portrait that threatens to destroy the illusions of its creator yet becomes the basis for an exploration of the power of the gaze to create and sustain meaning is Maggie's portrait of Amerigo in *The Golden Bowl.* In the novel's final scene, Maggie Verver gazes into Amerigo's eyes and recognizes that she cannot know or control her subject, rather, that to return his gaze is, in a sense, to become *his* subject:

> It kept him before her therefore, taking in—or trying to—what she so wonderfully gave. He tried, too clearly, to please her—to meet her in her own way; but with the result only that, close to her, her face kept before him, his hands holding her shoulders, his whole act enclosing her, he presently echoed: "See? I see nothing but you." And the truth of it had with this force after a moment so strangely lighted his eyes that as for pity and dread of them she buried her own in his breast. (580)

For most of the novel, Maggie has defined Amerigo according to her idealistic and controlling personal vision. When she realizes that Charlotte and Amerigo have begun to shape a private life quite contrary to her ideal image (she studies them in a portrait in which they look down on her from the balcony of her home, their gazes shaping her world), she redoubles her effort to maintain her vision and ultimately forces them to submit to it. On the surface, Maggie successfully incorporates her "subjects" into her personal vision, a fact illustrated by her penultimate assessment of Charlotte and Amerigo as figures in Madame Tussaud's museum. However, in the end, when Amerigo returns Maggie's gaze, an eerie moment arises and her ability to sustain her vision is challenged. Amerigo seems to be making a deliberate and arbitrary choice to exclude everything except what Maggie has chosen and to allow her gaze to define his reality. He tells her he will live for her meaning alone ("I see nothing but you"). Yet, Amerigo's acquiescence fills Maggie with "pity" and "dread." In a sense, the Prince assists Maggie in denying the lack that has hovered at the edge of her perceptions throughout the novel. He helps her to maintain the illusion that her own perceptions are whole and powerful. But although Amerigo grants her this power, it is his embrace that encloses her. Thus James leaves the reader with the important insight, one shared by Maggie and Amerigo, that there is a piece of each of their identities that cannot be defined or controlled by the other. At the same time, each tacitly recognizes that the gaze through which each shapes a portrait of the other is the only source of knowledge possible.

Perhaps the most highly evolved object of desire in James's fiction is the letter Milly Theale arranges to have sent to Merton Densher after her death at the end of *The Wings of the Dove.* Although the letter is unlike any of James's earlier art objects or portraits, in representing Milly herself, it embodies Densher's desire and thereby functions in exactly the same way other art objects do in James's fiction. The letter is important not only as a symbol representing that which Densher cannot relinquish but because it has the power to crystallize Densher's desire. With her death and with the subsequent destruction of the letter, Milly becomes completely inaccessible. Just as Densher's desire for Kate was constructed around the impossibility of "having" her, now his desire for Milly comes into being in the wake of her death and her silence. Densher's decision not to open the letter but rather to give it away allows him to hold on to all the possibilities of Milly's act, to keep the very construction of its meaning open. The contents of the letter are defined anew each time he conjures up his memory of Milly; her "real" feelings remain a mystery to him, but it is a mystery he cherishes:

> He kept it back like a favorite pang; left it behind him so to say, when he went out, but came home again the sooner for the certainty of finding it there. Then he took it out of its sacred corner and its soft wrappings; he undid them one by one, handling them, handling it, as a father, baffled and tender, might handle a maimed child. But so it was before him in his dread of who else might see it. Then he took it to himself at such

hours, in other words, that he should never know what had been in Milly's letter. (450)

When the letter is destroyed by Densher's fiancée, Kate, a "priceless pearl" (450) has been lost (and Densher does feel some of Othello's agony and responsibility for having destroyed Milly[13]), but, miraculously, as the construction of meaning is effectively shifted back to him, the beauty and mystery of Milly's gift expands in emotional content: "the turn she would have given her act . . . had possibilities that, somehow, by wondering about them, his imagination had extraordinarily filled out and refined" (450). Kate, like the young wife in "The Last of the Valerii," recognizes that she has lost Densher ("Her memory's your love. You want no other" [456]), and she is right. In this poignant moment, Densher embraces the mystery of Milly completely, relinquishing the desire to know and to possess his subject. Yet, for the first time, paradoxically, we may say that he has succeeded in "having" his object of desire.

III

An ability to enlarge meaning, to accept ambiguity, may be seen as an important step in the evolution of James's epistemology of desire. It suggests that there may be a way to hold on to one's ideal even while recognizing the limits of personal vision. In the late novels, James's characters struggle more directly to bring what lies outside their private images into the realm of their conceptualizing. When they make this effort, they must, in one sense, fail, for their portraits embody primarily their private vision or ideal and can only point to that which must remain outside it. But James's characters do begin to glimpse what Maggie apprehends in Amerigo's gaze. It is the very impossibility of gratifying one's desire in conventional terms: of ever truly, thoroughly, defining or possessing another. Merton Densher's solution, to keep the definition of one's desire open and to accept the impossibility of its literal realization, is thus James's most far-reaching attempt to recognize and in a sense to "name" the unnameable: the mysterious Otherness that lies at the heart of all being.

Objects of desire in the early stories announce some of the most important themes in James's fiction. The idealized object (or subject) appears with extraordinary consistency, and, through it, characters confront central questions about human subjectivity: what is the nature of desire? How is it engendered and sustained? What does it mean to "know" another subject? How is the individual forced to recognize the limitations of personal knowledge? What are the consequences for the individual of this awareness? With such knowledge, how can the individual sustain his/her faith in the integrity of human relations? As objects of desire in the early stories evolve into complex and multilayered portraits in the late novels, Jamesian characters confront the limitations of their ability to name accurately or to control effectively what they see. The object constructed by a character is always a misreading, and this is not only because of an inevitable need to believe in an ideal. As James's characters confront their own illusions, they discover that here is a fundamental irreducible mystery about their knowledge of others, something that cannot be named and that can be glimpsed only briefly before it must be repressed. This mystery may be understood in Lacanian terms as a "piece of the real" because it points to that which lies outside the symbolic order created by language. Lacan explains this concept thus: "I always speak the truth. Not the whole truth, because there is no way to say it all. Saying it all is literally impossible: words fail. Yet it is through this very impossibility that the truth holds onto the real" ("Television," 7). In other words, the "real" is that which is always beyond symbolization and that which reminds us of the limitations of language: "The real . . . stands 'behind' the reality constituted in and by our use of language and only hints at its operative presence in the variety of failures or ruptures or inconsistencies that mark this symbolic reality" (Lee, 136). This notion of the "real" in Lacan is directly parallel to the definition of desire reflected in James's fiction: desire is always that which retains its mystery, which cannot be fully understood or gratified or it would cease to be our desire.

From the early stories to the novels of the major phase, James's characters push the boundaries of their understanding until they come face to face with their failure to achieve the control we associate with "objective" knowledge. This moment has important consequences; it shatters the perceiver because it forces him to see that he is not whole, complete, powerful, that perceptions are mere illusion, that wholeness is also an illusion, a construct of consciousness. They remind the individual character of the frailty of perceptions. In the later novels, James's characters struggle consistently with the notion that the individual is something less than whole, complete, and powerful, that, like the objects and subjects that they endow with this illusion of wholeness, Jamesian perceivers, themselves, are shattered, fragmented.[14] In response to this encounter with the "real," an ethic grounded in personal vision tacitly emerges in the late James, suggested by his characters' acknowledgment of personal responsibility and, at the same time, their unquenchable faith as they recognize the limitations inherent in the compulsion to name, to judge, to impose the coherence of a single meaning and to allow others to be in their complexity, ambiguity, and richness.

Notes

1. For critical interpretations of works of art, analogies to specific artistic movements, and the function of the work of art in James, see Anderson, Hopkins-Winner, Tintner, and Torgovnick.
2. Sheridan, Lacan's translator, explains Lacan's epistemology of desire: "Desire is a perpetual effect of symbolic articulation . . . it is essentially eccentric and insatiable" (*Concepts,* 278).
3. Many of James's characters base their life choices on a fundamental but illusory belief in the "perfection" of their chosen object of desire, including Isabel Archer, Milly Theale, Lambert Strether, and Maggie Verver, and each, in some sense, remains committed to this ideal to the end.
4. Berkson argues persuasively that Count Valerio's obsession is based on erotic repression; his goddess embodies both his suppressed erotic fantasies and his need to see woman as a dehumanized "empedestaled goddess of virtue" (84).
5. The final exchange between husband and wife in "The Last of the Valerii" anticipates, both structurally and thematically, a much more ambiguous moment of commitment at the end of *The Golden Bowl* between Maggie Verver and Prince Amerigo, discussed later in this essay.
6. More than a decade later, James returns to the situation of the couple in "The Last of the Valerii," once again using the international theme (American wife, European husband) to explore conflicting values and desires. In "A Modern Warning" (1888) the object of desire that distracts the husband is not a sculpture but a manuscript that his wife has forbidden him to complete. As in the earlier story, James suggests that one character can fulfill desire only at the expense of the other. However, in "A Modern Warning," the ending is reversed. Realizing that she is losing her husband's affection, the wife encourages him to write his book. On the eve of its publication, however, she kills herself.
7. Madame de Mauves has constructed a portrait of her partner (long before she has met him) that meets her romantic ideals: "It was the portrait of a gentleman rather ugly than handsome, and rather poor than rich. But his ugliness was to be nobly expressive, and his poverty delicately proud" (130). Compare Isabel's romantic characterization of Osmond: "She had carried away an image from

her visit . . . the image of a quiet, clever, sensitive, distinguished man"; "What continued to please this young woman was his extraordinary subtlety" (*Portrait of a Lady,* 256).

8. See McLean for parallels between "Madame de Mauves" and *The Ambassadors,* especially the two heroines: "If one is adamantly virtuous and the other an adulteress, both are children of bad marriages, raised in French convents, and unhappily wedded to French counts; and both are pursued by the protagonists, from whom they desire comfort and help rather than an 'emotional friendship'" (448).

9. Lacan maintains that "the only thing of which one can be guilty is of having given ground relative to one's desire" (*Seminar,* 319).

10. A full discussion of *The Portrait of a Lady* here may seem like a conspicuous omission: there is no question that Isabel's idealization of Osmond fits the pattern I am discussing and that in her "midnight vigil" she confronts the nature of her illusion and the fact that her portrait of him has been, in large measure, her own construction: "She had a vision of him . . . a certain combination of features had touched her and in them she had seen the most striking of portraits" (393). However, Isabel's insights do not extend much beyond those of characters in the stories I have discussed; I have chosen, therefore, to focus on three later novels in order to examine the ways James extends his exploration of this theme.

11. There are several parallels between this early story and James's late novel, including a scene in each of the two works in which the narrator-character finds the ambiguous "Madonna" in a church: the narrator in "The Madonna of the Future" discovers the artist's Madonna, Signora Serafina, in the church of San Lorenzo in a scene that anticipates Strether's discovery of Madame de Vionnet in Notre Dame.

12. See, for example, Ellmann, who argues that Strether's "only logic" is "the logic of loss" (104).

13. "Then must you speak . . . of one . . . / whose hand . . . threw a pearl away / Richer than all his tribe" (*Othello,* 5.2.406–7).

14. Lacan claims that the subject can never be anything but "split," "alienated," "divided from himself" (*Ecrits,* 288); that is, the individual can never know himself completely because speech (symbolization) divides the subject, locates him in language and alienates him from himself. Foucault claims that the "shattering of the philosophical subject" (which he attributes to Bataille) "is one of the fundamental structures of contemporary thought" (42).

Works Cited

Anderson, Charles R. *Person, Place and Thing in Henry James's Novels.* Durham: Duke University Press, 1977.

Berkson, Dorothy. "Tender Minded Idealism and Erotic Repression in 'The Last of the Valerii' and 'Madame de Mauves.'" *Henry James Review* 2 (1981): 78–86.

Ellmann, Maud. "'The Intimate Difference': Power and Representation in *The Ambassadors.*" In *Henry James: Fiction as History.* Ed. Ian F. A. Bell, 98–113. London: Vision, 1984.

Foucault, Michele. "A Preface to Transgression." In *Language, Counter-Memory, Practice: Selected Essays and Interviews,* 29–52. Trans. Donald F. Bouchard and Sherry Simon. Ed. Donald F. Bouchard. Ithaca: Cornell University Press, 1977.

Hopkins-Winner, Viola. *Henry James and the Visual Arts.* Charlottesville: University Press of Virginia, 1970.

James, Henry. *The Ambassadors.* 1903. New York: Washington Square Press, 1963.

———. *The Golden Bowl.* 1904. New York: Penguin, 1987.

———. "The Last of the Valerii." In *"The Madonna of the Future" and Other Early Stories,* 223–53. New York: New American Library, 1962.

———. "Madame de Mauves." In *The Complete Tales of Henry James,* 3: 123–209. Ed. Leon Edel. Philadelphia: Lippincott, 1962.

———. "The Madonna of the Future." In *"The Madonna of the Future" and Other Early Stories,* 185–222. New York: New American Library, 1962.

———. "Osborne's Revenge." In *The Complete Tales of Henry James,* 2:13–60. Ed. Leon Edel. Philadelphia: Lippincott, 1962.

———. *The Portrait of a Lady.* 1881. New York: New American Library, 1963.

———. "The Story of a Masterpiece." In *"The Madonna of the Future" and Other Early Stories,* 87–121. New York: New American Library, 1962.

———. *The Wings of the Dove.* 1902. Baltimore: Penguin, 1986.

Lacan, Jacques. *Ecrits: A Selection.* Trans. Alan Sheridan. New York: Norton, 1977.

———. *Four Fundamental Concepts of Psycho-Analysis.* Ed. Jacques-Alain Miller. Trans. Alan Sheridan. New York: Norton, 1978.

———. *The Seminar of Jacques Lacan.* Ed. Jacques-Alain Miller. New York: Norton, 1988.

———. "Television." Trans. Denis Hollier, Rosalind Krauss, and Annette Michaelson. *October* 40 (1987): 5–50.

Lee, Jonathan Scott. *Jacques Lacan.* Amherst: University of Massachusetts Press, 1991.

McLean, Robert C. "The Completed Vision: A Study of 'Madame de Mauves' and *The Ambassadors.*" *Modern Language Quarterly* 28 (1967): 446–61.

Tintner, Adeline. *The Museum World of Henry James.* Ann Arbor: UMI Research Press, 1986.

Torgovnick, Marianna. *The Visual Arts, Pictorialism and the Novel.* Princeton: Princeton University Press, 1985.

Joseph Wiesenfarth

METAFICTION AS THE
REAL THING

Henry James's stories of writers and artists are stories about composing as well as reading, stories about the production and reception of literary and other kinds of art. They interest themselves in the situation of writers and readers, single and married, with and without children. Spouses and sons and daughters not only affect life and death but also, while a writer or artist lives, they affect how well he, only seldomly she, can fulfill his vocation and how well the critic can understand the artist. Family affects whether the artist will create a masterpiece or a potboiler. Will the writer or artist be a genius or a lion? Will he live like a monk in a small but knowing circle a life devoted to perfection? Or like a butterfly flit from town house to country house, from dinner to cigars, from adulation to exploitation among the opulently vulgar crowd? These stories define a sacred brotherhood and sisterhood of writers and their attentive readers who understand and appreciate the work of a Mark Ambient, a Dencombe, a Neil Paraday, a Hugh Vereker, a Paul Overt, a Ralph Limbert. They are decidedly different from the vulgar crowd, who worship the likes of the "jaunty Juvenal" who makes statues of men and women looking like cats and monkeys in amorous poses;

of a Guy Walshingham, the woman who writes as a man; of a Dora Forbes, the man who writes as a woman; of a Jane Highmore, who writes "tremendous trash"; of a Greville Fane, who dies with "her fine blindness unimpaired," having written "stories by the yard" but never "a page of English." James's stories invoke the sacred ground of Henry St. George's studio against the profane ground of Mrs. Weeks Wimbush's estate. These stories seek to define the world in which the artist labors and the relation of his work to that world. They seek to understand representation in the context of self-expression and the relation of each to intensity in art. So Henry James's stories of writers and artists are a series of imaginative meditations and wry observations on every aspect of the artistic process. Taken together, intertextually, they are metafiction: fiction about fiction. In James's story entitled "The Story in It,"[1] Colonel Voyt, who is having an affair with Mrs. Dyott, argues with Maud Blessingbourne about the subject of fiction. He maintains that the only proper subject of fiction is an illicit romance or an adventure. Maud, who loves Voyt but doesn't manifest her love, maintains that the good woman can be the subject of good fiction. Each reminds us that, of the reader as well as of the writer, it can be said that "the deepest quality of a work of art will always be the quality of the mind of the producer" (*Essays on Literature,* 64). And because Maud is the subject of James's story, James actually dramatizes his answer to her debate with Voyt. The good woman not only can be but, at the moment that they speak, also is the subject of good fiction. Virtue has its place in fiction and need not yield it to vice. James's stories of writers and artists are more nearly about the Maud Blessingbournes than about the Colonel Voyts—more, as one unravels the puns in the names, about limited blessings than about voids and die-outs. "The Story in It," consequently, is a parable that tells us that metafiction can be the subject of fiction—that metafiction can be the real thing.

James's story "The Real Thing"[2] proves the point. It contains neither illicit romance nor extravagant adventure. It is a self-contained dramatization of every aspect of the artistic process. It is a story about making books, and to that end it contains an artist, his models, his problems of representation and form, a critic, a publisher, reflections on failure and success, and a theory on which the story itself is built. There is no character in the story who is not related to the artistic process of production, representation, expression, and reception. There are two subplots in the story—one concerning amateurs and one concerning professionals—that are united by a single action. Major and Mrs. Monarch are an impoverished aristocratic couple who are looking to make ends meet by serving as models for an artist who is illustrating a book about ladies and gentlemen. They are the real thing that the unnamed artist need only copy to succeed. But the Monarchs are amateurs, unlike the Cockney Miss Churm and the immigrant Italian Oronte, who are professionals. All four models are trying to make ends meet. So is their employer: "My 'illustrations'," he says, are "my pot-boilers" (*Complete Stories 1892–1898,* 34). Indeed, the action of the story is to keep the pot boiling, and its subplots involve amateurs and professionals competing to do so. And just to make the point unmistakable, James has them at different times all boil water and serve tea. The artist, with the help of Jack Hawley, a brother artist with a "fresh eye" (51), realizes that he cannot keep his pot boiling unless he gets a contract for a series of pot-boilers—for a series of novels with which, by illustrating, he can make money enough to support himself while he works at his serious painting. That, of course, never does pay at all. He realizes that he will lose his contract for the novels if he continues to keep the Monarchs as models. They are "types," and he can't make individual characters out of them. They allow his imagination no scope. "They have no pictorial sense. They are only clean and stiff and stupid," James says in his *Notebooks* (103). They are what he calls in the preface to *What Maisie Knew* "ugly facts" (*Art of the Novel,* 141). It's only when the imagination can transform ugly facts that art succeeds. The Monarchs as the real thing of life allow the artist no scope to produce the real thing of art. Oronte and Miss Churm, however, stimulate his imagination and make his illustrations wonderfully individual. Therefore, Hawley says of the Monarchs, *"Ce sont des gens qu'il faut mettre à la porte"* ("These folks must be shown the door") (52).

The real things then are put outside the artist's studio, and the door is closed upon them. This is a reversal of the Platonic doctrine of art. In *The Republic,* Plato put the artists outside the gates of the city because they could not tell the truth about the real thing, the Platonic idea. James puts the real things outside the door of the artist's studio because they are no good at realizing the artist's idea. The business of the artist is not to imitate life slavishly, to reproduce the ugly facts. The business of art is to arrive at what James calls in the *Maisie* preface "the *best* residuum of truth"(*Art of the Novel,* 141), which the ugly facts too often obscure. Thus in *Maisie* the destruction of a little girl in a divorce case that gave James the germ of the novel is not as true as allowing Maisie to thrive in a squalid moral atmosphere because James's imaginative alternative gets at a truth that the ugly facts hide, which is this: "No themes are so human as those that reflect for us, out of the confusion of life, the close connexion of bliss and bale, of the things that help with the things that hurt, so dangling before us for ever that bright hard medal, of so strange an alloy, one face of which is somebody's right and ease and the other somebody's pain and wrong" (*Art of the Novel,* 143). It is out of this imaginative process of seeing the truth in the ugly facts and projecting it in a picture of life that, as James told the uncomprehending H. G. Wells, art makes life: "It is art that *makes* life, makes interest, makes importance . . . and I know of no substitute whatever for the force and beauty of its process" (*Letters,* 2:490).

Art makes life in "The Beldonald Holbein,"[3] for example, when Paul Outreau shows that, like Jack Hawley of "The Real Thing," he has an "eye." He sees the plain and aging Mrs. Brash and declares, "She's the greatest of all the great Holbeins" (*Complete Stories 1898–1910,* 388). The narrator and his fellow artists agree with Outreau, and Mrs. Brash becomes a "succès fou" (389): "She was, in short, just what we had made her, a Holbein for a great museum" (395). Suddenly, then, this neglected old woman from small-town America who has come to London specifically to live in the shadow of her cousin, the beautiful, ageless Lady Beldonald— "She looks *naturally* new, as if she took out every night her large, lovely, varnished eyes and put them in water" (384)—takes on an intense life of her own that her cousin's vanity cannot endure. Whereas Lady Beldonald can be a model, Mrs. Brash cannot: "she's not a model, hang it," the narrator tells Outreau, "she's too good for one . . . she's the very thing herself" (396). Lady Beldonald cannot tolerate such competition, and she sends Mrs. Brash home. Taken out of her element and separated from Outreau and the artists who have admired her, Mrs. Brash dies for want of an "eye" to appreciate her: "It wasn't—the minor American city—a market for Holbeins, and what had occurred was that the poor old picture, banished from its museum and refreshed by the rise of no new movement to hang it, was capable of the miracle of a silent revolution, of itself turning, in its dire dishonour, its face to the wall" (401–2). Without the artist's imagination to give her life, Mrs. Brash cannot be a Holbein; she can only be dead.

The goal of the artistic process in all of James's stories is to give life to "the *best* residuum of truth" that the artist's imagination finds means of expressing and to do it with the greatest possible intensity. That is perfection. The artist/narrator of "The Special Type"[4] achieves it in his portrait of Frank Brivet, whom he catches in the "freshness of his cheer" (*Complete Stories 1898–1910*, 302). Alice Dundene, who loves Brivet enough to have helped him with his divorce, admires the portrait he originally meant for his new wife but which the artist/narrator, who admires her more than the new Mrs. Brivet, insists is for her:

> She was amazed and delighted. "I may have *that?*"
> "So far as I'm concerned—absolutely."
> "Then he had himself the beautiful thought of sitting for me?"
> I faltered but an instant. "Yes." Her pleasure in what I had done was a joy to me. "Why, it's of a truth—! It's perfection!"
> "I think it is." (304)

Asked by Mrs. Brivet to repeat perfection, the artist insists that he cannot. With his divorce accomplished, Brivet, grown accustomed to his cheerfulness after it, cannot be caught again in the "freshness of his cheer." What inspired the artist to perfection is gone: "my best was my best and . . . what was done was done" (305). Such perfection, the artist's holy grail, has few Galahads of the pen and brush to threaten it.

Stuart Straith, the painter, and Mrs. Harvey, the writer, however, do seek it. "Broken Wings"[5] is the story of these affined lovers who once upon a time failed to speak their love to each other. But they get a second chance to do so, catching a glimpse of each other at Mundham during a country-house weekend there. Each once thought the other too grand—too successful as an artist and too rich as the result of that success—to approach as a partner for life, and each still sees the other that way at Mundham. But the truth is that Straith has been reduced to designing costumes for plays and that Mrs. Harvey has been reduced to writing a "London Letter" for a provincial paper. Although both once knew success, both are now failures: "One had but one's hour, and if one had it soon—it was really almost a case of choice—one didn't have it late" (*Complete Stories 1898–1910*, 341). Now, alas, it is late for them both. Once high flyers, each has broken wings.

"Broken Wings" shows Straith and Mrs. Harvey—long a widow—

coming to understand each other, to embrace each other, and, strengthened by their love, to embrace their art again by getting back to work. The story is developed in parallel scenes that emphasize their affinity. Its five-part structure shows (1) Straith seeing Mrs. Harvey at Mundham as too grand for him to speak to, (2) her seeing him at Mundham as too grand for her to speak to, (3) our seeing them as equals at the theater, (4) at his studio, (5) at her flat: "He took her in his arms, she let herself go, and he held her long and close for the compact" (344).

With this compact embrace James again invokes the shade of Plato, who in the *Symposium* supplies the primary text for the discussion of affined love. Aristophanes postulates the original androgynous human condition of man-woman to explain desire and love. Zeus, he argues, split the original entity into two sexes because he feared that man-woman was strong enough to overthrow the gods themselves. Affined lovers in consequence seek in each other the primal unity of their original androgynous creation. The servants of Mammon at Mundham keep Straith and Mrs. Harvey apart because they cannot take from the Straith-Harvey entity what they can take from them individually:

"We can't afford the opulent. But it isn't only the money they take."

"It's the imagination," said Mrs. Harvey. "As they have none themselves—" (343)

Straith and Mrs. Harvey are "sensitive souls of the 'artistic temperament'" (340), and they find in themselves and their work strength beyond the gods of Mundham—*opulentus mundi*. They differ from the rich wholly and from each other hardly in the amount of money they earn: he four shillings six pence for his costume designs and she three shillings nine pence for her London letters.

"Broken Wings" is a story with a familiar Jamesian structure of choice and understanding.[6] First, they choose to avoid approaching each other and thereby create misunderstanding. Then he chooses to speak to her at the theater, where they become the show itself during the intervals of the play, dramatically understanding the unhappiness of their single, separated state. Finally, she chooses to go to his studio, and he chooses to go to her flat, where they understand they should be together and work at their art for it-self, not for others. The story, therefore, is about artists who only gradually learn to read each other; who become better readers when they understand they misread each other; who become the best readers when they understand it is their choice to be happy in love and work.

Their embracing of love and of art dramatizes their having previously played badly the role of successful artist. Their stage has been Mundham, which is twice called "the real thing." Mundham is the real thing because it is theater. They talk about Mundham as theater when they meet in a West End theater. Straith tells Mrs. Harvey the truth: he is there to see his costumes. Then she tells him the truth: she is there to write her London letter. Both admit to working for a pittance. The theater, then, is their place of truth; Mundham is their place of illusion: "For Mundham *was,* theatrically, the real thing; better for scenery, dresses, music, pretty women, bare shoulders, everything—even in coherent dialogue; a much bigger and braver show, and got up, as it were, infinitely more 'regardless'" (334).

What Straith and Mrs. Harvey do after their reconciliation at the theater is lay bare his studio and her flat, where the drama of their artistic souls is lived out. As unsuccessful artists—because their art, genuine though it is, is not the kind that Mundham pays for—they become the real thing for each other.

> "We're simply the case," Straith familiarly put it, "of having been had enough of. No case is perhaps more common, save that, for you and for me, each in our line, it did look in the good time—didn't it?—as if nobody *could* have enough." With which they counted backward, gruesome as it was, the symptoms of satiety up to the first dawn, and lived again together the unforgettable hours—distant now—out of which it had begun to glimmer that the truth had to be faced and the right names given to the wrong facts. (343–44)

And why did this happen? Because at one end of the spectrum, "the people want such trash" (338), and at the other "the opulent take the imagination. . . . As they have none themselves" (343). In a word, caught between the Philistines and the Barbarians, to use Matthew Arnold's terms,[7] artists become the Aliens and must cling to each other (they embrace) and their art (they work).

> Here they had together—these two worn and baffled workers—a wonderful hour of gladness in their lost battle and of freshness in their

lost youth; for it was not till Stuart Straith had also raised the heavy mask and laid it beside her own on the table, that they began really to feel themselves recover something of that possibility of each other they had so wearily wasted. (342)

That is to say, Straith and Mrs. Harvey take off the mask of success[8] they wear to act their parts at Mundham and find gladness in life as comrades in battle. This is all important because, as James said in writing of Turgenev, "Life *is,* in fact, a battle. On this point optimists and pessimists agree. Evil is insolent and strong; beauty enchanting and rare; goodness very apt to be weak; folly very apt to be defiant; wickedness to carry the day; imbeciles to be in great places, people of sense in small, and mankind generally, un-happy" (*Literary Criticism,* 998). Straith and Mrs. Harvey lament their folly, renounce great places like Mundham, and seek an enchanting and rare beauty in each other and their art. That, they know, is their only chance for happiness as the battle rages.

A story published in 1900, "Broken Wings" might well be more than a story of Stuart Straith and Mrs. Harvey. It might be a story told of Henry James's dramatic years. The novelist who was once a resounding success with *Daisy Miller* was unsuccessful when he put Daisy on stage—to say nothing of Guy Domville. It is not an accident that Straith and Mrs. Harvey meet at a theater showing *The New Girl,* a play not nearly as interesting as their own story, itself so elegantly and carefully rendered. The Henry James who acts in the social drama of country-house weekends and dinners out was no stranger to acting the successful author. But he chose finally to dramatize the society he saw through in stories like this one. He even dra-matizes his own anxiety as an artist among people without imagination who want only trash. Unable to give it to them, James returned to fiction, where the real thing, as "Broken Wings" shows, is love and work grounded on imaginative truth.

But the artist, no matter what his anxiety, must work if he is to fight the good fight. The artist who does not work is the subject of "The Madonna of the Future,"[9] in which Theobald, after years of trying, is unable to put even one brush-stroke on his canvas because his idea of what a madonna should be is beyond his capacity to translate it into line and color. He has what Peter Baron in "Sir Dominick Ferrand" calls "the creative head without the creative hand" (*Complete Stories 1892–1898,* 164). Raphael's "Madonna of the Chair" is for Theobald the perfect painting because "graceful, human, near to our sympathies as it is, it has nothing of manner, of method, nothing almost of style; it blooms there in rounded softness, as instinct with harmony as if it were an immediate exhalation of genius" (*Complete Tales,* 3:19). In a shorter formulation Theobald says that "this *is* Raphael himself" (3:20). Translated into aesthetic principle, this means that the perfect artwork is a total expression of the artist's self that gives the impression of effortless realization. The model is a "vulgar fact" that keeps the artist in touch with life while, simultaneously, liberating his genius. With imaginative inspiration, then, the artist transforms facts into the truths of life. Thus, Theobald says, "No one so loves and respects the rich realities of nature as the artist whose imagination caresses and flatters them" (3:21).

When Theobald comes to admit to himself his total failure to realize his idea, he simply withers away and dies. Unless the artist develops a technique to translate his idea into a perceptible medium, he cannot be an artist at all. The creative head without the creative hand is the artist's greatest torment. It is the torment that defines Theobald decisively. The artist must nonetheless not be so absorbed by the world that he has no vision of his own: his hand must not work without his head working too. The hand without the head produces a "jaunty Juvenal" who can find one thing only: "Cats and monkeys, monkeys and cats, all human life is there!" (3:52).

The object of the quest, then, is the artwork that achieves a balance between the world's facts and the artist's imagination—intensely. That is what Paul Overt, the author of *Ginistrella,* his highly regarded first novel, seeks to achieve in his next work.[10] But as in quests of old, to achieve his goal he must overcome temptation and renounce sex and money. Money would come by writing works with popular appeal. Sex would come with marriage to Marian Fancourt, the extraordinarily beautiful and intelligent young woman Overt loves. But Overt renounces marriage under the tutelage of Henry St. George, the author of *Shadowmere,* an exquisite novel of a master craftsman. But that was St. George's last exquisite novel; the rest have been clever imitations of it written to make money to support his wife and sons in an imposing upper-middle-class way of life. The fallen knight advises the squire not to be like him. Meanwhile, when his own wife dies, St. George marries the woman Overt loves. Overt is not a little bit suspicious of St. George's motives. But "The Lesson of the Master" distinguishes motive from doctrine. St. George's advice is sound even if he himself is not. Overt's new novel is better than *Ginistrella*. By living a monk's life he has become every inch an artist. He has achieved an intensely real incarnation of life in fiction. He has achieved perfection.

James's stories are filled with the vocabulary of perfection. Perfection is the goal of the artistic quest. It is all that his civilization has left of godliness. For the artist, like Yahweh in the Scriptures, is a creator who makes and peoples a world. Thus a story like "The Next Time"[11] is not atypical with its vocabulary of "Parable[s]" and "miracles," "sinners" and "human weakness," "the brotherhood of faith" and the "Trappists, a silent order," "imperturbabil[ity]" and "impeccabil[ity]," the "act of faith" and "the wisdom of the serpent," "pure glory" and the "fiery hearted rose." Here the writer Ray Limbert "belongs to the heights—he breathes there, he lives there, and it's accordingly to the heights" that the critic "must ascend" (*Complete Stories 1892–1898*, 517). This is the vocabulary of medieval romance that James uses to tell the story of the modern artist. The knight-errant, as the product of a decidedly different kind of discursive formation than the civilization of Victorian England, provides James with a vocabulary that gives an ascetic quality to the artist who lives in a filthy-rich society more friendly to journalists than to craftsmen. The quest for the perfection of the artwork thereby attains a certain purity of process as well as of intention.

Like Childe Roland who to the dark tower came, the artist must go through the desolate landscape of modern life as he pursues perfection. Just how desolate that landscape is James makes clear in "John Delavoy."[12] A brilliant novelist recently dead, Delavoy led an intensely private live, convinced, as his sister remarks, that "He *was* his work" (*Complete Stories 1898–1910*, 22). The public, however, wants to know nothing about his art and everything about his life: the editor of *The Cynosure* wants his sister's "reminiscences."[13] She tells Mr. Beston that Delavoy's is a "great literary figure" because "he wrote very great literary things" (30); but Beston wants "anecdotes, glimpses, gossip, chat" (22–23). The great editor will not publish any of Delavoy's fiction or anything about his fiction; he will only publish "something horrible" (22). He argues that because his readers are not "conscious" of Delavoy's art, he refuses to be conscious of it either. He will give his readers nothing but trash.

When, similarly, in "The Real Right Thing,"[14] George Withermore tries to do something more delicate and refined by writing Ashton Doyne's biography, the dead novelist does not allow him to do so. Doyne's ghost stands guard over his papers to frighten his biographer away. As Withermore comes to see, the dead Doyne thereby saves his life because "the artist was what he did—he was nothing else" (*Complete Stories 1898–1910*). If Doyne's work lives, Doyne lives as well. A biography is consequently useless. James drives this point home in "The Private Life,"[15] where there are two Clare Vawdreys: one, rather dull, circulates in society and is unexceptionably ordinary; the other, intensely brilliant, lives his real life in the pool of light that surrounds his writing desk. There it is that Vawdrey lives his only real life—the private life that can be glimpsed in his works only.

Mr. Beston's *Cynosure* thrives on a public that "isn't anybody" (33) and has no private life. The same is true in "Sir Dominick Ferrand"[16] of the *Promiscuous Review,* whose readers are mindless: "as if the public *had* a mind, or any principle of perception more discoverable than the stare of huddled sheep!" (*Complete Stories 1892–1898,* 171–72). In such circumstances, the artist seeks perfection while all around him seek success. The *Cynosure* and the *Promiscuous* and similar publications are happy to sell out the artist in order to sell out an issue of the magazine. They are simply symptomatic of a public that refuses to be conscious—a public that has the aspect of *la belle dame sans merci* whether she is inside or outside the artist's house.

She may be a Mrs. St. George, who burns "one of her husband's finest things" (*Complete Tales,* 7:219). She may be Mrs. Ambient, who wants books like her husband's *Beltraffio* to teach, not delight.[17] She may be a Mrs. Paraday, who is not interested in her estranged husband's novels but only in his earnings. Or she may be Mrs. Weeks Wimbush and a Princess, who lose the manuscript of Neil Paraday's masterpiece and allow their lion to die in an unheated den in Prestige, the Wimbush estate.[18] Between them they kill both the writer and his work. Thus "Neil Paraday" is a pun on the words "kneel" and "parody." Indeed, Neil Paraday's story is a parody of pretending to kneel before artists as gods while actually being a story about lion hunters and zookeepers. "The Death of the Lion" is another protest on James's part against the intemperate interest in the artist as a personality rather than in the art of the artist. It is all of a piece with "The Aspern Papers," where the duplicitous search for the treasure hoard of Jeffrey

Aspern's papers finds his overly zealous biographer branded with the label of "publishing scoundrel."[19]

The ideal reader, therefore, is someone like Fanny Hurter, who renounces the opportunity to meet Neil Paraday. She makes it a sacred obligation never to look upon the divinity of the artist, but she has a proper reverence for his works. She is the kind of reader who keeps the author alive after his death. She is not unlike Gwendolen Erme, who becomes Mrs. George Corvick, in "The Figure in the Carpet."[20] Gwendolen's husband helps her to appreciate their favorite novelist. Anything but a publishing scoundrel, Gwendolen, who learns from Corvick the secret of Vereker's fiction—"the organ of life" within it (*Complete Stories 1892–1898*, 581)—keeps it to herself as a matter of love and honor. The narrator's excavation of Vereker's fiction for that "buried treasure," however, destroys his appreciation of it. Instead of reading novels, he tries to solve riddles. Like Mark Ambient's wife, the narrator looks for something so particular that he misses the experience of reading altogether: "the special beauty (that is mainly the just word) that pervades and controls and animates" Vereker's fiction (*Notebooks,* 220).[21]

A Hugh of a different kind from Vereker appears in young Dr. Hugh of "The Middle Years."[22] This is a story about writing and reading that begins with the aging Dencombe meeting Hugh—that is, with the Writer meeting You—as each finds the other reading Dencombe's novel *The Middle Years.* Dencombe finds his greatest admirer in Dr. Hugh, who incurs the wrath of his elderly patient and employer, the Countess, and of Miss Vernham, her companion and nurse, who wants to marry the doctor after he inherits the Countess's fortune. But the doctor becomes more interested in Dencombe's health than in the Countess's. Dr. Hugh, supposedly, loses all around because the Countess disinherits him and Dencombe dies. But he also wins, not simply because Miss Vernham drops him, but because he has taken his chance and submitted to "the madness of art" (*Complete Stories 1892–1898,* 354).

This story once again puts women in opposition to art. Not only the jealous Countess and the mercenary Miss Vernham but even Dencombe's dead wife (and son) because he could hardly have written *The Middle Years* if he were a devoted husband and father. Henry St. George's wife and sons are fair warning. So also is the worthless Leolin, son of Greville Fane, who works his mother to death as her fiction goes from bad to worse to support him.[23] And Mark Ambient's wife allows her son to die rather than have him live in a world that her husband's fiction all too perceptively realizes in his novels. Ironically, only after suffering her son's death does she come to appreciate Ambient's art. But that death also loosens Ambient's own hold on life, and he shortly follows his son to the grave. Even the entirely sympathetic wife of Ralph Limbert and their children drive him ever harder to write something popular in "The Next Time" and shorten his life. Limbert always thinks that the next time he writes he will write a popular novel. But his gift of genius is his fate: he cannot write anything but masterpieces. Therefore he has only the smallest of audiences. He doesn't sell well, and his family doesn't live well.

There is no "next time" for Dencombe or Dr. Hugh in "The Middle Years." The principal thematic element of the story turns on the word *chance*. Dencombe would like to have the chance to write something even better than *The Middle Years*. The title corresponds to his own age and suggests that there might be a "next time" for him. But he is really too sick to expect to have another chance. He and Dr. Hugh meet by chance. Both are reading the same book by chance. Finally Dencombe says, "A second chance—*that's* the delusion. There never was to be but one." But with that one chance, he has made Dr. Hugh care: "The thing is to have made somebody care," Dencombe says to Dr. Hugh. "You happen to be crazy, of course, but that doesn't affect the law." Being crazy has to do with "the madness of art": "We work in the dark—we do what we can—we give what we have," says Dencombe. "Our doubt is our passion and our passion is our task. The rest is the madness of art" (354).

The madness of art returns us to Plato, who in the *Ion* tells the rhapsode he is mad when he recites Homer's poetry. Certainly there is a touch of that madness in a prolific storyteller like Henry James. His stories quite clearly reflect anxieties about women, the vulgar crowd, and the corrupting power of money—of which he sought a lot and gained only a little. These flaws in James's rational make-up are all too obvious to doubt them. But so what? In spite of them—indeed, perhaps because of them—he made writing his life. The madness that affected him and that Plato condemns, he celebrates. The madness of art makes life worth living. The madness of art makes "The Middle Years" the story of two men (a writer and a reader) rather than the story of a doctor and an invalid and a nurse. It turns it from being a story that has an unhappy ending because there is no bride and no inheritance into one that has a happy ending because the story of three people (Dr. Hugh, the Countess, and Miss Vernham) has become the story of two people (Dencombe and Dr. Hugh). The story of marriage and money, therefore, becomes the story of writing and reading. The madness of art kills a melodrama and gives life to a metafiction. The madness of art, like Plato's *pharmacon*—the drug can both kill and heal—brings death but gives life as well. If, as in Dencombe's case—or as in James's—madness is sanity, metafiction is the real thing.

Notes

1. "The Story in It" was first published in the *Anglo-American Magazine* in January 1902. James noted its subject in his *Notebooks* in 1899 as *"L'honnête femme—n'a pas de roman* story," where it was tentatively entitled "The Publisher's Story" (275–76).

2. "The Real Thing" was first published in *Black and White*, 16 April 1892. James recorded the donnée for this story—"the way superficial, untrained, unprofessional effort goes to the wall when confronted with trained, competitive, intelligent, *qualified art"*—in his *Notebooks* on 22 February 1891 (102–4).

3. "The Beldonald Holbein" first appeared in *Harper's New Monthly Magazine,* October 1901. James recorded the germ for this story—"little old ugly, or plain (unappreciated) woman, after dull, small life, in 'aesthetic' perceptive 'European' 'air'"—in his *Notebooks* on 16 May 1899 (290–91).

4. "The Special Type" first appeared in *Collier's Weekly,* 16 June 1900. James's "germ of the *point de départ* of something" (recorded on 21 December 1895) is quite different from the story: Alice Dundene is not a *"demi-mondaine"* whom Frank Brivet uses "to force his virago of a wife to divorce him" (*Notebooks,* 232).

5. "Broken Wings" first appeared in *Century Magazine* in December 1900. James set down the germ of the story in February 1899 as that of "2 artists of some sort—male and female—I seem to see them—as a writer and a painter—who keep a stiff upper lip of secrecy and pride to each other as to how they're 'doing,' getting on, working off their wares, etc., till something sweeps them off their feet and breaks them down in confessions, AVEUX, tragic surrenders to the truth, which have at least the effect of bringing them for some consolatory purpose, together" (*Notebooks,* 282).

6. On the typicality of this structure of knowing and choosing in James's fiction, see Wiesenfarth (130–32).

7. James praised Arnold in his January 1884 article, "Matthew Arnold," in the *English Illustrated Magazine,* finding him "more than anyone else, the happily-proportioned, the truly distinguished man of letters." James praised "the luminosity of *Culture and Anarchy,*" calling it Arnold's "most ingenious and suggestive production" (*Essays on Literature,* 719–731, esp. 728, 731).

8. "Success" is highly problematic for the artist, as George Dane indicates in "The Great Good Place" (*Complete Stories 1898–1910*):

> "I just dropped my burden—and he received it."
> "And was it very great?"
> "Oh, such a load!" Dane laughed.
> "Trouble, sorrow, doubt?"
> "Oh, no; worse than that!"
> "Worse?"
> "'Success'—the vulgarest kind!" And Dane laughed again.
> "Ah, I know that, too! No one in future, as things are going, will be able to face success." (162)

9. "The Madonna of the Future" first appeared in the *Atlantic Monthly* in March 1873, and subsequently in *A Passionate Pilgrim* (1875), James's first book. No notes for it appeared in the *Notebooks,* which James began keeping in November 1878.

10. "The Lesson of the Master" first appeared in the *Universal Review,* 16 July–15 August 1888 and became the title story of *The Lesson of the Master* (1892). James's story is a brilliant reworking of its donnée in the *Notebooks* (5 January 1888), where he sees Alphonse Daudet writing inferior works due to his marrying. "So it occurred to me," James writes, "that a very interesting situation would be that of an elder artist or writer, who has been ruined (in his own sight) by his marriage and its forcing him to produce promiscuously and cheaply—his position in regard to his younger *confrère* whom he endeavours to save, to rescue, by some act of bold interference" (87).

11. "The Next Time" first appeared in *Yellow Book* in July 1895. James's germ for the story, which he set down on 4 June 1895, is "the notion of the little drama that may reside in the poor man of letters who squanders his life in trying for a vulgar success which his talent is too fine to achieve . . . BUT do what he will, he can't make a sow's ear out of a silk purse" (*Notebooks,* 200).

12. "John Delavoy" first appeared in *Cosmopolis* in January–February 1898, reprinted in *Complete Stories 1898–1910,* 1–35. The story sprang from R. U. Johnson's rejecting for *Century Magazine* an article by James on Dumas as "shocking their prudery"; the event, James noted on 13 February 1896, "strikes me as yielding the germ of a lovely little ironic, satiric tale—of the series of small things on the life and experience of men of letters, the group of

the little 'literary' tales. Isn't there an exquisite little subject in [Johnson's] sentence about their calculation that my article on A. D. would have been unobjectionable through being merely personal?" James goes on to note that "they desire the supreme though clap-trap tribute of an *intimate* picture, without even the courage of saying on what ground they desire any mention of him at all" (*Notebooks*, 245–46). Clearly energized by such nonsense, James wrote "John Delavoy."

13. When James reviewed Ernest Daudet's book on Alphonse, *Mon Frère et Moi*, he remarked that "there is little to please us in the growing taste of the age for revelations about the private life of the persons in whose works it is good enough to be interested. In our opinion, the life and the works are two very different matters, and an intimate knowledge of the one is not at all necessary for a genial enjoyment of the other. A writer who gives us his works is not obliged to throw his life after them, as is very apt to be assumed by persons who fail to perceive that one of the most interesting pursuits in the world is to read between the lines of the best literature" (*Literary Criticism*, 214–25).

14. "The Real Right Thing" first appeared in *Collier's Weekly*, 16 December 1899. James noted on 7 May 1898 that August Birrell told him that when he was writing the life of Frank Lockwood "soon after his death" that he had the "feeling as if he [Lockwood] might come in" (*Notebooks*, 265).

15. "The Private Life" first appeared in *Atlantic Monthly* in April 1892. James indicated on 27 July 1991 that the story began as a "little tale founded on the idea of F. L. and R. B." (*Notebooks*, 109)—of Frederic Leighton and Robert Browning, the one as President of the Royal Academy having, seemingly, only a public life; the other as the author of *Men and Women* having, along with his public presence, an intensely private life.

16. "Sir Dominick Ferrand" first appeared as "Jersey Villas" in *Cosmopolitan Magazine*, July–August 1892. James grasped the story fully in a note he made on 26 March 1892 (*Notebooks*, 117–18) and wrote it almost immediately, seeing completely the outline of a conflict between publishing private papers to make a lot of money and destroying them on principle.

17. "The Author of *Beltraffio*" first appeared in the *English Illustrated Magazine* in June and July 1894. James jotted down the donnée in his *Notebooks* on 26 March 1884, cautioning himself that it "would require prodigious delicacy of touch" to bring it off (58).

18. "The Death of the Lion" first appeared in *Yellow Book* in April 1894. James wrote a lengthy entry in his notebook on the subject on 3 February 1894, remarking that "the phenomenon is the one that is brought home to one every day of one's life by the ravenous autograph-hunters, lion-hunters, exploiters of publicity; in whose number one gets the impression that a person knowing and loving the thing itself, the work, is simply never to be found" (*Notebooks*, 148).

19. "The Aspern Papers" first appeared in the *Atlantic Monthly* in March–May 1888. James recorded the germ for the story—Captain Silsbee's seeking, in Florence, the letters of Byron and Shelley from the aged Claire Clairmont by moving into her house—on 12 January 1887 (*Notebooks*, 71–73).

20. "The Figure in the Carpet" first appeared in *Cosmopolis*, January–February 1896. James's very excited and exciting note on the story turns into a plot summary that insists that the game is indeed worth the candle (*Notebooks*, 221–24).

21. The whole sentence reads: "He has such qualities of art and style and skill as may be fine and honourable ones presumably—but he himself holds that they don't *know* his work who don't know, who haven't felt, or guessed, or perceived, this interior thought—this special beauty (that is mainly the just word) that pervades and controls and animates them" (*Notebooks*, 220).

22. "The Middle Years" first appeared in *Scribner's Magazine* in May 1893. James's note of 12 May 1892 (*Notebooks*, 121–22) epitomizes the story as he has written it, even to mentioning "a young doctor, a young pilgrim who admires him."

23. "Greville Fane" first appeared in the *Illustrated London News*, 17 and 24 September 1892. James wrote a very complete note for this story on 27 February 1889 in which he describes Mrs. Stormer, whose pen name in Greville Fane, her snobbish daughter, and her sponging son (*Notebooks*, 93–94).

Works Cited

James, Henry. *The Art of the Novel: Critical Prefaces*. New York: Scribner's, 1953.

———. *Complete Stories 1892–1898*. Library of America. New York: Literary Classics, 1996.

———. *Complete Stories 1898–1910*. Library of America. New York: Literary Classics, 1996.

———. *The Complete Tales of Henry James*. Ed. Leon Edel. 12 vols. Philadelphia: Lippincott, 1962–64.

———. *Essays on Literature, American Writers, English Writers*. Library of America. New York: Literary Classics, 1984.

———. *The Letters of Henry James*. Ed. Percy Lubbock. 2 vols. New York: Scribner's, 1920.

———. *Literary Criticism: French Writers, Other European Writers, the Prefaces to the New York Edition*. Library of America. New York: Literary Classics, 1984.

———. *The Notebooks of Henry James*. Ed. F. O. Matthiessen and Kenneth B. Murdock. New York: Oxford University Press, 1947.

Wiesenfarth, Joseph. *Gothic Manners and the Classic English Novel*. Madison: University of Wisconsin Press, 1988.

Daniel R. Schwarz

MANET, "THE TURN OF THE SCREW," AND THE VOYEURISTIC IMAGINATION

I

Phoenix-like, the relationship between literature and its contexts has been reborn as the field of cultural studies—a field that stresses power relationships among genders, races, and classes. New Historicism and its child, cultural studies, have been skeptical of the older historicism's positivistic stories of "A" influencing "B" and of reductive drawings of the boundaries that divide foreground and background. Although it has sought to see literature as one of many cultural artifacts, the artifacts usually are seen in terms of socioeconomic production. But the stress on micropolitical and macropolitical relations should not prevent this welcome return to mimesis and to historical contexts from attending to other kinds of cultural frames. Specifically, the return from the formalism of deconstruction to mimesis should be a catalyst for examining and juxtaposing figures and movements without regard to simple patterns of influence. What I am interested in is the process of examination of cultural figures in configurations that put new light on cultural history. My goal is to isolate essential ingredients of modernistic culture, ingredients that spill over the borderlands between genres and art forms. Although we have learned in recent years to be wary of locating essential or transcendent themes, it is still necessary to understand the genealogy of modernism and the figures who contributed to the modification of the cultural genetic code—particularly because these modifications live with us now in contemporary art and literature. Specifically, I am going to frame contextually an odd triptych: Edouard Manet, Henry James, and Thomas Mann; as I weave a narrative from particular strands of similarities, I shall inquire into what cultural forces produced this configuration.

From our vantage point now, we can see that the cultural revolution known as modernism originated as much with the paintings of Picasso and Matisse, and before that with Manet and Gauguin, as with literary figures. Modernism questioned the possibility of a homogeneous European culture even as it sought to propose diverse and contradictory alternatives. As John Elderfield puts it, "history was not always thought to be quite possibly a species of fiction but once comprised a form of order, and might still" (203). One might recall James Clifford's comment that in 1900, "'Culture' referred to a single evolutionary process. The European bourgeois ideal of autonomous individuality was widely believed to be the natural outcome of a long development, a process that, although threatened by various disruptions, was assumed to be the basic, progressive movement of humanity" (92–93). The major modernists felt estranged from orthodox political and historical assumptions and from the cultural values in which they were educated. Yet artists and writers paid homage to the very traditional ideas of art from which they were departing by their strong response to their predecessors and their need to modify and transform them.

Modernists often tried to insulate art from history and to apotheosize the aesthetic. Indeed, New Criticism was not only a response to modernist texts but originated in part from modernist aesthetics, such as Eliot's objective correlative, Joyce's concept of epiphany, Lawrence's insistence that we believe the tale not the teller, and James's emphasis in his prefaces on the inextricable relationship between the aesthetic and ethical (see Schwarz, chapter 1). But the recent emphasis on historicism seems to be particularly apt for modernism, which was shaped by World War I, the Depression, the women's suffrage movement, and the disappointments in the promise of industrialism and urbanization. English modernism questions the mythical idealized Victorian family; European artists were also addressing bourgeois expectations and myths. As we shall see, in keeping with my hedge-hoggy integrative spirit that eschews foxlike linearity, my account of the genealogy of modernism will include varied data, such as the sexual repression of the governess in "The Turn of the Screw" (1898), the paintings of Manet, and that strange bachelor novel of Thomas Mann, "Death in Venice," which owes much to Huysmans. All address the question, "What shall we do about loneliness?" For the need to be noticed, seen, and read relates to a pervasive sense in the late nineteenth century that each human is a separate island, disconnected both from his or her fellow humans and from any transcendent order or teleology. I shall be focusing on how seeing and being seen is related not only to the cosmic loneliness of the modern world but to the social and personal loneliness of bachelors and spinsters—and of governesses and prostitutes—who become metonymies in modern literature for all humankind. In other words, for otherwise insignificant humans, the act of seeing and being seen becomes a desperate part of the quest for meaning.

Modern literature and modern painting valorize what is represented as an intensified and illuminating version of reality. Although self-consciously and knowingly using a web of signs, artists affirm that what they see is a version of the essential nature of things. Following romantic antecedents and compensating for the dissolution of shared beliefs and emptiness within themselves, artists respond to nature in a way that reflects an often desperate quest of an intuitive, powerful imagination. Modern artists deeply desire the capacity to see beyond the rest of us but have difficulty convincing themselves and others that they have done so. This leads to the wearing of masks, ventriloquism, role playing, and multiple ways of seeing the same phenomenon, for instance, "Thirteen Ways of Looking at a Blackbird." Yet the very process of role playing—experimenting with diverse styles, with rapidly changing voices—was an essential part of modernism. Role playing was crucial to Manet, James, and Mann. In a world where a systematic world view is impossible, *inclusiveness of possibility*—of multiple ways of seeing—is an aesthetic and a value. Is not the essence of cubism the insistence that we need not restrict perspective and that reality depends on the angle of vision?

Earlier artists drew upon other artists' subjects and inspiration, but modernism began to take art more seriously. Modernism's turn to intertextuality and metonymy relates to the loss of belief in the traditional Christian plot stretching from the Creation to the Apocalypse. The works of humans, like the world of humans, take on stature and importance once the painter no longer feels compelled to record the high points of the teleological Christian plot, such as the Incarnation, the birth of Christ, or the crucifixion, or to record the portraits or deeds of secular potentates.

The invention of photography, the breakdown of accepted moral certainties in religion and politics, the Darwinian revolution, modern physics, Freud, Nietzsche—all these about which I and others have written—played a role in the shaping of new aesthetic assumptions. We need to understand and reconfigure the affinities between modern painting and sculpture and modern literature—affinities that at times take the form of influences, at times cultural parallels, at times unconscious responses. The experiments of James, Conrad, Joyce, Woolf, Eliot, and Stevens that challenged orderly narrative and consistent point of view have their parallels in, and at times owe the challenges to mimesis to, Matisse, Picasso, and Klee, whose experiments in color, line, space, and abandonment of representation often provided a model for the experiments of modern writers. Juxtaposing disparate elements in collage certainly anticipated and was later affected by the disjunctions in modern narrative. The stress on form and style in Eliot, Woolf, Stevens, Joyce, and James is a correlative in literature to Matisse's stress on patterning and the decorative. In *Dance II* (1909) and *Music* (1910), Matisse subordinates individuality and character to the purpose of design. His art is at once a triumph of self and form. Turning to modern literature, is there a more patterned book than *Ulysses* (1922), a more choreographed one than *Mrs. Dalloway* (1925) or *The Wings of the Dove* (1902)? In *Ulysses*, particularly in the later chapters, Joyce's experiments in style are a version of the decorative; indeed, his assigning colors to each chapter recalls Kandinsky's color theories. Yet, as Joyce discovered in "Sirens" and in "Oxen of the Sun," language resists the decorative because we recuperate it in terms of meaning.

By the 1880s, we have Nietzsche's *Gay Science* (1882–87) with his contention that God is dead as well as Krafft-Ebing's revolutionary texts on sexuality, and we also have the beginnings of modern physics in the work of J. J. Thomson. Cézanne carried the revolution away from the convention further when he deconstructed and undermined the idea of a single perspective. He subordinated details to the demands of a grand design without sacrificing specificity of his eye. Cézanne knew that we see in context and that an object takes its meaning from that context. Like Joyce, he stressed that the identity and meaning of any given object or person depend upon its proximity to other given objects. Like Bergson, who wrote in *Les Donnés immédiates de la conscience* "we have to express ourselves in words, but more often we think in space" (quoted in Russell, 31), Cézanne was concerned, like Conrad and James, with the act of cognition and with the perception of spatial-temporal relations. We can see a direct line to Picasso and Matisse, both of whom reinvented the world according to their imaginations.

In this paper I want to examine the importance of seeing and being seen. When Conrad wrote eloquently in the preface to *The Nigger of the "Narcissus"* about his purpose as a writer, he wrote with the fervor of a man who believed in the capacity of art to shape our responses to life: "My task which I am trying to achieve is, by the power of the written word, to make you hear, to make you feel—it is, before all, to make you *see*" (708). He was speaking of the power of the written word to create within the reader's mind an experience—visual experience—that would be the reader's own but still a version of Conrad's:

> Fiction—if it at all aspires to be art—appeals to temperament. And in truth it must be, like painting, like music, like all art, the appeal of one temperament to all the other innumerable temperaments whose subtle and resistless power endows passing events with their true meaning, and creates the moral, the emotional atmosphere of the place and time. (707)

In many ways, "To make you see" is the subject of James's "The Turn of the Screw"; the governess learns how to see differently in part because of her need to be seen; Douglas wants to be the center of attention as narrator, and James is using his tale to discuss the subjective nature of optics. Using the governess as a paradigm of what happens when reality becomes subordinated to self-indulgence, James explores the way a teller becomes a painter of souls whose telling always has a strong autobiographical dimension. It may be that the governess—the unreliable narrator whose perceptions are psychotic—is a self-parody of extreme and self-indulgent aestheticism.

I want to discuss "The Turn of the Screw" among the mindscapes of modernism, specifically in reference to a number of the novellas of the period—notably, "Heart of Darkness," "Death in Venice," "The Dead," "The Secret Sharer," and "Metamorphosis"—as well as to the paintings of

Edouard Manet. James published "The Turn of the Screw" in 1898, the year Conrad published "Heart of Darkness." James's and Conrad's experiments with the dramatized narrator show how modernism has shifted the emphasis to the subject as interpreter, to the perceiver's mind in action, to the observer as subject as much as to *what* he or she observes. With some complaining irony, Woolf remarked in "Mr. Bennett and Mrs. Brown," "where so much strength is spent on finding a way of telling the truth, the truth itself is bound to reach us in rather an exhausted and chaotic condition" (117). In the modern period, "finding a way"—the quest for values and the quest for the appropriate style and form—becomes the subject. And is not finding our way another version of seeing?

What James has done in "The Turn of the Screw" is to provide an alternative to the spiritualized Victorian woman's narrative; as Beth Newman eloquently writes: "[I]t might be possible to hear in her willingness to endure such 'exposure' a disguised expression of her desire to be seen, a wish that she could best exercise her supervisory duties and prevent the children from seeing the ghosts by in some way 'exposing herself'" (61). The governess's desire to be seen, recognized, and validated runs throughout her narrative:

> Caught between two definitions of ideal femininity—one valuing the inconspicuous but vigilant woman, the other representing the desirable woman as an object of visual pleasure—she consciously chooses the former. But she cannot divest herself of her unconscious desire to be seen, which influences her insistent seeing and possibly—if the ghosts are hallucinations—the content of what she sees. (Newman, 61)

The task set upon her by the master who hires her is a desexualizing one "denying her participation in the libidinal economy of seeing and being seen" (Newman, 61)—the economy that, as we shall see, is so much a part of Manet's world. But she finds sublimated ways to participate in that economy.

II

I turn rather abruptly to Manet's *Déjeuner sur l'Herbe* (1863), a parody of the pastoral as seen from an urban perspective. Two young urban males—the tasseled cap was worn by students—are picnicking with a naked woman.

Meanwhile, in the background—recalling ironically Botticelli's *Birth of Venus*—a woman emerges from a stream. But the flat background landscape might be another picture ironically commenting on the foregrounded picnic. Or we might say the middle-grounded picture because foregrounded on the left is a still life; only the still life has a sense of depth. Is not Manet calling attention to his ability as a painter to mix genres however he pleases and to defy—like the naked woman—conventions of genre and perspective?

Neither woman—the one sitting on her wrap or the one emerging from the stream—pays attention to the men or to each other. Each is in her own space. Note how the naked woman is unself-consciously looking away from her companions, perhaps to catch the attention of other men or women who are not within the scene. In a sense, we the audience are engaged frankly by her as voyeurs in a libidinal interchange in which she both looks and is looked at. If we think of "The Turn of the Screw," the middle-grounded woman is the governess's suppressed libidinal self, whereas the self-absorbed and mysterious woman in the background is the embodiment of the governess's conscious level. We follow the phallic cane as it calls attention to her nakedness. As Françoise Cachin notes, "The still life accentuates the nudity of the woman, who becomes, in the presence of this heap of fashionable raiment, undressed rather than nude" (*Manet: 1832–1883*, 169). Yet the picnic lunch, with its cherries of June and the figs of September, is not realistic. We see the influence of Titian's *Concert Champêtre* and Raimondi's engraving—inspired by a Raphael composition, *The Judgment of Paris*. (Manet would have enjoyed the classical echo of his city's name.) But in Manet's realistic Paris sexual frankness dominates.

In the woman emerging from the lake, Manet ironically refers to Botticelli; yet Manet reminds us that the current Venus in contemporary Paris is the middle-grounded nude woman—perhaps but not necessarily a prostitute—who can do with her body what she wishes. Indeed, from one perspective, the painting is gender-inscribed both as a masculine fantasy and as a text to show woman's control over her body, sexuality, and mood. She will *decide* on the sexual stakes and not tolerate abuse. By using his two brothers for his models of the males, Manet shows his own participation in the fantasy. We are reminded of how modernism's energy derives, in a time of moral and historical transition, from the artist's self-creating, or, as Stevens put it in "Tea at the Palaz of Hoon," "I was the world in which I walked, and what I saw / Or heard or felt came not but from myself; / And there I found myself more truly and more strange" (65). In its deference to Old Masters, the painting respects canon; in its provocativeness and parody, it opens the curtains to modernism. Indeed, the background could be a stage backdrop for a Japanese screen. So unrealistic is the background, its very artificiality undermines the verisimilitude of a scene in open air, and, in fact, it was painted in a studio. The trees on the left and right suggest a framing curtain and anticipate Matisse's *Bonheur de Vivre* (1905–6) and Picasso's *Les Demoiselles d'Avignon* (1907).

Let us think about Manet's modernism. In subject matter, he freed— to the dismay of many conservative critics of his day—the female nude from any pretensions of idealism and planted her squarely in the world of sexuality. Could Joyce have had this painting in mind when he created Molly and Bloom's great moment of uninhibited intercourse during a picnic on the Howth in the "Lestrygonians" section of *Ulysses?* And Manet addressed the urban world of the city from fashionable life (*Music in the Tuilieres*, 1862) and from the life in cafés to the outsiders, such as the prostitute in *Olympia* (1867). He depicted women as sexual figures without sentimentalizing them. Manet explores various kinds of possibilities that thwart, offend, and undermine bourgeois family values. As in his pictures of Berthe Morisot, he also depicted women as coequal humans with a full range of emotions. And these two innovations—the focus on the painter and the perceiver, the opening up of subject matter—are related.

Manet's paintings—not only *Déjeuner sur l'Herbe*, but *The Bar at the Folies-Bergère* (1881–82), *The Plum, Olympia*, and *Nana* (1877)—are narratives of voyeurism that anticipate the preoccupation in James's "The Turn of the Screw" with seeing and being seen. Just as James penetrated the gloss and style of English aristocracy to discover darker truths, so does Manet address Parisian society. Manet's oeuvre is like a novel; each painting is an episode or chapter in an unfolding saga of life in Paris. Manet's city paintings remind us of Joyce's vignettes of the modern city in *Dubliners* and in *Ulysses*, particularly "The Wandering Rocks" section. Just as episodes organize vignettes and pieces of dialogue and action, and chapters organize episodes into larger narrative elements and, finally, parts or volumes of novels organize chapters, so single paintings form series that pertain to one subject, and several series of paintings might form larger organizing groups. Of course, what we organize into series and groups depends upon our perceptual interest. In this way we can regard Manet's paintings of Paris and its inhabitants as collectively forming a saga composed of a concatenation of narrative episodes: *Young Lady in 1866 (Woman with Parrot), Gypsy with Cigarette* (1862), *Young Woman Reclining in Spanish Costume* (1862), *The Street Singer* (1862), *Masked Ball at the Opera* (1873–74), *Lola de Valence, Olympia,* and *Déjeuner sur l'Herbe.* In one group, including *Déjeuner sur l'Herbe, Woman with Parrot, The Plum, Olympia,* and *Nana,* he is fascinated with changing sexual mores. For example, in *Woman with Parrot*—which alludes to Courbet's *Woman with Parrot*—the parrot is a metonymy for sexuality; the parrot sees his mistress undressing and knows her secrets—and perhaps could reveal fragments of them that it had overheard. Certainly the woman in the peignoir who is holding a monocle that could be a man's—her lover's—combined with the discarded orange—image of her being used and discarded by the absent male, image of her open vagina—is not idealized. The orange anticipates the untouched plum, itself metonymic of sexuality, in *The Plum* (1878?). (Does not the plum suggest Joyce's use of the plum as a sexual and political symbol in *Ulysses?*) The woman is either a prostitute or a *grisette,* a working-class woman who often dressed above her station and visited places of public entertainment. Manet understands that the way women are looked at and how they look at others creates their identity in a man-controlled world. Like James's governess, these women are often in their own space, on their own island and dependent on others to give them identity.

Manet is the painter of the contemporary life of his era, and his competitors were photographers such as Félix Nadar, who showed how no two people are alike, notwithstanding that he used a few simple props and a planned background for his portraits. Like Manet, Nadar neither idealized his subjects nor made them coarse and indecent. What Joyce did for Dublin and Damon Runyan did for New York, Manet did for Paris. Manet's oeuvre displays his exuberant response to the variety of the city, its range of classes, its stories of seeming insignificance, its energy and complexity. He sees the spontaneity of human actions—including its ugliness and foolishness—of Paris's inhabitants, and he understands their impulse for self-survival in an indifferent environment. The very order, splendor, and glamour that Baron Haussmann brought to Paris had not improved the lot of the working person. Beneath the glitter was another Paris; the high rents drove workers into the new slums that replaced those in the central city. Manet delights in the physical presence and quirks of his figures and deftly balances empathy with objectivity. He enjoys the impudence of the *gavroche* in the *Masked Ball at the Opera*. Influenced by Ribera, he depicted the outsiders, the disadvantaged, and the lower classes with gusto and sympathy in turn, he showed the way for Picasso to do the same. Indeed, Picasso's Paris—and Joyce's Dublin, which in the "Circe" section of *Ulysses* and in the bargirls snapping their garters in "Sirens" is often Paris-mediated—owes much to the influence of Manet. Picasso's old guitarist might have been a response to Manet's *The Spanish Singer* (1860).

In *The Bar at the Folies-Bergère*, what is most striking about the bar is that the image in the mirror does not reflect the scene out front; it is as if the viewer who is absent has taken the place of the man whom the barmaid is serving in the reflection. The painting calls attention to the viewer even while reminding us that the woman is more perceiver than participant. We should see something of him in front of her, but we do not. Her story is ambiguous; she is detached and something of an intermediary between the perceiver and the world of the Folies-Bergère as if she were an artist watching the world in which she participates. Like James's governess, she is an insouciant outsider—reflective about her life but somewhat oblivious to the world she inhabits. It is as if Manet were stressing the double selves, the inward and outer selves, both the man and woman have. The mirror—another glass plate—no longer holds up an image to nature but in a process of metaphoricity distorts, controls, undermines, and projects. We recall the epiphanic moment in "Circe" when Stephen and Bloom look into the mirror in the whorehouse and see Shakespeare. In "Asides on the Oboe," Stevens describes the poet as the man of glass: "The impossible possible philosophers' man, / The man who has had the time to think enough, / The central man, the human globe, responsive / As a mirror with a voice, the man of glass, / Who in a million diamonds sums us up" (250). The modern artist holds the mirror up to nature, but what it gives back is an illuminating distortion. The mirror in *The Bar at the Folies-Bergère* insists that art give us more than it sees. But ironically, the woman bartender withholds herself from both. The artificiality of the perspective stresses the importance of art.

Manet exalted in the energy of the modern city even as he understood it as both promise and problem. Like Bakhtin, Manet understood the possibility of a multitude of voices in any discourse and visually represented them. He presents the spontaneity of human actions without pontificating or moralizing, and this includes *Woman in the Tub* (1878–79), *Olympia,* and *Nana.* Of course, Manet painted in the context of the French naturalists. In 1877, Zola had introduced Nana in *L'Assommoir* but had not yet begun serializing *Nana,* and would not do so until 1879. Later, when Degas and Toulouse-Lautrec became fascinated by the prostitute, not only would Degas's figures be of a lower class than Manet's, but both artists would be more judgmental and ironic than the accepting, detached Manet.

Manet's characterization of Nana dominates the space of the painting of that name—a departure from the expectations of genre painting—and the voyeuristic male client (like James's master in "The Turn of the Screw") is reduced to a supernumerary who is treated mockingly if not contemptuously. It is as if Manet conceived the two figures on a different scale. *Olympia* is also about the art of watching, in this case a naked woman who flaunts her sexuality. In *Olympia*—a pose adopted from Titian's *Venus of Urbino*—he uses the black cat, the black servant, and the black ribbon. He uses eccentric details—illuminating distortions—to make his point. The huge bouquet, opened by the black servant, suggests a gift from an admirer but calls attention to her sexual parts and her propensity to make them available; the flowers—echoed in the blue trim of the slippers and in the red and green of the embroidery—become a metonymy for her sexual mysteries within the wrappings (or vagina lips) that enclose them. The bold placement of the bed in the foreground emphasizes the subject figure's uninhibited boldness, and the details of the sheets and pillows recall the sumptuously dressed portraits of prior eras, including Van Dyke's. Her head is hardly modeled, as if her head were less important than her body, while the black ribbon and the blue slippers stress her eroticism. Finally, the viewer is complicit in the art of voyeuristic gazing. What Manet had done is not only provide an alternative to the spiritualized Victorian woman narrative but also raise questions about bourgeois expectations and myths; he created a link among desire, eroticism, and loneliness in a world where God's presence in a post-Darwinian cosmos is a matter of doubt and anxiety.

III

From Manet's Paris to James's London is not such a long journey. Governesses, life models, and prostitutes belong to no social class. What makes the governess uncomfortable is that she is being looked at by one man as she herself fantasizes about being desired by another man, her employer. As Newman puts it: "It is as though the governess's earnest, conscious desire to be the ideal domestic woman (the better to please her employer and perhaps gain his love) forces her into a sharper, more stringent surveillance" (60). And at all times the governess is most conscious of being watched by the master, by the children, and by the spectres. Quint, as Tadzio does for Aschenbach in Mann's homoerotic version of "The Turn of the Screw," represents, as Newman remarks, "the return of the repressed, with all the uncanniness—that combination of strangeness and familiarity—such a return implies" (53). The desire to be seen, recognized, validated, desired—the result of her isolation—runs through the governess's narrative.

"The Turn of the Screw" develops out of nineteenth-century obsessions about looking and about being seen; "The Turn of the Screw" parodies the reductive dichotomy—inculcated by Victorian cultural conventions—between reason and passion, between id and super ego, while examining how paralytic self-consciousness can result from repression and displacement. What I want to argue is that erotically charged seeing is understood by looking at Manet and that texts like "The Dead" and "Death in Venice" partake of the same phenomenon. And it is Manet, I am contending, who is partly responsible for bringing the looking at of unidealized sexual beings out into the open.

Quint emerges for the governess as a sexual object in invidious form that challenges her fantasy as a wife; and perhaps she understands at some level that Quint is her rival for her master's affection. After all, she is "young and pretty" and, like the naked women in *Déjeuner sur l'Herbe*, there to behold when she meets her Master. She was "carried away" by her employer. Like those women Manet presented in *Olympia* and *Déjeuner*, the governess is an erotic and ironical comment about the sexualization of women. It is as if James—doubtless familiar with Manet's painting and with naturalism in literature—were trying to see if the genre of sexuality can be put back in the box of Victorian propriety. For the bachelor-patron struck the governess as "gallant and splendid" (631),[1] and she "saw him all in a glow of high fashion, of good looks, of expensive habits, of charming ways with women" (631). When she took the job, the greatness of the country contrasted with her "own scant home" (635). Her service is erotic and hints of the master-slave variety. Lonely, sublimated, and ingenuous—the very epitome of modernist isolation—she feels joy in giving pleasure "to the person to whose pressure I had responded" (646).

James's "The Turn of the Screw" is about seeing and being seen. So is the tradition of still life, which plays such an important role in impressionism and post-impressionism and is a source of the miniature episodes that comprise "The Turn of the Screw." As we have been noticing, *the act of observing* is a crucial point in modernism; borrowing from astronomy, Joyce makes central to *Ulysses* the theme of parallax—how the same phenomenon looks different from a different angle, or perspective or by extension, human events look different to a different perceiver: cubism is about the need to see from multiple perspectives. Manet, like James, was interested in how the exceptional and diurnal rub against one another. Manet wrote, "the heroic image and the image of love can never hold their own with the image of pain. This is the essence of humanity, its poetry" (*Manet: 1832–1883,* 275). And James's rendering of the governess is a rendering of a character in excruciating pain. For Quint is something of a rake but more than that, a man of insidious vice, sexual insistence, putative perversion; moreover, in the economy of erotics, the governess has imagined herself as the object of his gaze. What the frame technique does is empower the reader's gaze by making the reader—through her/his metonymic relationship with both speaker and governess—a perceiver, a crucial figure.

Because Manet does not provide us with the rhetoric to tell one story, the audience is called upon to complete the painting. In other words, Manet requires a "reader-oriented" response because the "doesness"—the structure of effects—is underdetermined. When the gaze—how one looks at things—becomes the subject, the perceiver's gaze enables the subject to become object. Although the impulse to make oneself the subject of one's own art includes Rembrandt's self-portraits, the impulse crystallized in the nineteenth century with Courbet's *L'Atelier, The Real Allegory Determining a Phase of Seven Years of My Artistic Life (1845–55)* with its intense focus on Courbet at work. In the middle of that painting is a god-like Courbet with a model—if I may quote Julian Barnes—"reinventing the world. And Courbet with a model—perhaps this helps answer the question of why Courbet is painting a landscape in his studio rather than *en plein air:* because he is doing more than reproducing the known, established world; he is creating it himself. From now on, the painting says, it is the artist who creates the world rather than God" (3). Does not this description recall Stephen's argument about what the artist found in the "Scylla and Charybdis" section of *Ulysses?* "He found in the world without as actual what was in his world within as possible."

I want to think of the governess's telling in "The Turn of the Screw" as a self-portrait. The governess sees herself as if she were a painting, an object, or text requiring another to bring her to life. Thus the governess's telling is part of a genre of nineteenth-century self-portrait in which the gaze of the perceiver completes and realizes the subject, but it is also a repressed and displaced version of Manet's erotically charged gaze, a version shaped by the anxiety of the paralytic self-conscious speaker. We understand that her perspective results from an idealized, mysticized sexual culture where—unlike the world of Manet—passions and libido are denied. We might recall Lacan's insight about the painter's gaze as a way of linking our parallel between James and Manet:

> The painter gives something to the person who must stand in front of his painting which, in part, at least, of the painting, might be summed up thus—*You want to see? Well, take a look at this!* He gives something for the eye to feed on, but he invites the person to whom this picture is presented to lay down his gaze there as one lays down one's weapons. This is the pacifying, Apollonian effect of painting. Something is given not so much to the gaze as to the eye, something that involves the abandonment, the *laying down,* of the gaze. (101)

Like Gabriel Conroy, the governess often regards herself as strangely detached, the object of her own gaze, a kind of painting that she might observe on the tastefully decorated walls of the house she inhabits. The governess speaks of her experience as if it were a series of paintings: she seeks to depict "a credible picture of my state of mind" (664). She is both a fictionmaker and a participant in the fictions of others. If Quint is a spectator, is she creating her own viewer/narratee? The governess lives in a world of pictures; "The Turn of the Screw" is James's version of *Pictures at an Exhibition*. She wants to see allegorized, uplifting pictures and conceives herself in those terms—terms borrowed from nineteenth-century British representations of women in painting. Her mental pictures are the kind of misty allegorized pictures of the pre-Raphaelites such as John William Waterhouse's *Hylas and the Nymphs* (1896) or Ford Madox Brown's *The Last of England* (1860) or the paintings of Rossetti or Burne-Jones. But with her eyes she *sees* scandalous pictures produced by French lubricity.

Put another way, "Turn of the Screw" is a museum piece because the vignettes are visual. The governess arrests narrative moments and perceives them spatially as if they were museum pieces. Early on, Flora is compared with "one of Raphael's holy infants" (636). The children create a "spectacle" in which she participates as an active admirer: "I walked in a world of their invention" (665). Does not "The Turn of the Screw" call attention to the aesthetic, the fantastic, the romantic, the gothic, and the performative? To the governess, Quint looked "like an actor" (658). Her imagined reality refuses to be constrained or contained by day-to-day reality. The governess lives in a pictorial gallery of her own making: "Someone [the man who hired her] would appear there at the turn of a path and would stand before me and smile and approve" (647). For her, optative becomes indicative.

But what intrudes is a modernist nightmare worthy of Munch: "the man who looked at me over the battlements was as definite as a picture in a frame" (648). In her head is a dialogue between two pictures: the fantasy vision that the appealing bachelor who hired her will appear to sweep her away and the rakish corrupt figure that haunts her: "What arrested me on the spot—and with a shock much greater than any vision had allowed for—was the sense that my imagination had, in a flash, turned real. He did stand there!" (647). Of course, to the figure staring at her, she is the aesthetic object. It is as if she were looking in the mirror, but like Stephen and Bloom in "Circe," what she sees is "other," but other as a version of self: "[E]ven as he turned away [he] still markedly fixed me" (649); or: "I applied my face to the pane and looked, as he had looked, into the room" (654). In a sense, Quint and Miss Jessel represent the aesthetic and the fantastic, wooing the children from the world of doing.

To a resistant reader, the governess's sexual obsession and hysteria have undermined her capacity to take care of the children as surely as in Conrad's "The Secret Sharer" (1911) the captain's obsession with Leggatt has undermined his capacity to command his ship. The governess has no sexual self-confidence and thinks of women as the "inferior sex." She doesn't summon the Master—Flora's and Miles's uncle—because she believes that he will think that she "had set in motion [machines] to attract his attention to [her] slighted charms" (695). She is loyal to the absent uncle—her chosen "master" to whom she submits her will—with whom she has an erotic obsession, and her judgment about his behavior is skewed:

> He never wrote to them—that may have been selfish, but it was a part of the flattery of his trust of me; for the way in which a man pays his highest tribute to a woman is apt to be but by the more festal celebration of one of the sacred laws of his comfort; and I held that I carried out the spirit of the pledge given not to appeal to him when I let my charges understand that their own letters were but charming literary exercises. (700)

These children are in need of social services, and a contemporary reader might ask ironically why has not someone, maybe Mrs. Grose, called the Hotline to complain of a neglectful uncle as well as abusive servants. Is the governess paranoid? Sexually hysterical? She considers appearances of the dead to be "molestations" of her person; when they do not appear she says: "I continued unmolested" (698). But her real issue is a desperate need to be attended, objectified by the gaze of others, and filled with the plenitude of recognition. Without realizing it, she is one of what, in chapter 27 of *Moby-Dick*, Melville calls *Isolatóes*, those who "not acknowledging the common continent of men . . . [live] on a separate continent of [their] own" (117).

We think of Huysmans and of the aesthetes, such as Wilde and Beardsley, when the governess refers to her perceptions in aesthetic terms, as if they were pictures in a gallery: "This picture comes back to me in the general train" (650). Her views of the apparition resemble the experience of coming upon disturbing paintings, for like paintings the apparition does not do anything or respond or take part. That may be the reason, among others, that James spoke of the story in a letter to F. W. H. Myers as "a merely *pictorial* subject" (Rahv, 623). As in Conrad's "The Secret Sharer"—which also emphasizes looking and seeing as a mode of perception that reveals the inner workings of character—loneliness half creates what she sees. Let us recall when she sees Miss Jessel: Miss Jessel is described as "a woman in black, pale and dreadful—with such an air also, and such a face!—on the other side of the lake" (668). After looking—but not speaking or moving toward the female figure, her other self, a woman mysteriously and helplessly sexually corrupted by Quint or perhaps the initiator of corruption herself—she looks at the young girl in her charge. That her predecessor had been corrupted and seduced is both a source of fear and sexual hysteria that she displaces and projects onto the children; to be sure, she fears for them, but isn't the threat a projection of her own psyche? In her mind she paints still lifes, portraits, and weird landscapes from her fantasies.

Miles and Flora are desperate for love, for they are orphans, virtually abandoned by their uncle, who has consigned their upbringing to servants. What Quint and Miss Jessel offer apparently is initiation into sexual mysteries with a homosexual orientation. (That such an offer proffered by an older man is rejected by the young boy in Joyce's "An Encounter" shows that this theme recurs in the period, and James in "The Pupil" explores the homosexual undertones between mentor [Pemberton] and pupil [Morgan].) Quint wears the master's clothes the way Leggatt wore the captain's. Here we have the governess as a third party who—repressed, lonely, and increasingly hysterical—must distinguish between the master and servant, the living and the dead, the innocent and the corrupt (in the matter of the children's complicity), the spectral appearance and the real. Are not the curses of Miles and Flora an aestheticism, compulsive self-reflection, and narcissism? Like Tolstoy's Ivan, they can't feel and are caught in a web of their own selfishness. (Apparently the reason Miles was asked to leave school is that he spoke about sex to the fellows he "liked" [746], but does he not often seem anaesthetized?) And the sexual undertones emphasize this; note how, after Flora and Mrs. Grose depart, Miles takes the place of a male companion when he and the governess sit together in the schoolroom "as silent, it whimsically occurred to me, as some young couple who, on their wedding-journey, at the inn, feel shy in the presence of the waiter" (738). After Flora leaves, he no longer can see Quint, as if the charm depended upon her.

Among other things, autoeroticism is a metaphor for the inversion of art. In a sense the apparitions, particularly Miss Jessel, become the governess's secret sharer, and she speaks of Quint as a stranger the way the captain-narrator spoke of Leggatt in "The Secret Sharer." Particularly to a contemporary reader, does not the male bonding in Conrad's story have a homoerotic aspect? After all, they are in bed together and communicate like lovers: "And in the same whisper, as if we two whenever we talked had to say things to each other which were not fit for the world to hear, he added, 'It's very wonderful'" (688). Note the parallel with the unmarried governess when she encounters her predecessor—or, rather, her ghost—in the schoolroom: "[S]he had looked at me long enough to appear to say that her right to sit at my table was as good as mine to sit at hers" (707).

Walter Benjamin observed, "The city is reflected in a thousand eyes, a thousand lenses . . . [M]irrors are the immaterial element of the city, her emblem" (quoted in *Manet,* 482). Mirrors always distort, for we see only what we, the perceivers, want to see; we only see the part of the body on which we focus. We might recall the mirror in *The Bar at the Folies-Bergère.* In "The Secret Sharer," the captain observes: "The shadowy, dark head, like mine, seemed to nod imperceptibly above the ghostly gray of my sleeping suit. It was, in the night, as though I had been faced by my own reflection in the depths of a somber and immense mirror" (657–58). In "The Turn of the Screw," the governess sees herself for the first time "from head to foot" in the mirror in the long, impressive room to which she is assigned (635). Identity is dependent on what one sees, on *how* one sees, and on how one is seen. And does it not focus on ourselves creating what we see and thus call attention to the self-reflexivity of reading in the modern era and to the continuity between reading texts and reading lives? Are not Manet and James inviting us to ask questions about the way we see in mirrors—and texts—what we bring to them? Do we not inadvertently, like the governess and Aschenbach and Manet's women, make texts into sites for our own constructions? Spectre experiences may reveal that the character is perceiving myopically or perspicaciously.

"The Turn of the Screw"'s self-reflection and narcissism are troped in its style. The "I" not as a *subject* of ego but as the *object* of service becomes the subject:

> I used to wonder how my little charges could help guessing that I thought
> strange things about them; and the circumstance that these things only

made them more interesting was not by itself a direct aid to keeping them in the dark. I trembled lest they should see that they were so immensely more interesting. Putting things at the worst, at all events, as in meditation I so often did, any clouding of their innocence could only be—blameless and foredoomed as they were—a reason the more for taking risks. There were moments when, by an irresistible impulse, I found myself catching them up and pressing them to my heart. As soon as I had done so I used to say to myself: "What will they think of that? Doesn't it betray too much?" It would have been easy to get into a sad, wild tangle about how much I might betray; but the real account, I feel, of the hours of peace that I could still enjoy was that the immediate charm of my companions was a beguilement still effective even under the shadow of the possibility that it was studied. For if it occurred to me that I might occasionally excite suspicion by the little outbreaks of my sharper passion for them, so too I remember wondering if I mightn't see a queerness in the traceable increase of their own demonstrations. (678–79)

Do not, as perceived by the governess, both Miles and herself have demonic posts of service? And are not those posts erotically defined by the act of seeing? Are they not both fixed by the governess and by the reader, and—as we shall see—by Douglas, as objects of voyeurism?

IV

Let us now examine "The Turn of the Screw" from another perspective. In James, as in Huysmans, a sometimes inverted bachelor needs to create his own company and routines; as in "The Pupil," we see lonely male figures reaching out for empathetic others. Something of the kind is at work in the group—men and women—at the country house scene in the opening of "The Turn of the Screw." As does Huysmans, James depicts lonely, repressed, emotionally stifled figures who create their own needs. (Ishiguro draws upon this tradition in *The Remains of the Day*, a different kind of ghost story narrated by a post–World War II Douglas.) The governess's story is told within a predominantly male and apparently bachelor circle, although there are a few ladies present. Douglas, the narrator, shares the manuscript of the governess with his friends, a manuscript entrusted to him after he had earned her confidence because they shared a relationship one summer. She had been his sister's governess; they had spent a summer together and clearly enjoyed each other's company. The teller, the first narrator, is also a bachelor who seems to find the presence of women a nuisance: "The departing ladies who had said they would stay didn't, of course, thank heaven, stay" (631). That Douglas leads his audience as if he were conducting a Socratic dialogue implies a homoerotic dimension. Of course, given how many of James's bachelors find confidence in a "safe" married woman—as in "The Aspern Papers"—it is possible that the first narrator is a woman or that James is deliberately ambiguous about the sex of the frame narrator. Yet I hear a voyeuristic male voice replicating not only Douglas's curiosity and sexual interest but also perhaps the Master's.

The governess's hysteria is related to the sexual excitement aroused by the bachelor-master who hired her to tutor his young charges. Why does the master make such a misjudgment? Because Quint is described as the master's "own man," is it not implied that those two bachelor figures were lovers? Could he also have been corrupted by Quint? Does that explain his pathological need for distance? Quint, who appears as an apparition to the governess, is dissolute but "handsome" (658), according to the housekeeper, the aptly named Mrs. Grose. He is a bachelor who preys on the innocence of his victims. As a bachelor he is as capable of corrupting her as he did her predecessor. Quint seems to be a pederast, sexually corrupting Miles while Miss Jessel—with whom he apparently had a liaison—corrupts Flora. The second apparition—Miss Jessel, her predecessor—is to the governess "an alien object in view—a figure" (666). And she thinks that Miss Jessel looks at her in the same way. The governess is sexually attracted to Miles, whom she calls "my boy," and gives him far more attention than she gives Flora.

As Richard Sieburth notes, the bachelor has no place in a culture oriented toward family:

> The bachelor cuts a somewhat pathetic figure in a nineteenth century given over to the ideological consolidation of the social and economic virtues of family life. Sexually, he is viewed with both condescension and trepidation, for while his legitimate recourse to prostitution is more or less condoned, he nonetheless threatens the social order as a possible agent of adultery, criminal seduction, or unnatural perversion.

Economically, he is considered at most a marginal entity, for he plays
no role in the transmission of property through inheritance or dowry.
Civically, he is seen as an embarrassment to community values, a case
of arrested development, narcissistically clinging to the prerogatives of
his self-centered individualism. (5)

And, of course, the governess is a female counterpart of the bachelor. Is not
this shift to self—this narcissism—on the part of master, governess, and
Douglas appropriate for the self-contained unit of bachelorhood?

It is not accidental that Joyce's "Stately, plump Buck Mulligan" recalls
Oscar Wilde, the ultimate bachelor figure although married. In Joyce,
Stephen is a desperate young man who must resist homosexuality, and
Bloom has been reduced to a caricature of a bachelor by his dysfunctional
marriage. The bachelor motif plays a role in the sea tales of Conrad and in
the male bonding between Marlow and Kurtz and, in particular, between
the Captain and Leggatt, where the word "secret"—which, as in *My Secret
Life,* implied to the Victorians one's sexual life—gives the story a strong
sexual implication.

Huysmans's and Wilde's bachelors anticipate the frame narrator and
Douglas of "The Turn of the Screw" and the Marlow who narrates to a fellow group of males in "Youth," "Heart of Darkness," and *Lord Jim,* as well
as, of course, Mann's and Kafka's bachelor. Sieburth notes "Huysmans's
aestheticism," his "encyclopedic compost," his interest in the occult, his
rapid alternation between nightmare and reality—what Sieburth calls his
"laconic montage technique" (5). And the qualities, I think, anticipate the
techniques both of Conrad—particularly in his Marlow tales where the discourse controls the story—and James. Marlow, like the governess, becomes
imprisoned by the Kurtz nightmare of his choice: Kurtz and Quint are demonic figures who destabilize the central narrators—Marlow and the governess—and undermine their assumptions.

The James tale also takes place in a world that challenges Western assumptions about reality and its concepts of order and logic: "The answer to
my appeal was instantaneous, but it came in the form of an extraordinary
blast and chill, a gust of frozen air and a shake of the room as great as if, in
the wild wind, the casement had crashed in" (715). The governess sees an
"apparition" of the dead servant, Quint—"the thing was as human and

hideous as a real interview: hideous just because it *was* human, as human as to have met alone, in the small hours, in a sleeping house, some enemy, some adventurer, some criminal"—and seeing derives from her paralytic self-consciousness about being seen (682). That the narrator of each tale tells the story of atavistic energy within a frame—the listeners on shipboard in the Conrad tale, the listeners to Douglas reading in a drawing room—enacts the attempt of so-called civilization to control primitive energy—a manifestation of Kurtz's reversion to savagery and megalomania and to Quint's and Miss Jessel's sexual license—and understand it in terms of the culturally accepted norms.

One wonders if Gauguin's depictions of spirits—such as among the spirit, the girl, and the artist "Manao Tupapau"—influenced James because in that painting, the ambiguity about who is imagining and gazing at whom is essential. Gauguin eulogized the primitive in the 1892 *Fatata te miti,* which transforms the Golden Age of traditional painting—Titian, Fragonard, Courbet, Corot—to Tahiti. Because "The Turn of the Screw" is about obsessiveness, trauma, and catatonia, it is appropriate that time stands still. In "The Turn of the Screw," Miles and Flora—and the governess, who is tutored, mentored, and metamorphosed by them—are condemned to a perpetual present haunted by ghosts of Quint and Miss Jessel—and the implication of initiation into sexual perversity—that will not fade; as with Kafka's nightmare fable "The Hunter Gracchus," past and present inhabit conterminous space. Time can be an imprisonment when obsessions intrude and arrest time, leaving the obsessed in a perpetual present. Note how the story moves from June to November, from late spring to approaching winter: the twenty-four chapters emphasize the ghostly claustrophobic ticking of a clock as well as call attention to the time of the listeners to Douglas's story. The twenty-four short chapters—like hours on a clock—emphasize the tick-tock of passing time and the logical progressive temperament of the Western reader as he or she—like the governess—faces challenge to the known.

V

Let us turn to our parallel text, "Death in Venice" (1912), indeed a text that makes more explicit the underlying themes that we have been discussing in

"The Turn of the Screw": "Death in Venice," like "The Turn of the Screw," is about erotic aestheticism; Aschenbach's narcissism, paradoxically, was implicit in his ascetic denial of life, in his obsession with control, and in his conception of heroism—in a work such as his *The Abject*—as persevering in the face of exhaustion. Paradoxically, the governess's *service*—abject service—becomes a kind of narcissism, and her self-abnegation is a cause of a kind of nervous collapse. Mann suggests that asceticism and aestheticism share a narcissistic base (as does Kafka in "Metamorphosis"). When Aschenbach meets Tadzio, he transfers his passive-aggressive behavior from art to life. Just like Kurtz and the governess, Aschenbach erases the boundaries between self and other.

Fearing the bourgeois careerist in himself and knowing his own ambition and his own desire for a comfortable life focused on his work, Mann totemized his concerns in the figure of Aschenbach. Mann's narrator is an example of the vestigial omniscient narrator who, in the guise Mann gives him, seems to present an analysis derived from a particular point of view but who really presents a multilayered perspective. His is a thick, rich reading of Aschenbach's behavior, an allegory of the impossibility of the univocal view. As in *Lord Jim,* a character feels himself enclosed by an abyss from which the quirks and idiosyncrasies of character prevent him from escaping. Yet the narrator does with Aschenbach what Aschenbach does with his own work: with rage the author here rejects the rejected, casts out the outcast—and the measure of his fury is the measure of his condemnation of all moral shilly-shallying. Explicitly he renounces sympathy with the abyss, explicitly he refutes the flabby humanitarianism of the phrase *"Tout comprendre c'est tout pardonner"* (13). Aschenbach's pathological control is the quintessence of the European temperament, which Mann associates with an enervated culture.

Aschenbach perceives Tadzio as a work of art in a different medium than in the one in which he works:

> His face recalled the noblest moment of Greek sculpture—pale, with a sweet reserve, with clustering honey-coloured ringlets, the brow and nose descending in one line, the winning mouth, the expression of pure and godlike serenity. . . . It was the head of Eros, with the yellowish bloom of Parian marble, with fine serious brows, and dusky clustering ringlets standing out in soft plenteousness over temples and ears. (25, 29)

The irony is that the seeming classically Apollonian statue intrudes the Dionysian element into Aschenbach's life. He also perceives Tadzio in terms of Botticelli's *The Birth of Venus* (1480). "The sight of this living figure, virginally pure and austere, with dripping locks, beautiful as a tender young god, emerging from the depths of sea and sky, outrunning the element—it conjured up mythologies, it was like a primeval legend, handed down from the beginning of time, of the birth of form, of the origin of the gods" (33). That Aschenbach rejects modernism—futurism, fauvism, post-impressionism, the blue rider school in Germany—for the classical tells us something about him and his art. His is a poignant effort to resist the juggernaut of modernism, for has he not in Munich also tried to turn his back on contemporary urban life, industrialism, psychoanalysis, modern science as well as sexuality and passion? Compare Aschenbach's world with that of Manet or Joyce. He imagines himself as an heir to the Platonists, including and especially their pederastic tendencies. He is as indifferent to modernism as he is to contemporary politics and history; the narrator begins in 1912 with how "Europe sat upon the anxious seat beneath a menace that hung over its head for months" (3). Aschenbach embodies the spirit of Europe at a time when it has lost its sense of purpose, but we the audience respond with a polyauditory ear that hears other echoes. Aschenbach identifies with those who are exhausted and persevere in spite of enervation. Is Aschenbach not the "creator of that powerful narrative *The Abject*, which taught a whole grateful generation that a man can still be capable of moral resolution even after he has plumbed the depths of knowledge" (8)? Tadzio—and Venice—represents all that Aschenbach—and the rest of Europe—has repressed and excluded: Asia, the unknown, the other, passion, and the insidious moral illness that is undermining its health. In art, Venice is color, decoration, diffused light, relaxation. For him in Venice, Tadzio's presence—his presence as Eros—becomes an inspiration, but the inspiration is libidinous and passionate, as the speaker ironically remarks: "Verily it is well for the world that it sees only the beauty of the completed work and not its origins nor the conditions whence it sprang; since knowledge of the artist's inspiration might often but confuse and alarm and so prevent the full effect of its excellence" (46–47).

The bachelor motif is central to Mann's "Death in Venice." Aschenbach has resisted and repressed his libido until it relentlessly emerges in the

form of a catastrophic passion for Tadzio, a young boy at the edge of ado-
lescence. Is not "Death in Venice" not only about the dangers of the narcissism of art—the retreat into the self that makes the creator oblivious to
history and morals—but about the narcissism of bourgeois life as well?
Kafka's "Metamorphosis" is about inversion caused by self-denial and self-
effacement, about a kind of emotional masochism, about the starving of
one's soul that is a not-too-distant cousin of narcissism. And this bachelor
motif is applicable not only to Birkin and Gerald in *Women in Love* and to
Tom Brangwen in *The Rainbow* before he meets Lydia, but to single
women as well in the early twentieth century, including Ursula in *The
Rainbow* and Lily in *To the Lighthouse*. Marriage is *supposed* to happen. Do
we not see a kind of female counterpart to bachelorhood in Lawrence's Ursula, in Woolf's Lily, and in Gerty in *Ulysses,* as well as in *Dubliners*—in the
title character of "Eveline," in Maria in "Clay," and in the three spinsters
and Molly Ivors in "The Dead"? The singleness of women of marriageable
age is an embarrassment to the women and is conceived by women as a
problem to solve. In "The Turn of the Screw," is not "the spring of a beast"
(646) that the governess feels in part originating in her psyche?

   Aschenbach's relation to Tadzio has a strong affinity with the governess's relation to her master and to the way it shapes her response to the children as well as with Bloom's relation with Stephen. Joyce's "Hades" section
in particular recalls Mann's text. The carriage in which Bloom rides recalls
Charon's boat—the gondola that takes Aschenbach through Venice to his
house. Stephen Dedalus needs to eschew the Platonism that Aschenbach
embraces; in the "Scylla and Charybdis" section in *Ulysses,* to imply the
threat of Greek homosexual male bonding with his audience, Joyce has
Stephen both echo and parody the Socratic dialogues and Wilde's version
of those dialogues in *The Decay of Lying*. And so must the governess eschew
Platonism, for are not the ghosts visitations of prior forms? Aschenbach's
associations with the strangers he meets are examples of the double secret-
sharer motif. Travel for Aschenbach is discovery of *other,* an area beyond
his control, and once he leaves Munich he lives in no man's land, on the
margin along with Joyce's Bloom and James's governess.

   Art has become service, control, a check on Aschenbach's feelings and
has exhausted him, in part because of the efforts of repression, displacement, and artistic discipline that have used up these libidinous energies:

This yearning for new and distant scenes, this craving for freedom, release, forgetfulness—they were, he admitted to himself, an impulse towards flight, flight from the spot which was the daily theatre of a rigid,
cold, and passionate service. . . . So now, perhaps, feeling, thus tyran-
nized, avenged itself by leaving him, refusing from now on to carry
and wing his art and taking away with it all the ecstasy he had known
in form and expression. (6–7)

Mann's Aschenbach looks forward to Kafka's Gregor, who, like the governess, has no way of escaping the service of a functionary; Gregor gradually surrenders his humanity to insecthood, where he paradoxically finds his
humanity, and goes to another state than that of insect: death. In a word, art
has become *resistant* to living passionately, fully, imaginatively. Cosmetically
decorated—wearing red necktie and straw hat—Aschenbach becomes his
others—those rakish, solipsistic hedonists who are indifferent to others. He
becomes a figure in Veronese rather than a North European figure of a Mem-
ling or the Cranachs. In journeying from Germany to Italy—from Munich to
Venice—he journeys from nineteenth-century emphasis on neo-classic and
Apollonian virtues of control and reason to modernist romantic and Dionysian possibilities—including color, decoration, and self-expression in which
one's art reflects one's life. Passionately obsessed, he remains in Venice, notwithstanding his knowledge of the plague.

VI

Where then does our inquiry take us? When the omniscient narrative perspective, based on measuring behavior against an assured perspective,
breaks down, the reader becomes the one who gazes, and literary works become, like modern paintings, dispersions of impressions for another perspective. Such openness is seductive and compelling and requires us to
respond to the surface with our own narrative of meaning. When Hardy
spoke of *Jude the Obscure* (1895) as a "series of seemings," he was acknowledging that neither mimesis nor point of view need be consistent. He uses
different modes of mimesis—Jude is a representative figure, Sue an idiosyncratic figure, Father Time an allegorical figure, and his omniscient narrator a vestige of the objective ironic voice now transformed into an

engaged partisan of Jude. Yet, notwithstanding the apparent single point of view, the novel contains multiple and contradictory explanations for its characters' behavior until we realize that Jude's and, particularly, Sue's behavior are partially *obscure* to the narrator whether intended or not. Such a technique—at once so sure of its conclusions and yet so tentative—empowers the reader, makes the reader's odyssey part of the agon of the artistic work. I take this agon to be a principal feature of modernism for visual artists such as Rodin, Picasso, and Matisse, as well as for the modern authors that I have been discussing. Modernism is the story of the artist's quest more than it is of the finished work. As Barbara Rose notes of twentieth-century American painters, "usually, that subject was their own sense of self, their own intensely personal conception of the world and nature and their own feelings and responses to that world" (61).

Conrad thought of his technique of catching characters within the gaze of a narrative presence and rendering the perceiver's response as *impressionism;* for him, dramatizing the reason for the narrator's interest—the psychic and moral reason for that interest—was more real than the tradition of filling in a character's appearance in a story with essential background information, for instance, "Jim was born in . . . he went to grammar school . . . he joined the merchant marines." Like "The Turn of the Screw," *Lord Jim* is, among other things, a search for perspective; in Conrad's novel the omniscient narrator, Marlow, Stein, and Brierely—even Gentleman Brown, Doramin, and Dain Waris—gaze at Jim, but we gaze at these characters trying to understand Jim and also, in part because of Conrad's efforts to undermine traditional linearity, to arrange spatially the configurations of the figures in a cognitive pattern within our mind. That pattern of meaning that our mind retains after our reading is as much out of time as that of a painting. Much as in modern painting, the reader's gaze weaves a pattern of meaning to complete the meaning. (Recall the pictorial view of Jim on the shore that Marlow describes as he leaves Jim after his visit on Patusan, which itself is more an aesthetic realm than a real one.)

What I am suggesting is that I want to think of cultural criticism more as a verb than a noun. I want to stress the activity of inquiry, not announce the ends of the inquiry before it begins. The kind of narrator James uses in "The Turn of the Screw" as an instance of the modernist focus on the gaze resituates not only the governess's telling as subject but makes her an object—as much or more than her tale—of our gaze. For in the governess do we not see a model of the self-creating narcissist who imagines forms of transference and courts transference with her observers, listeners, and readers? I am suggesting that this has implications for the perceiver-reader who, released from the strong rhetorical control of the author or painter, reconfigures the subject as he or she chooses according to his or her own epistemology. And we readers, voyeurs, like the governess, create in our reading our self-portraits and our doubles—whether it be the governess as sexually hysterical or as the victim of ghosts, or those who play the psychoanalytic role for her, the master, Douglas, Douglas's audience, and us readers.

Our gaze is a way that we define ourselves as subject, give meaning to objects, and control the not-I world in which we live. Our gaze is shaped by our psyche and by our values, and our psyche and values are modified by it. Without a gazing observer, the painting does not live. But, just as when we read, we move beyond the gaze to cognition and to reflection on what we have seen and have subsequently understood in terms of what we know. And when we reread, we are gazers—voyeurs—and yet also we are in the position of being tempted to lay down our gaze and to participate. And for this reason also we find not only a strong kinship between literature and the visual arts but in our response to these art forms. For modernism depends not on a fixed perspective but on what Joyce calls parallax or what we might call polyperspectivism—and so does its study because we successors to modernism are self-consciously aware of our place in a dynamic and temporal framework; and we, like the modernists, know that fixed time, stable viewers, and an object that has only one meaning are no longer possible.

Notes

A version of this essay appears in Daniel R. Schwarz, *Reconfiguring Modernism: Explorations in the Relationship between Modern Art and Modern Literature* (Basingstoke: Macmillan, 1997).

1. I have used the original 1898 edition reprinted in Philip Rahv's *The Great Short Novels of Henry James* rather than the more stylistically uniform New York edition.

Works Cited

Barnes, Julian. "The Proudest and Most Arrogant Man in France." *New York Review of Books,* 22 October 1992, 3.

Clifford, James. *The Predicament of Culture: Twentieth Century Ethnography, Literature and Art.* Cambridge: Harvard University Press, 1988.

Conrad, Joseph. *The Portable Conrad.* Ed. Morton Dawen Zabel. New York: Viking, 1975.

Elderfield, John. *Matisse in Morocco.* Washington: National Gallery of Art Press, 1990.

James, Henry. "The Turn of the Screw." In *The Great Short Novels of Henry James.* 627–748. Ed. Philip Rahv. New York: Dial, 1944.

Joyce, James. *Ulysses.* 1922. New York: Vintage-Random, 1986.

Lacan, Jacques. *The Four Fundamental Concepts of Psycho-Analysis.* Ed. Jacques-Alain Miller. Trans. Alan Sheridan. New York: Norton, 1981.

Manet: 1832–1883. New York: Metropolitan Museum of Art Press, 1983.

Mann, Thomas. *Death in Venice and Seven Other Stories.* Trans. H. T. Lower Porter. New York: Vintage, 1936.

Melville, Herman. *Moby-Dick.* 1851. Ed. Charles Child Walcutt. New York: Bantam, 1967.

Newman, Beth. "Getting Fixed: Feminine Identity and Scopic Crisis in *The Turn of the Screw.*" *Novel* 26.1 (1992–93): 49–63.

Rahv, Philip. Comments [on "The Turn of the Screw"]. *The Great Short Novels of Henry James,* 622. Ed. Philip Rahv. New York: Dial, 1944.

Rose, Barbara. *American Painting: The Twentieth Century.* New York: Rizzoli, 1969.

Russell, John. *The Meaning of Modern Art.* New York: Museum of Modern Art Press, 1981.

Schwarz, Daniel. *The Humanistic Heritage: Critical Theories of the English Novel from James to Hillis Miller.* Rev. ed. London: Macmillan, 1989.

Sieburth, Richard. "Dabbling in Damnation: The Bachelor, the Artist and the Dandy in Huysmans." *Times Literary Supplement,* 29 May 1992, 3–5.

Stevens, Wallace. *Collected Poems.* New York: Knopf, 1965.

Woolf, Virginia. *"The Captain's Death Bed" and Other Stories.* New York: Harcourt, 1950.

Contributors

Kristin Boudreau, an assistant professor of English at the University of Georgia, has published essays not only on James but on Ralph Waldo Emerson, Louisa May Alcott, Rebecca Harding Davis, and Toni Morrison. She is completing a study on American modernism, *Philanthropic Mush: Sympathy and Sentiment in Jamesian America.*

Adam Bresnick teaches at the Collegiate School in New York City and occasionally as an adjunct at Fordham University. He is a frequent contributor to the *Times Literary Supplement.* An earlier essay of his on James's "Private Life" was awarded Honorable Mention for the 1992 Don Holliday Prize and appeared in *The Henry James Review.*

Joseph Dewey (see Editors)

Rory Drummond teaches at Christ's Hospital School, England. He is currently completing his doctoral thesis, "An Intellectual Adventure: Henry James on England, 1888–1903," from which this essay is taken.

Annette Gilson is an assistant professor at Oakland University. Her dissertation examined lines of influence between male and female writers of the modernist era. She has also completed an influence study of John Ashbery and Emily Dickinson, forthcoming in *Twentieth Century Literature.*

Brooke Horvath (see Editors)

Daniel Kim is completing postgraduate work in postmodern theory at the University of Toronto. This essay marks his first publication.

Jeraldine Kraver is an assistant professor of English at the University of Texas, San Antonio. Her previous work has appeared in *L.I.T.* and in

Studies in American Jewish Literature. She is completing a study of Latino literature, *Paris South: Expatriate Writers in Post-Revolution Mexico.*

Patricia Laurence, a professor of English at the City College of New York, has published widely on modernism and postcolonialism. She has published, among other works, *The Reading of Silence: Virginia Woolf in the English Tradition* (1991) and has recently completed *Lily Briscoe's Chinese Eyes: Bloomsbury, Modernism and China.*

Lomeda Montgomery completed her postgraduate work at the University of Texas at San Antonio. This essay, a revised version of a paper delivered at the American Literature Association Symposium on Women Writers, marks her first publication.

Michael Pinker is the author of numerous articles on twentieth-century poetics and prose that have appeared in, among other places, *The Review of Contemporary Fiction* and the *Denver Quarterly.*

Jeanne Campbell Reesman is a professor of English at the University of Texas, San Antonio. Her essays have appeared in numerous periodicals, including *American Literary Realism* and the *Kenyon Review.* In addition, she is the editor of *Speaking the Other Self: American Women Writers* (1997) and the author of *American Designs: The Late Novels of James and Faulkner* and the revised Twayne volume on Jack London.

Earl Rovit, emeritus professor of English at City College of New York, has a long and distinguished record of publications on modern American literature, including studies of Hemingway, Bellow, and Elizabeth Madox Roberts.

Daniel R. Schwarz is a professor of English and Stephen H. Weiss Presidential Fellow at Cornell University. A significant contributor to contemporary theoretical debate, he has written a dozen books, including seminal studies of Conrad, Joyce, and Stevens; *Reconfiguring Modernism: Explorations in the Relationship between Modern Art and Modern Literature;* and the recent *Imagining the Holocaust.* His *Rereading Conrad* will appear in 2001.

Karen Scherzinger is a senior lecturer at the University of South Africa.

Her essay is drawn from her doctoral dissertation on James and Jacques Lacan, completed at the University of the Witwatersrand, Johannesburg.

Phyllis van Slyck is professor of English at Fiorella LaGuardia Community College, Long Island City, N.Y. Her essay is drawn from a study she is completing entitled *Knowledge and Representation in the Work of James,* another part of which has appeared in *The Henry James Review.*

Molly Vaux recently completed her doctorate at the Graduate Center of the City University of New York. Her dissertation was a study of the prefaces of Child, Hawthorne, and James.

Joseph Wiesenfarth is the Nathan S. Blount Professor of English and the Sally Mead Hands-Bascom Professor of English at the University of Wisconsin-Madison. In addition to his many publications on a wide range of nineteenth-century British writers, he has published widely and with great distinction on Henry James since the 1963 release of his seminal study *Henry James and the Dramatic Analogy.* At present, he is completing a study of Ford Madox Ford and the Moderns.

Editors

Joseph Dewey (Ph.D. Purdue University), an associate professor of American literature at the University of Pittsburgh, has authored numerous articles on American fiction that have appeared in *Modern Fiction Studies, The Hollins Critic, Steinbeck Quarterly, The Review of Contemporary Fiction, Texas Review, Nuclear Texts and Contexts, AIDS: The Literary Response, Contemporary Gay American Novelists,* and *The Mississippi Quarterly.* A former editorial assistant at *Modern Fiction Studies* and currently the book review editor for *Aethlon: The Journal of Sport Literature,* Professor Dewey is the author of *In a Dark Time: The Apocalyptic Temper in the American Novel of the Nuclear Age* (1992) and *Novels from Reagan's America: A New Realism* (2000).

Brooke Horvath (Ph.D. Purdue University), a professor of American literature at Kent State University, has served as editor with *The Review of Contemporary Fiction, Aethlon: The Journal of Sport Literature,* and *Modern*

Fiction Studies. His work on American literature and culture has appeared in *Cimarron Review, American Literature, American Poetry Review, Rhetoric Review, Denver Quarterly, Missouri Review, Tar River, Southern Quarterly,* and in many other journals and books. Professor Horvath is also a frequent book reviewer for *The Cleveland Plain Dealer* and the author of two poetry collections: *In a Neighborhood of Dying Light* (1995) and *Consolation at Ground Zero* (1996).

Index

Le Spécialiste Junior

Chasseur d'insectes

Texte
Adaptation fr.

Gründ

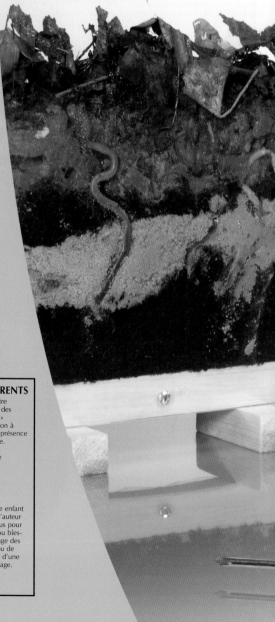

UN LIVRE DORLING KINDERSLEY

POUR L'ÉDITION ANGLAISE :
Bookwork Ltd :
Suivi éditorial : Louise Pritchard,
Annabel Blackledge
Suivi artistique : Jill Plank, Kate Mullins

Dorling Kindersley Ltd :
Création éditoriale : Fran Baines, Carey Scott
Création artistique : Stefan Podhorodecki
Responsable éditoriale : Linda Esposito
Responsable artistique : Jane Thomas
Graphisme de la couverture : Chris Drew
Textes de couverture : Adam Powley,
Carrie Love
Responsables de publication :
Caroline Buckingham, Andrew Macintyre
Direction artistique : Simon Webb
Directeur de la publication : Jonathan Metcalf
Fabrication : Erica Rosen
Iconographie : Sarah Pownall, Sarah Mills
PAO : Natasha Lu
Photographies : Dave King

POUR L'ÉDITION FRANÇAISE :
Adaptation française : Maura Tillay
Secrétariat d'édition : Élodie Chaudière

© 2007 Éditions Gründ
pour l'édition française
© 2005 Dorling Kindersley Limited
pour l'édition originale
sous le titre *Bug hunter*

ISBN 978-2-7000-1626-0
Dépôt légal : mars 2007
PAO : Nord Compo, Villeneuve d'Ascq
Imprimé en Chine
Loi n° 49-956 du 16 juillet 1949 sur les
publications destinées à la jeunesse
Éditions Gründ – 60, rue Mazarine –
75006 Paris www.grund.fr

ATTENTION ! AVERTISSEMENT AUX PARENTS

Certaines activités proposées dans cet ouvrage doivent être
effectuées sous le contrôle d'un adulte. Au fil des pages, des
symboles indiquent lesquelles. Les encadrés « **Attention** »
décrivent les risques encourus et les mesures de précaution à
prendre. Veillez à repérer quelles activités nécessitent la présence
d'un adulte, et surveillez votre enfant lorsqu'il s'y adonne.

 Cette activité doit être effectuée avec l'aide
d'un adulte.

 Soyez très prudents pour cette activité.

ATTENTION
Encadré mentionnant
si l'activité décrite
peut être salissante.
Suivez les conseils
proposés et n'effectuez
l'activité que dans
un lieu approprié.

Assurez-vous toujours que votre enfant
respecte bien les instructions. L'auteur
et l'éditeur ne peuvent être tenus pour
responsables de tout accident ou bles-
sure résultant d'un mauvais usage des
instructions, ni de toute perte ou de
tout dommage qui résulteraient d'une
activité proposée dans cet ouvrage.